THE DIVISION OF LITERATURE

THE DI|VI|SION

OR THE UNIVERSITY

OF LIT|ER|A|TURE

IN DECONSTRUCTION

PEGGY KAMUF

THE UNIVERSITY OF CHICAGO PRESS
CHICAGO & LONDON

PEGGY KAMUF is professor of French and comparative
literature at the University of Southern California.

The University of Chicago Press, Chicago 60637
The University of Chicago Press, Ltd., London
© 1997 by The University of Chicago
All rights reserved. Published 1997
Printed in the United States of America
06 05 04 03 02 01 00 99 98 97   1 2 3 4 5
ISBN: 0-226-42323-9 (cloth)
ISBN: 0-226-42324-7 (paper)

Library of Congress Cataloging-in-Publication Data

Kamuf, Peggy, 1947–
    The division of literature: or the university in
  deconstruction / Peggy Kamuf.
        p.   cm.
    Includes bibliographical references and index.
    ISBN 0-226-42323-9. — ISBN 0-226-42324-7 (pbk.)
    1. Criticism.   2. Literature—Study and teaching (Higher)
  3. Universities and colleges—History.   4. Deconstruction.
  I. Title.
  PN81.K338   1997
  807'.1'173—dc20   96-20255
                                                    CIP

♾ The paper used in this publication meets the minimum
requirements of the American National Standard for Information
Sciences—Permanence of Paper for Printed Library Materials,
ANSI Z39.48-1984.

C O N|T E N T S

A C|K N O W L|E D G|M E N T S

Versions of several chapters have appeared previously in print: the introduction was first formulated as a review essay for *Diacritics* 25, no. 2 (1995), published by Johns Hopkins University Press; chapter 1 first appeared in *Logomachia: The Conflict of the Faculties,* edited by Richard Rand (Lincoln: University of Nebraska Press, 1992); a partial version of chapter 5 is included in *Deconstruction is/in America,* edited by Anselm Haverkamp (New York: New York University Press, 1995). Permission from the publishers to reprint this material is gratefully acknowledged. In addition, "Melville's Credit Card" is adapted and translated from an essay published in French, in *Passages des frontières, autour du travail de Jacques Derrida,* edited by Marie-Louise Mallet (Paris: Galilée, 1994). I also wish to recall here that the starting point for this project was an invitation to deliver the Ida Beam Visiting Professor Lectures in 1991 at the University of Iowa, which resulted in the substance of chapter 3. I want to thank Herman Rapaport, as well as all those whose generous invitations prodded me to fill out the design of this book. Finally, I am grateful to the students in my graduate seminars at the University of Southern California, who have known not only how to question but how to respond.

INTRODUCTION | CATACHRESIS AND INSTITUTION

IN 1857 Charles Baudelaire cited, among the many reasons to admire Edgar Allan Poe, the latter's denunciation of a certain "heresy":

> But there is another heresy which, thanks to the hypocrisy, clumsiness, and baseness of certain minds, is even more formidable and has even greater chances of surviving—an error that is even harder to get rid of. I am speaking of the heresy of *teaching,* which includes as inevitable corollaries the heresies of *passion, truth,* and *morality.* Masses of people imagine that the aim of poetry is to teach some kind of lesson, that it must either fortify the moral conscience or, finally, *demonstrate* something useful. Edgar Poe maintains that Americans especially have sponsored this heterodox idea . . . .[1]

Although Baudelaire does not let stand the claim about the special affinity Americans show for didactic poetry ("Alas!" he adds, "one does not have to go to Boston to encounter the heresy in question. We are besieged by it right here"), he also concedes that the qualities he most respects in Poe are all the more admirable for having surfaced against the countercurrents of hypocritical American moralism. It is already hard enough, observes Baudelaire, to practice poetry nobly and profitably in a moderate monarchy or a regular republic, but "it becomes almost impracticable in a kind of shambles where every petty official polices public opinion to the profit of his vices—or his virtues, it's all the same" (36). And yet, Baudelaire concludes that the "bad criticism of good poets is the same in all countries" and in France, no less than in America, an "antipoetic race" imposes its mediocre opinions to the detriment of poetic perfection. As example, he cites the popular Victor Hugo, "who only managed to be forgiven his lyric genius by forcefully and brutally introducing into his poetry what Edgar Poe considered to be the chief modern heresy: teaching" (47).

Baudelaire's term, which I have twice translated by "teaching," is *enseignement.* With that word, he probably meant to render "moral," as in the moral of the story.[2] The translation I have given, on the other hand, tends to confuse things somewhat since, more than a century after Baudelaire wrote in praise of Poe, "teaching" no longer denotes, first and foremost, reading off the moral lessons of tales. In the course of that century, the notion of a scientific, scholarly education has displaced many of the moralistic connotations that, for Poe and Baudelaire, remained attached to teaching. Neither of them, for example, would have likely intended the "teaching of poetry" to mean that which goes on principally in the literature departments of our institutions of higher education, for the simple reason that, in the 1850s, such departments had largely yet to be invented. Thus the translation proposed is faulty because it invites a misunderstanding through a kind of anachronism. We miss Poe's and Baudelaire's point if we understand teaching as the "chief modern heresy" of poetry in any sense other than the moral lesson.

Perhaps, however, if there is a risk of misreading this *enseignement,* it is less a fault of the translation than of a persistent, shared reluctance to acknowledge the way in which teaching remains "heretical" to poetry in precisely the sense Baudelaire meant. If so, then the context of recent debates in the American literary academy about what should or should not be taught, principally in the undergraduate literature curriculum, may offer one of the best opportunities to examine this reluctance since the "scientific" study of literature first began to be instituted late in the last century. For few could deny that, in these debates, the moralistic claim for literature and for its teaching has come once again to the fore. My translation will have merely confirmed the continuity of this will to moralize literature as a vehicle of teaching.

All the same, it is clear that when Baudelaire spoke of *enseignement* as a formidable heresy for poetry, he had in mind a doctrine promoted by critics writing for literary journals and gave but little thought, if any, to the teaching of poetry that was then current in the *lycées* and at the university, which is to say to instruction in rhetoric and classical languages. Poe likewise was exclusively concerned with the "heresies" as professed in the prominent literary journals of the day. Each judged the doctrine of didacticism or the moral utility of poetry from the standpoint of a poet writing largely for the same journals as and under the critical eye of that doctrine's advocates. And both, of course, were severely judged in their turn. In what seems a marked contrast, our contemporary debates about the "uses of literature" aim less to determine whether poetry or literature should *teach* than whether some poetic work or other should *be taught*. The second question, unlike the first, supposes the existence of a specific teaching institution, the school or the university. More than that, it is a question posed to the possible *limits* of this institution, that is, to the definition of what is and what is not to be comprehended within that institution's determination of itself. Clearly, therefore, the invention and intervention of this institution has to be taken into account when translating what it has meant over the last century, for poetry, to teach and be taught.

Such an account might begin by pausing to wonder about this question that literature and the teaching of literature pose to the institution. As we have just remarked, when one asks what literary works should (or should not) be taught, another question is implied: what are the limits of the institution "within" which something called literature ("great literature," "the canon," "the literary tradition," and so forth) is supposed to be taught? Why does the first question entail the second? And why does the question that *literature* poses to itself put in question this other institution that is the university? While no doubt the historical and scientific disciplines (the disciplines of the "fact") have undergone considerable shifts in the determination of their own boundaries, the *fact* is that, since the establishment of the modern, scientific university, none of these redefinitions has been understood or perceived as touching upon some essential foundation of the university institution. However profound the reordering of these disciplines has been, the principle of *universitas* has accommodated, indeed welcomed, the innovations as proof of the soundness of the central tenets of its own credo: the advancing frontiers of knowledge, the retreat of error, the objectivity of science, and so on. When there has been public debate about what should or should not be taught in these disciplines (creation science, negationist history, branches of sociobiology), scientific criteria are generally thought to remain in place to adjudicate the dispute. As for questions about the kind of scientific research carried out with university support (for example, weapons research, experimentation on animals), these are ethical questions posed to society at large and not just to the university as such. In other words, it still seems possible to judge these and similar controversies that have arisen out of university scientific teaching or research by referring either to *intramural,* scientific criteria or to *extramural,* ethical standards—even if such criteria and such standards never simply present themselves. But in all these cases— and this is the point—the *division* of intra- from extra- by which the institution is established is not itself in question. Whereas when one asks: what do we teach *as* literature? the question seems to go to the very border along which an institution, here the university, sets itself off from some outside. And this means that, with the question of literature's institution, a space may be opened up for the *remarking* of institutionality in general, a space that is neither inside nor outside some pre-given (instituted) boundaries. This "space" of the neither-nor, which is precisely not marked out by spatial or conceptual boundaries, constitutes something like a reserve of possible transformation for the stabilized, but never thoroughly stable institutions that draw on it. It is the reserve, therefore, of these institutions' historicality, by which is meant both that they have been bequeathed to us by a specific history and are not naturally occurring phenomena, and that whatever stabilized forms they may assume in the present remain open to the transformations of a future.

In advancing this notion of "literature" (in quotation marks for reasons that will become clear) as such a reserve in excess over its past or present institutions, we are reiterating and reaffirming one of the principal reasons deconstructive thought has had the far-reaching and often remarked influence on literary studies and theory in the English-speaking university. We thus seem to take little account of the persistent announcements, most often accompanied with some expression of relief, that that influence has waned and need no longer be reckoned with. On the contrary, however, the fact that such announcements have persisted for so long has to intrigue any interested observer of the scene. She or he may recall Paul de Man's description in 1982 of the receding wave of foreign-influenced literary theory after a fifteen- or twenty-year period of interest in the United States. He then remarked, with the characteristic detachment that often infuriated his many adversaries: "Such an ebb and flow is natural enough, but it remains interesting, in this case, because it makes the depth of the resistance to literary theory so manifest."[3]

Almost fifteen years later, we could add that the ebbing has persisted into a strange afterlife, by which we do not mean only the survival of writings de Man himself signed. This is not a prelude to yet another analysis of the fury unleashed in 1987 when the rediscovery of de Man's wartime journalism for Nazi-sympathizing newspapers was made public, for that, too, seems to have ebbed, although clearly not because the questions raised there have since been resolved.[4] In this waning twilight, one can nevertheless still frequently discern the sentiment that "deconstruction" (more or less personified) ought to be banned from critically, historically responsible debate about the future of our literary institutions. One must have few illusions about the likelihood of persuading those who share such a sentiment to think otherwise; nonetheless, I wish to make clear at the outset that if all the analyses put forward in this study rely, tacitly or explicitly, on deconstructive thought, and in particular the writings of Jacques Derrida, for indications of how to continue to encounter the texts of our tradition, it is because they attempt to take account of concrete effects emanating from the deconstructive reserve across all the institutions of a culture's history, especially the institutions of "literature." These analyses, then, are carried by the belief that any future of that institution, which can only be something other than its present, something other, therefore, than "literature," is given its best and indeed only chance by this deconstructive reserve.

With the notion of reserve, then, we mean that which precedes, exceeds, or is not fully drawn down by instituted divisions of meaning, and still less by the ebb and flow of controversy over these divisions. When Derrida coined the term "differance" to designate "the playing movement that 'produces'—by means of something that is not simply an activity—these [linguistic] differences, these effects of difference,"[5] he acknowledged that it "lends itself to a certain number of nonsynonymous substitutions, according to the necessity of the context." One such substitution, explicitly mentioned in this essay, is "reserve" (12). The provisional use of the term in this introduction would attempt to activate its necessary associations with our context, which is the specifically textual tradition of "literature." The latter has come to designate that which is set aside, or reserved, from within writing in general, according to a shifting set of nonformalizable criteria and by means of the decisional practices of numerous institutions.[6] Precisely because these criteria cannot be formalized or made systematic and also, therefore, because the institutions that invoke them in their decisions are themselves historical—that is, transformable—the reserve of "literature" designates as well the possibility of tapping the "literary" resources of texts that had been neglected, forgotten, or dismissed by a critical tradition. This possibility, which is anything but remote and of which new examples come to light every day, is itself often to be accounted for by yet another sense of "literature" as reserve: the sense in which a literary text holds sense in reserve, does not exhaust the possibility for meaning in an indicative or transitive relation to a referent. Such texts, we can say, are reserved, that is, they hold back from a full and present disclosure of sense, not because they conceal a secret that can eventually be uncovered (although this structure of reserve cannot easily be distinguished from the structure of secrecy in the ordinary sense) but because the reserve shelters that which cannot be simply presented in the present and that which was never presentable in the past. It is the reserve of a time radically other than the present or the past present, the radical other we call, hopefully or in trembling, the future.

For the moment, these assertions regarding the reserve, in all the senses just enumerated, will be left to stand by themselves, abstracted from their support in the concrete, step-by-step elaborations of a text written under the literary reserve clause. We will come back to these elaborations later, in the second division, when we approach a certain *closet* that opens the text of Melville's *The Confidence-Man*. It opens that text, in other words, it marks the place of beginning, but also it opens or breaches the textually marked limits of a beginning and an end, the confines of the literary fiction. All of this it does without opening its own door on any secret of the sort that can be hidden in a closet. Which also means that this textual closet, this bottomless reserve, does not open onto a revelation of identity—a character's, a narrator's, an author's, a reader's, some subject's; rather, it gives a threshold onto which another may step, an other-than-identity in all its infinite difference.

But, leaving this reserve in reserve, we must try not to get ahead of ourselves and remain for a while still on this side of the fictional threshold that divides this study between "history" and "literature." It is this fictional division, a division *in* fiction, that we will call the division of literature: a division that continues to divide. By way of introduction (but we are already writing from that division, which therefore does not wait to be introduced), we will set down some other terms with which to name, provisionally, the deconstructive reserve we call "literature."

It is tedious to write repeatedly "literature" in quotation marks. Before, however, we reduce the tedium by erasing those marks, we should try to recall what the punctuation awkwardly signals by convention. By convention, or rather by a large set of conventions, we may speak of literature as the instituted name of a set of traditions, practices, conventions, and evaluations, which set, however, is of indeterminable dimensions. This indeterminability of what is (or is not) literature, of what properly belongs to the set called literature, is not a contingent condition but a necessary one of continuing to call "literature" by that name. The name, in this sense, has not been around very long, as everyone knows. Despite its short life (the first occurrence given in the OED is from 1812: "Their literature, their works of art offer models that have never been excelled"[7]), the instituted name has accumulated the weightiest determinations and appropriations in the realm called "ideology." To a large extent "literature," so determined and overdetermined, has ceased to be a useful term for it can no longer designate an open set and, thereby, the opening beyond itself, beyond the self that that same "ideology" has appropriated. "Literature" is "ideology," so they say, an assertion that is, by definition, unfalsifiable because it does not so much assert a state of things as perform and produce that which it asserts. But this performative, which has so largely installed the effective "truth" that literature equals ideology in departments of Literature in the English-speaking world (but the limits of the "English-speaking world" are more than ever uncertain), in effect leaves once again unnamed and unclaimed the indeterminability that "literature" had, for a time—but perhaps always in a past—served to evoke. In other words, the determination of "literature" equals "ideology" does not, we must believe, reduce the indeterminable margins of those cultural formations, for example, the modern, scientific university, *within* which "literature" has been assigned a certain place or space or value. Otherwise, we would have to believe that these same formations or institutions had achieved their final and destined stability, that they were historically finished off. Manifestly, however, the concerns with which we accompany and assist the closure of "literature's" institutions are carried by the force of a belief that there is still history to come, beyond the announced closure. And we—for this belief is also and perhaps first of all the belief in a "we"—now look for new names with which to call what is coming, to call it, precisely, to come.

The closure in question, therefore, will not have happened to "literature" simply from without; it is rather the closure *of* its historical institutions, the very movement whereby those institutions have had a history. Such, at least, is the supposition we propose to examine in the samplings from successive periods of that history which follow. These samplings are selected according to a progressive narrowing of the focus on "literature" as that which can and should have a determined place in the modern, scientific university. Whether (or not) literature can be instituted, whether (or not) its uncertain borders can be closed: these questions come to be posed from the place of that other institution that is the university, although in that process the sense in which the latter is simply other will itself be opened to questioning. As questions, they concern the possibility of knowing—and therefore teaching—what is called literature.

Our own tracking through this process, however, takes its point of departure from a somewhat different set of questions. They ask: What if the institution of literature, which sets it up through a decision within writing in general, which divides the latter and sets aside a reserve, were a gesture that must itself be repeatedly performed? What if each instituting decision carried over the very mark of division as a kind of surplus that belongs on neither side of the division it marks? If so, could we then say that what is instituted is "literature" *as* division, as the mark of division, a mark that can always be re-marked? In that case, its institutional status would never be fully assured or self-evident because, under the name of literature, it is this divisionality, if one may coin such a word, that is put in place, a "place" of division wherein all institutions are founded. Such a speculative description is made more concrete when it is referred to the inclusion of departments of literature in the university. At the same time, however, that inclusion itself provides a distinctive trait of the modern versus the classical university. In other words, it is a matter less of inclusion or incorporation within the modern university than of a constitutive act of the latter's institution. What we are describing, and only very tentatively for the moment, would take the form of an absolute, and therefore impossible, division, the university as the institution of totality (of knowledge) without remainder or reserve, without relation. Nevertheless, it is perhaps just such an impossible institution that has been dreamt from the moment "literature" is installed there, not merely as one division among others but *as* divisionality; from the moment, in other words, that the university includes departments of literature among its divisions, it attempts in effect to comprehend its own *founding* within its borders, that is, its own separation from what it is not.

The impossible topology we have just described would trace a limit *while at the same time* including the traced limit itself within what is thereby set apart and separated. This topology can be analyzed, as Jean-Luc Nancy has done, as a contradiction within the constitution or institution of the ab-solute, that is, within that which would be perfectly detached, "distinct and closed, without relation."

This ab-solute can appear in the form of the Idea, History, the Individual, the State, Science, the Work of Art, and so on. Its logic will always be the same inasmuch as it is without relation. A simple and redoubtable logic will always imply that within its very separation the absolutely separate encloses, if we can say this, more than what is simply separated.

Which is to say that the separation itself must be enclosed, that the closure must not only close around a territory (while still remaining exposed, at its outer edge, to another territory with which it thereby communicates) but also, in order to complete the absoluteness of its separation, around the enclosure itself. The absolute must be the absolute of its own absoluteness, or not be at all. In other words: to be absolutely alone, it is not enough that I be so; I must also be alone in being alone—and this of course is contradictory. The logic of the absolute violates the absolute. It implicates it in a relation that it refuses and precludes by its essence. This relation tears and forces open, from within and from without at the same time, and from an outside that is nothing other than the rejection of an impossible interiority, the "without relation" from which the absolute wants to constitute itself.[8]

We are advancing, then, the notion that the institution of literature in the university, or even, the institution of literature *as* the university, would have repeatedly inscribed this impossible topology of absolute division. We earlier called the latter a dream, implying thereby a dreamer, an agent, albeit an unconscious one. What about this question of agency?

To this point, we have understood "the institution of literature" solely in the objective sense of the genitive, literature, therefore, as *that which* is instituted, set up, framed, decided, cut off, put in reserve, and so forth. This passive syntax, however, leaves open or unspecified the position of the *agent* of these instituting acts. Such an opening seems to be an invitation to fill in the empty position with that ready construct that is the anthropomorphic subject. It seems, in other words, fairly natural to assume that human institutions are of human design. This assumption need not issue in the explicit positing of a conscious, willing agent, either individual or collective. The "literature equals ideology" thesis, for example, in its most prevalent current forms, generally invokes an Althusserian definition of ideology, which, like earlier versions of "false consciousness," does not attribute ideological formations to agents of fully conscious decisions. However, even this unconscious agency retains the features of a human subject, which is why it can be inserted into the dialectical relation of ideology to science, that is, to the achievement of a conscious awareness, rather than a misrecognition, of real relations to the conditions of that subject's existence. For this account as well, then, the apparently "natural" assumption of human agency remains in place, although no doubt less complacently and with less assurance

than in accounts offered by more or less heroic versions of humanism, which never figured out what to do with evidence of the unconscious other than be embarrassed by it.

But this difference does not dispel the problem that shows up
within a syntax of agency, especially when that syntax is pressed into
the service of narratives of the subject's *subjection*. It is the problem
identified by Nancy of the in-dividual or the ab-solute, of an institution of self that would *also* be a self-institution. The difficulty can be
stated in what seem to be the most strictly logical terms: If indeed
the self or subject is instituted, constructed out of a division, then to
what is owed this constitutive act? If the subject is the result and the
end of an institutional process (the process of "subjectivation,"
which, in fact, must constantly be begun again), how can it also set
that process in motion? And if such questions are avoided, does one
not then risk taking the subject for *granted* even as one also works to
show its constructed, restricted, constrictive nature? In the interest
of and in view of changing the subject, lifting its restrictions and its
exclusions, an initial exclusion would thereby be accepted, assumed,
and ratified: the exclusion of that *granting* instance which is not itself
subject to the order of the subject it installs. By not even recognizing
this prior assumption, one closes off at the very outset any possibility
of taking into account the effects such a limitation may produce.

That assumption, however, is made to appear when we turn to
the other, as we say *subjective* sense of the genitive in a phrase like
"the institution of literature." Read in this sense, "literature" (here
the grammatical subject) *institutes*. But it institutes what? And what
is "it" if that which we call literature is only the *result* of a process
of division, restriction, in short, institution? In order to spell out the
syntax of the subjective genitive, in other words, it would seem we
have to anticipate the predicated outcome: an instituted literature.
Putting subject and predicate together, we end up with an almost
perfectly circular or pleonastic sentence: "literature" institutes literature. This is almost, but not altogether, a pleonasm because the quotation marks around the subject of the sentence would be the marks
of a suspended nomination, the sign that a familiar, that is, *instituted*
name has been "borrowed" to designate that which has no ready,
proper name. Without its quotation marks, literature is a catachresis.
And it is the necessity of this catachresis that inscribes the redundant
sentence, a necessity that can easily be effaced simply by dropping
the marks that distinguish "literature" from its instituted and no
longer catachrestic name, literature. With that gesture, however, one
effaces as well the mark of a certain *outside* that no institution of

literature (without quotation marks) can simply include. This effacement is recorded by our sentence in the shift from an instituting
"literature" to literature that is instituted.

Let us try once more, then, to spell out this troublesome syntax:
"Literature" (writing in the general sense of a movement that inscribes
an outside or other in the mark of differentiation and division) *institutes literature* (writing in a restricted sense, for example, "writing
which has claim to consideration on the ground of beauty of form
or emotional effect," in the OED's definition). It is this restricted
sense that has been made to work for the subject, consolidating the
subject, and representing subjectivity to itself. But as an instituting
force, as institutionality or divisionality, "literature," writing in the
general sense, is *not* a subject, an agent, or even an agency without
agent; it is, rather, withdrawn from the subject/object relation. Nevertheless, it is this divisional movement without name and without
face that the generative grammar of the subjective genitive can also
inscribe according to its own genetic code. According to this code,
"literature" would be a kind of *agencer,* to invoke a French verb
infinitive that has no equivalent in English.[9] In its current sense, it
means to arrange by combining elements, to organize a set by a
combination of elements. Formerly, however, the verb also meant
to embellish or to adorn, a sense it would have derived from the
medieval Latin use of *genitus* to mean, not just born or engendered,
but well-born. The well-born is that which demands or appeals to
preservation, reproduction, repetition, that is, institution. It is
through this overlay of the genetic code, the measure of division and
reproduction of life, that one has to try to hear the "institution of
literature" in another, altogether *unfamiliar* sense, a sense that has
become effaced or restricted by one of its own most apparently successful inventions: the agent or the subject in whose name(s) the
copyright or patent protecting originality is applied for and issued.
It has become effaced, that is, by the face, that arrangement of elements or features in which the human comes to reproduce, represent,
and recognize itself. Force is instituted as (beauty of) iterable form.[10]

Our "syntactic" analysis of the literary institution suggests why
it should be the case that divisionality gets remarked in the literary
disciplines of the university. The setting up and setting apart of literature *itself* requires that a certain marked relation to an outside, to a
not-itself, be effaced, which we represented by the disappearing quotation marks. Yet this movement of effacement is countered by the
very discipline it installs: the discipline of the *letter* of the text, the
habit of re-marking the specific mode of inscription in a language.

For this discipline, the effacement of the marks of division and difference is itself a mark that can be re-marked.

But all this seems beside the point if indeed literature is being written out of the American university. What does it matter whether it is written out with or without its quotation marks on? Very little, in fact; however, does it follow that what is thereby dispensed with is the catachrestic excess, or reserve of indeterminability, which "literature" has re-marked? For reasons we have already evoked, we cannot hope that to be the case. Despite that, however, perhaps a version of an old dream is discernible in the will to replace the literality of "literature's" name with some other institutional convention.

Let us take as an example one symptom of this de-literalization that will have the advantage of making a connection to our earlier remarks about the ebbing interest in a literary theory marked by foreign influences. If it generally seems to be the case that—to use a very sloppy kind of shorthand that the academic institution not only tolerates but prefers and proliferates—"French theory" has been forced back into some kind of retreat from the shores of humanities and particularly literature departments in the United States, then this retreat has not occurred without leaving behind an offshoot that is usually called simply "theory." "French theory," in other words, may have been put under some kind of general ban, but "theory" without the qualifier has won what, for the moment at least, seems to be a respected place in catalogues of graduate literary studies. This development is no doubt a healthy one if it can be understood as denationalizing a general, theoretical reflection on literary objects and other cultural inscriptions. One could also argue, quite justly, that the "French" qualifier was always a misnomer that disguised the extent to which the production so labeled depended on other traditions of thought, particularly German, for many of its raw materials. Because labels of national origin are merely a shortcut when applied to "products" such as these, there is little reason to regret it when they are abandoned by those who, in theory at least, submit their analyses to stricter standards.

But this sanguine view will have to be supplemented by a rather different evaluation as soon as one looks more closely, as most professors of literature have daily the occasion to do, at some of the actual institutional effects of this renaming or resituating of a specifically theoretical concern within the expanded or exploded field of literary studies. One may remark, for example, that the renaming has permitted the formation of something like a parallel "canon" of works considered indispensable to any understanding or appreciation of this field, a canon that, however it may figure on some list, is now called (just) "theory." I was once shown such a list for a doctoral program in English in which "theory" was one of seven or eight designated options for examination. Of the titles listed, a significant percentage were works originally written in French (as I recall, by Barthes, Derrida, Foucault, Irigaray, Kristeva, Lacan, and Metz) while the remainder of the list was composed exclusively of texts written in English and for the most part American English within the last ten years. Now, this symptomatic artifact would not deserve much attention were it not the case that the doctoral program that produced it (for one should insist that such "texts" are authored, as it were, first of all by the institution itself) is administered solely by an *English* department, that is, by one of the places in which the division of literature in the university continues to designate itself by national origin, national language, or at least a particular language. One immediate consequence of this for our (just) "theory" list is that all the works, no matter how many different languages they may represent in the original (but, in fact, in our example these would be only two: French and English) will be rendered into and read in just one language: English.

If works in translation can be required reading in an English doctoral program in (just) theory, then one implication of this symptom is that, unlike the other divisions or subdivisions of literature (or perhaps we must say of just English), (just) theory can be taught and learned and "canonized" without allowing or accounting for matters of language difference, idiomaticity, cultural and historical specificity, originality of expression, and so forth. This is in itself an interesting development. It points to the persistent tendency to distinguish thought from language, that is, to maintain the very idealist concepts of thought and language that so much of the "theory" in question (notably the work of those "French" writers included—in translation—on our sample list) has sought to displace in various ways. Now, one of the most important or at least most pertinent of these ways is the recourse to "literature" in the materiality of its letter, literature, therefore, as an inscription that resists the idealization of thought that would somehow take place before, beyond, or without language, without its difference and specificity. From this point of view, the symptom we are considering represents a significant retreat from the most acute form of this resistance, a retreat that is all the more difficult to read as such or whose symptom is all the more difficult to diagnose because it occurs in the very place designated by the institution for this "theory"; indeed, it occurs in the name of (just) "theory."

This kind of symptom arises out of the tendency to perform and to maintain a certain idealist reduction of the difference of language or the literality of the letter.[11] One could cite numerous similar superficial symptoms across a whole range of instituted practices of literature.[12] But while we should not ignore such bureaucratized endproducts, their value is at best limited as symptomatic indicators of what is going on at the juncture of "literature" and institution. Fortunately, we do not have to approach that question from scratch because it has received probing and sustained attention in a large number of recent studies. Indeed, these are so numerous as to suggest that one thing that is definitely going on is a preoccupation with what is going on: what is going on with the teaching of "literature"? Or as Poe might have put it: what is the current heresy of "The Didactic"?

We noted above that, for the catachrestic discipline of the letter of "literature," the institutional effacement of marks of division is itself a mark that can be re-marked. It is, therefore, not simply an effacement or not fully effaced; one could say, following Samuel Weber, that such a mark records *ambivalence*. Although Weber relies to a certain extent on Freud for an understanding of this term (it entails, he writes, "not merely the static opposition of conflicting emotions, but rather a constantly shifting dynamic of drive and prohibition"[13]), he finds as well in Kant's Third Critique the traces of that ambivalent institution called the humanities. In an appendix to the Analytic of the Sublime ("On the Methodical Doctrine of Taste"), Kant notes that presumably the humanities are so called "because *humanity* signifies on the one hand the universal *feeling of taking-part* [*Teilnehmungsgefühl*], and on the other, the power of being able to *impart oneself* [*mitteilen*] in the most inward and universal manner; which properties in combination comprise the *sociability* of human beings, by which they distinguish themselves from the limited character of animality" (143). As at once a *participation* in the general social order and an *imparting* of the particular, this sociability is in fact a partiality that, as Weber notes, is only partially effaced in the totalizing concept of "humanity" (for Kant is interested above all in this passage with the feature that can distinguish humanity from animality). Weber then comments:

Kant's invocation of the "humaniora" here serves not so much to reaffirm the traditional notion of the humanities as a socializing force, as to bring to the fore the ambivalent character of such socialization. This can help explain why in recent years the humanistic disciplines have manifested an increasing interest in their institutional status and in institutional issues more generally. Such an interest would not simply be an empirically contingent response to "external" factors. Rather, it would be inscribed in the aporetic project of the humanities as described by Kant: that of *imparting the particular*. Questions involving "the institutionalization of knowledge" reflect the desire to come to terms with the partiality of the project, but they have generally tended to avoid rather than to address the difficulties discussed. (144)

That it should be Kant who is shown to have so precisely named "the aporetic project of the humanities" is likely to encounter a skeptical response among many who have shown "in recent years" the increasing interest in the institutional status of the humanities to which Weber refers. This is because, as Weber doubtless realizes, much of this work has proceeded from a refutation or at least a dismissal of Kant's *Critique of Judgment* and in particular the restrictive conditions Kant places on aesthetic judgment. We will discuss two such efforts in some detail below.[14] Although Weber is clearly unconcerned here to mount such a refutation, neither can we take his analysis as simply a confirming commentary on Kant's thought. Quite pointedly, his point turns around the literality of the text: "If I have rendered *Teilnehmungsgefühl* and *mitteilen* more literally [than J. H. Bernard, who translates the words as "sympathy" and "communication"], as "taking-part" and "imparting," it is in order to render legible what the two German words used by Kant have in common and what I take to be the distinctive feature or 'property' of the humanities as he invokes them here: *partiality*" (143). What the two words have in common is the *Teil* or the share; between them they divide *teilen*, dividing, they parcel out the act of parceling out the particular. It is this partial particular that Kant's text re-marks when it carries over the division of the *teilen* from one sense to the other of humanity's divided meaning. In this fashion it

> calls attention to the conflictuality of a sociality in which the particular can never be entirely transcended, and yet in which it can also never simply persist in its isolated partiality.
>
> The *Third Critique* can thus be read as inscribing the cultivation or culture of the humanities in precisely the place where the partiality of man partakes and imparts itself by a process of self-effacement that is

never entirely successful and that—like Freudian repression, to which it is related in more than one way—always leaves traces. (144)

If we were to presume an addendum to this exemplary reading, it would be merely the particle word "of" so that the first sentence might then situate "the cultivation or culture of the humanities in precisely the place where the partiality of man partakes *of* and imparts itself by a process of self-effacement." This precise place of the "humanities" is thereby named by the self-effacing, dividing syntax that spaces out the -part- not only between part-ake and im-part, but also between the particles, thereby pulling these actions into the self-effacing movement that only partially effaces itself. It is named "humanities" and that name is in the same movement set beneath erasure.

That Kant should have so precisely named the place of the "humanities" perhaps gives us to think in another way about the place to which the Kantian text is assigned by the modern—i.e., *post-Kantian*—tradition of the "humanities." The extent to which Kant continues to lend his name to this place of division between a modern and a classical tradition would point now to that "aporetic project" of reducing a division that continues to divide at the point of the cut.[15] This is also Weber's conclusion, for he attributes the increasing interest in the question of the humanities' institutional status to the aporia in which they are inscribed. He adds, however, that the way this question is approached tends "to avoid rather than to address the difficulties discussed." An aporia is, precisely, a difficulty, that which halts passage or cannot be passed over or passed through. The "humanities" are so difficult because they re-mark and recall the end of the particular, its only partial passage into a general and ideal humanity. As Melville put it, with the great economy of his art: "Ah Bartleby! Ah humanity!" (The name of Melville is here put in reserve, to be drawn upon again in the second division.) At the same time, however, "humanities" would also designate the place where difficulties are more often than not avoided. Such avoidance would be the price—or the prize—of continuing to invoke that name with any assurance as to its generality, rather than partiality.

We will take several partial indications of this difficult passage from the rather vast current literature on "humanities" and institution.

Gerald Graff's widely discussed *Professing Literature: An Institutional History* documents very thoroughly the series of conflicts that have mobilized and divided the teachers of literature in the United States since the final quarter of the last century, the period that he refers to as the early professional era. While many who are heirs to this history may have some notion of its general outline—the demise of classical rhetorical study, the rise of philology and literary history, the implantation of New Criticism, the advent of "theory"—the considerable merit of Graff's study is to fill in this outline by recalling in detail the positions of all the parties to the various conflicts and differentiating them carefully. Basing himself on this research, he is able to undermine quite persuasively the argument according to which various innovations in literary study over the last two decades or so have robbed that discipline of a former unity of purpose. On the contrary, Graff argues, the history with which he is concerned can in no sense be described as the disintegration of a former consensus concerning the general humanistic or cultural value of literature and its study. Rather, the notion that the earliest professional teachers of literature once "had a shared idea of their rationale that had somehow got lost along the way"[16] has functioned like a myth, a myth that remains dear to the most alarmist critics of literary theory. As myth, it dissimulates or denies the conflicts that have never ceased to divide and redivide the ground upon which literary study is instituted.

Graff's demythification leads him in his conclusion to propose certain modifications to the current organization of most academic literary curricula, on the grounds that these curricula tend to perpetuate a dissimulation of the conflicts that have produced them. These proposals have now been sloganized with the catch phrase "teaching the conflicts." Here, in part, is how Graff first advanced the idea:

> That there is no agreement over how the cultural text should be understood, or whether it should come into play at all in the teaching of literature, seems to me an argument for rather than against a more explicitly historicized and cultural kind of literary study that would make such disagreements part of what is studied. The important thing, in any case, is to shift the question from "Whose overview gets to be the big umbrella?" in which form it becomes unanswerable, to "How do we institutionalize the conflict of interpretations and overviews itself?" (258)

Such proposals have indubitably much to recommend them. Without question, students of literature are still too often permitted and even encouraged to believe in the myth of the great consensus. Yet, several features of both his diagnosis and the remedy he prescribes, as formulated in the above passage and elsewhere,[17] could give one pause. To begin with, one might wonder about the posture that, it is implied, stands outside the "conflict of interpretations and overviews" without proposing to adjudicate among them, but merely so as to give them a stage on which to disagree. There is no assurance, of course, that such exteriority to the conflicts has been or can indeed be reached. The good intentions of Professor Graff (which, it goes without saying, are not at all in question here) will not be sufficient in this regard. And if these proposals do not emanate from a transcendent position, then from what partial place *within* the field of conflicting forces could they be issued that would not mark them as part of and party to those conflicts as described?[18] Literary study, Graff argues, has been instituted only at the price of a denial of the conflicts that divide its understanding. On his own analysis, then, must not the vision of institutionalizing "the conflicts of interpretations and overviews itself" participate in this denial even as Graff proposes to overturn it or correct it? Does it not, in other words, put forward a notion of consensual neutrality that masks a conflict of another order? This is to suggest that, despite his denial, Graff is reaching for that device he calls an umbrella, that is, for a position above the fray that takes it all in and merely keeps the playing field dry, if not level, for the participants. In doing so, the movement of demythification ends up reinstalling a new, apparently dehumanized version of the myth it has dismantled.

The principal reason Graff's account cannot prevent this repetition of the error he diagnoses seems to lie in his conception of the institution—i.e., the university—as, precisely, a kind of umbrella. According to this conception, the university as institution is of purely functional design and its principal function is to define a space within which to disagree, among other things, about the meaning and importance of literature. By means of this notion of a neutral frame that is not part of what it frames, Graff draws a limit around this conflictual space and designates, in effect, a point at which the conflict is neutralized, at which partisan discord dissolves into a common ground *without* division. His own discourse strives less to represent this point or this ground (for he knows it is unrepresentable) than to occupy it, to speak for or from that point while claiming his is not just a position among others. Such a positionless position that comprehends all others is, of course, the ground that any discourse will strive to occupy in order to prevail over adversaries and impose itself, not as interpretation but as something like reason itself. But it may be that, if Graff's recommendations sound reasonable, it is because they preserve a certain *interpretation* of the institution and the university as ground of consensus upon which division and dissent are merely staged as in a theater. Such a theater would contain and limit this division; it would put in place an effective barrier to division beyond a certain point of indivisibility. Which is to say that, as one might naturally expect, this interpretation seeks above all to preserve itself from conflict with a contrary notion, such as the one proposed here, according to which any apparent institutional "neutrality" results from the effacement of marks of division. Holding this other notion at bay, Graff's proposal is simply silent about what it could possibly mean to "institutionalize," for example, a practice of literary interpretation that puts in question its own instituted status as well as that of "literature" and that pursues an analysis of institutionalization in general as a process by which such conflict is apparently neutralized or forgotten.

If this forgetting can affect even Graff's far-reaching effort to counteract it, if the division in question cuts across the very attempt to read some of its historical manifestations, then it would seem that it is not strictly containable. And that conclusion can lead us to ask questions other than those Graff wants to entertain here about literary teaching, specifically about what we are doing when we try to envision still a better way to impart a knowledge, rather than forgetfulness, of "literature." That Graff can analyze this amnesia with one hand as he performs it with the other should indicate clearly enough that the divisions he is speaking of are at best superficially described when they are understood principally in terms of disputing schools of thought or interpretations that have in their turn dominated the academic discipline of literature over its brief history. Yet I have suggested that the notion of the institution as a neutral "umbrella" is just such an interpretation, one that would attempt to comprehend all competing or conflicting interpretations and thereby impose itself in the guise of the overview of "reason." This description offers the perspective of the familiar agonistics in which another, similarly comprehensive interpretation would attempt to displace the first, and so forth. It is in effect this essentially static perspective that Graff, on one level, seems to want to escape by framing it or staging it in the terms we have just examined—the wager being, on another level perhaps, that once put on stage and exposed in this fashion, the dead end of such conflicts will become too apparent not to force everyone to seek a new exit and, who knows, maybe even a new consensus. The problem is—and once again we put aside whatever good intentions may motivate this scenario—that it always remains possible to *interpret* the proposed "institutionalization of the conflict of interpretations and overviews itself" *as interpretation,* and therefore *part* of the very conflict it purports to oversee. The stasis is not lifted but reinforced by this turning of the screw of interpretation. Indeed, the principal effect of such "institutionalization" has to be a stabilization because it projects that institution as finally a closed field, held within the circumference of an "umbrella."

Such effects of stabilization and closure are no doubt inevitable. But one should not forget that, in the recent attack on, principally, literary study in the American university, it was this question of the *closure* of the institution—to "nontraditional" ideas, fields, and methods as well as "nontraditional" students—that was at stake. As our brief analysis of Graff's contribution to the rethinking of literary studies can demonstrate, the model of conflicting interpretations, which may take the form of the liberal "marketplace of ideas" or a less ruthless eclectic pluralism, does not *in itself* provide the necessary critical leverage with which to counter effectively the urge to stabilize the university, and in particular literary studies, in a mythical consensus. And this despite Graff's considerable contribution toward debunking that mythical idea. In fact, one has to suspect that what has so alarmed the increasingly strident critics of the university's curricular and other reforms (despite what they say[19]) is not so much the vision of a conflict of interpretations, in which these critics would see traditional interpretations successfully challenged, as an obscurely grasped sense that this stable and stabilizing model is itself being displaced or overrun by something else. That is, something else, something more fundamentally destabilizing and detotalizing, has shown itself to be at work on the very borders of the institution. After all, as Graff has reminded us, the American university literature department, since its inception, has been the scene of constant strife in which "traditional" interpretations and methods of approaching literature have regularly given way to "innovations" without, for all that, breaking down the barriers that contain such debates safely within the bounds of the academic.

Graff's vision of the neutral or neutralizing institution has been— explicitly or implicitly—criticized on wholly different grounds than the ones I have so far discussed here. Since its publication in 1987, *Professing Literature* has been followed by an impressive number of studies that research a similar or parallel set of questions: the institution of literature, literary studies in the university, the discipline of "English," and so forth.[20] One of the most serious and provocative of these studies, John Guillory's *Cultural Capital* relies to a certain extent on Graff's research despite an explicit rejection of the liberal pluralist "umbrella" and a crucially divergent understanding of the institution as site of literary education. For Guillory, that site is anything but a neutral frame or stage; rather it is a central mechanism in the reproduction of class distinction through the preservation of controlled access to what he calls, following Pierre Bourdieu, cultural capital.[21]

Stated in such general terms, this description is neither novel nor particularly controversial, the sociology of academic reproduction having sometimes the sole and dubious merit of confirming the obvious.[22] But Guillory uses these conceptual tools with considerable assurance and to very worthwhile effect in analyzing what is called, in the book's second title, the problem of literary canon formation. In particular, he diagnoses the current debate in the American academy as premised on a false opposition: the distinction of canonical from noncanonical works, as these terms are commonly used, disguises the fact that both qualify subsets of a form of cultural capital that Guillory designates as "traditional," by which he means in this case a textual tradition maintained by the schooled practices of reading and writing certain languages as preserved or exemplified in textual models. But this form is traditional also in the sense that it is the cultural capital of a former dominant class, one whose distinction was to a considerable extent measured by its appropriation of textual and historical literacy. That this is no longer the case, that a "professional-managerial" class has acquired social and economic dominance over the traditional cultural elite indicates a "more historically significant split" (45) than the division between canonical and noncanonical: it is the split between two kinds of cultural capital, the textual tradition, which has lost most of its exchange value, and technical, scientific, or professional knowledge, which Guillory describes as "organic to the constitution of the professional-managerial class."[23] Hence the general "'capital flight'" from the humanities, the decline of its "market value," a condition that is addressed only symptomatically and in a displaced fashion when literary scholars concern themselves so single-mindedly and myopically with the problem of the canon's representativity. That this latter concern has come to absorb with such insistence the "progressive" political investments of teachers in literature departments is likewise a symptom of this displacement, representation in the "canon" serving as virtual alibi for political representation. The argument here (pp. 6ff.) is cogent and incisive, as Guillory shows how the alibi functions within what he calls "the field of 'imaginary' politics" (6). The point is not, he insists, that "imaginary" politics is *unreal,* but that it remains a politics that banks on "a hypothetical *image* of social diversity, a kind of mirror in which social groups either see themselves, or do not see themselves, reflected" (ibid.).[24] All the same, it is quite clear that for Guillory the *real* and overriding political question of the university is elsewhere and must be posed otherwise: if we are "to recognize the *real* relation between the humanities curriculum and the social forces which operate on it," then we "will have to raise the much larger question of what is at stake in the relation between the kinds of cultural capital" (445; emphasis added).

Now, what about this "much larger question"? Not surprisingly, Guillory has little to say specifically about "what is at stake in the relation between the kinds of cultural capital." This is not surprising because these stakes are in fact presumed to be evident in the very manner in which the stated relation is posed: at stake is the gradual liquidation through devaluation of "traditional" cultural capital. This eventuality follows from the identification of the split between two unequal or incommensurate forms that are related to each other only as heterogeneous concretions of the abstraction called cultural capital. (Guillory speaks, for example, of "the heterogeneous constitution of cultural capital" [47].) In other words, "the much larger question" is formulated in terms of a supposed heterogeneity in kind, which itself is not in question. From there to casting the heterogeneity in terms of an opposition, and the grounds of a political struggle, the step seems virtually automatic, to go without saying. The oppositional configuration leaves the analyst of "the real relation between the humanities curriculum and the social forces which operate on it" little option but to reassert the integrity of the so-named humanities curriculum. This Guillory does forcefully although somewhat enigmatically when he figures a certain taking back: "It is perhaps time for progressive teachers to take back the humanities curriculum—all of it—as an integrated program of study" (50); "Were the left/liberal academy to reappropriate the 'humanities,' that is, to take back the authority to define the cultural capital embodied in its curriculum of study, it would have to devise a rationale for an integrated curriculum of textual/historical study exceeding the laudable objective of affirming cultural diversity" (54). Is this to suggest that, despite the heterogeneity of the "traditional" humanities and the techno-scientific, professional-managerial curriculum, the former has somehow been expropriated by the latter? What exactly is one being urged to "take back" and from whom?

These questions have to wait for answers until the final pages of the book, in a chapter devoted to the "discourse of value." The expropriation in question would have been perpetrated at the beginning of the last century, in the hijacking of aesthetic judgment by the analogy to exchange value and thus to the logic of marketplace economics. The discipline or formalized discourse of aesthetics, as a result, became saturated by the misplaced notion of value, a condition that is to be seen chiefly in the confusion of aesthetic judgment with value judgment. In its latest avatar, this confusion or reduction accounts for the impasse currently experienced by advocates of curricular politics via the "representative" canon: aesthetic judgment, so long as it is thought in terms of value, remains tied to the values of a dominant class that only masquerade as universal. Accordingly, aesthetic judgment is found to be irredeemable as a tool of progressive political engagement in the university, and specifically for that part of the university that, formerly at least, defined and was defined by the humanities curriculum.

But it is precisely aesthetic judgment that, in Guillory's view, must be "taken back" by untying it from the discourse of value and by liberating it from its enclosure within a "pedagogic imaginary" where imagined totalities, called "communities," perform value judgments based independently on the defining characteristics of each community. The penultimate sentence of the book speaks of "an aestheticism unbound," by which is meant principally a generalization of aesthetic experience or pleasure, its unrestricted recognition as an autonomous category of existence. But such a generalization or unbinding also implies, therefore, that what counts as aesthetic experience (for producers no less than consumers) be "unbound" from those laws of the market that restrict access to cultural goods. Referring to Bourdieu's defense of the autonomy of intellectual and artistic production, which relies solely on "specifically symbolic distinctions," Guillory comments:

> The idea of production for the producers (which by definition entails *consumption* by the producers) projects onto a utopian screen the disarticulation of cultural capital from the system of class formation, and thus from "distinction" based on inequality of access to cultural goods. Bourdieu calls this condition "total autonomy from the laws of the market." Such a condition does not, however, prophesy the disappearance of cultural capital. The universalization of restricted production would rather transform cultural capital into pure "symbolic distinction." The cultural capital embodied in cultural products would then be judged (and also contested) on aesthetic grounds, as the products already are, but not on the basis of their inaccessibility, the restriction of access guaranteed by the educational system. . . . But social distinctions reinstated on such an aesthetic basis would have to be expressed in social relations as distinc-

tions in "lifestyle," in other words as a vast enlargement of the field of aesthetic judgment. (339)

To do justice to these assertions, it must be pointed out that Guillory here has claimed for them the relative immunity of what he calls, with pointed irony, a "thought experiment," one he has modeled on Marx and Engels's evocation, in *The German Ideology,* of communist society, which would put an end to the "exclusive concentration of artistic talent in particular individuals, and its suppression in the broad mass which is bound up with this." But because the immunity claimed here can only be relative, the reader of these lines is left to wonder about how to reconcile their vision of " 'total autonomy' " and "pure 'symbolic distinction' " for aesthetic judgment from an assertion made only three pages before, namely: "There is no realm of pure aesthetic experience, or object which elicits nothing but that experience. But I shall nevertheless argue that the *specificity* of aesthetic experience is not contingent upon its 'purity' " (336). Is this apparent contradiction resolved if we understand that in this latter instance, Guillory is explicitly setting aside the Kantian description of the pure judgment of taste, pure, that is, of any interest in the actual existence of the object and thereby pure as well of any sensuous pleasure? In the previous quotation, on the other hand, autonomy and purity are understood with regard to the hierarchies established by a market that restricts access to cultural products and contaminates aesthetic judgment with judgments of relative exchange value. Guillory himself, who is unlikely to have intended a simple contradiction, would perhaps underscore this point and maintain that between the two kinds of purity, the one he rejects and the one he endorses, there is a clear distinction without contamination of the one in the other. And perhaps he would reiterate that the argument is, after all, not about the purity of aesthetic experience; it is rather about its *specificity,* as his text emphasizes.

Yet what is the difference that is implicitly being invoked here? Can one deduce the specificity of an "experience" without, at some point, referring to a quality or aspect that characterizes that kind of experience and no other? In other words, to an essential trait that can be distinguished in its *purity* from every other trait of the same experience? In epistemological terms, the "specific" concerns a species and its specific difference from other species; it is said of that which has a nature proper to it. The condition of continuing to speak of the specificity of "aesthetic experience," therefore, is that a certain touchstone of purity or property remain available to conceptual language. The fact that Guillory, on the example of Bourdieu, rejects the purity of the aesthetic as Kant conceives it, the fact that Kant's aesthetic judgment is seen to be contaminated by class distinction and ultimately the cultural marketplace when it should remain totally autonomous of such forces, these facts do not override the condition under which Guillory continues to invoke *specific* aesthetic experience, be it thoroughly unbound or generalized: the condition of a certain purity, which in his text surfaces in the form, however utopic or only dreamed-of, of noncontamination by the laws of the market.

In Guillory's analysis, therefore, the specificity of the aesthetic persists and can continue to be identified regardless of the inmixture of all sorts of other pleasures, sensations, or calculations ("There is no realm of pure aesthetic experience"). Why, then, would the contamination by the laws of the market, with the pleasures and calculations one may suppose specific to it, threaten aesthetic specificity any more than some other "impurity," for example, in Bourdieu's words, the "bracketing of form in favor of 'human' content, which is barbarism par excellence from the standpoint of the pure [i.e., Kantian] aesthetic" (334)? If indeed there is no contradiction here, despite appearances, then it would seem to be because the *specificity* of the aesthetic is not at all at stake in the invocation of "total autonomy from the laws of the market" or "pure 'symbolic' distinction"; what is at stake is the availability of the aesthetic as a *politically* pure, or purged, category which can be "taken back" or reclaimed as the grounding specificity of the humanities curriculum. For recall that we earlier followed Guillory up to the point where, having opposed the two forms of cultural capital, he then argues for the integrity of the humanities, although one must await the "thought experiment" of the final pages before this integrity, or specificity, is given its rationale in the form of the reclaimed and rehabilitated aesthetic experience.

It is thus in these final pages devoted to the "thought experiment" that *Cultural Capital* fulfills the promise made in the preface to reimagine "the relation between the cultural and the economic in social life." The word is well chosen for the relation as reimagined is finally that of an imaginary specificity *without relation* of the aesthetic. The promise is thus less fulfilled by the thought experiment than relaunched as the promise of a specificity without relation: an experience of the "purely symbolic" aesthetic. To put it in the terms of the current university institution as described by Guillory, it is the promise of a reclaimed, integral humanities curriculum able to pose itself and present itself without relation to, without division by the technical training required by the "professional-managerial class." It is because "theory," as Guillory defines it,[25] failed to "reimagine" such a without-relation that its chapter is now closed in the American institution of literary studies. Guillory argues that de Manian deconstruction was an "unconscious" attempt to reposition or reauthorize literary studies in the new technobureaucratic organization of the university, an institution that increasingly reflects the hegemony of a new class: "technical/managerial specialists." "Theory," he writes, performs a "transformation of the work of reading into an *unconscious mimesis* of the form of bureaucratic labor" (257). What is unconscious or symptomatic is not the set of "technical" concepts or, as he writes, the "transforming of reading into a rigorously iterable *technical* procedure." No, it is rather that in so doing, "theory" did not recognize its reproduction or "mimesis" of the emerging interests of a new class that had redrawn the lines of force in the university. The implication throughout is that this unconscious mimesis constitutes, in effect, a capitulation to and consolidation of those interests, thereby advancing rather than resisting the erosion of the intellectual or professional autonomy of the literary curriculum. "If deconstruction," he writes, "no longer establishes the terms by which certain texts, of whatever provenance, can be integrated into the corpus of literary theory, that is preeminently because it no longer offers to the pedagogic imaginary a resolution to the problem of professional autonomy" (256).

According to Guillory, then, deconstruction failed to keep the promise to deliver a relation of no-relation, that "total autonomy from the laws of the market" without which the humanities curriculum is squeezed into obsolescence between its traditional and henceforth indefensible "humanist" rationale, on the one hand, and the "hegemonic rationality" of techno-marketocracy, on the other. But in fact the case of deconstruction is even worse than Guillory allows: it actually rescinded the promise of aesthetic specificity when it proceeded to deconstruct the very idea of that idea, the property of the concept of the no-relation. Deconstructive thought (to which we give a much larger extension than Guillory would allow) has, from the beginning and without reprieve, insisted on the *technicity* of the idea, on the iterability of the "proper," on the divisibility of any mark of division, and therefore on the necessary contamination of any posed or supposed purity. The very possibility of deconstruction comes down to the fact that, as Jean-Luc Nancy reminds us, the no-relation can never be posed in its absolute purity. One of the most consistently and insistently invoked "no-relations," indeed the one that could be said to inaugurate philosophy in the West, is the no-relation to the technical or the iterable. From the beginning and relentlessly, deconstructive thought has insisted that conceptual oppositions that situate the technical or the iterable as simply exterior or without relation to some other term (the natural, the human, the social, the cultural, the aesthetic, etc.) are all deconstructible. By which is meant not only are they deconstructible by some "thought experiment" or "in theory" but they are always, practically, in deconstruction. They are in deconstruction in their very institution. There is no institution of any sort, and first of all no institution of meaningful signs, and of course no "literature" and no "cultural" without iterability. Iterability is what we mean by institution and the reason we can mean anything at all. Not only, then, has deconstructive thought never promised an aesthetic or literary or humanistic, that is, *nontechnical* specificity in the name of which to "take back" the traditional disciplines of the humanities, it has explicitly and constantly urged a rethinking of all the oppositions structuring the metaphysical or idealist apprehension of the technical as the "other" of the properly human (or social or aesthetic, etc.).[26]

For these reasons, then, the thesis of two, heterogeneous kinds of "cultural capital" cannot provide the starting point for the necessary reconceptualization Guillory indicates and calls for: "the urgent need to reconceptualize the object of literary study" (265). If, as Guillory well knows, that "object" has never had the character of a simple "thereness," if the iterable character of the written mark both suspends "thereness" and divides whatever limiting trait is supposed to set off this "object" from nonliterary or technical objects, then this rethinking cannot begin by bracketing the very condition without which "cultural capital" of any sort could not even be accumulated, stored, retrieved, repeated, reproduced, transmitted, inherited, taught, appropriated, or transformed.

This is not an argument merely about the technologization of systems of "communication," although certainly these cannot be overlooked if one is serious today about rethinking the "object of literary study." Rather, the more fundamental point concerns whether or not we give ourselves the means to think a transformative capacity of the "literary" in relation precisely to its institution and to the various modes of its appropriation as "capital" or as "culture." But that of course is not all, since the "literary" here names only provisionally (in a historically determined fashion) the transformation in question, one to which all instituted meanings are subject. And yet, at least in the academic context, a certain privilege or exemplarity attaches to that name for the rethinking that is being called for. This is doubtless partially because a significant part of this task requires exploring, as Samuel Weber puts it, "the relation between the reading and writing of texts and the operations of the institution." Nevertheless, to focus upon the discipline of literary studies, he continues, is to acknowledge a

> limitation [that] is more a part of the *problem* addressed than of its solution. The fact that, in the English-speaking world at least, the question of representation . . . has been articulated most extensively within the disciplines of literary studies is an example of that institutional constraint without which nothing is possible, but which also tends to assimilate the practices it permits and to absorb their transformative potential.[27]

By "institutional constraint" here Weber understands the imposition of clear and exclusionary boundaries by means of which an iteration of meaning, and thus a cognition, is possible.[28] Concerning the institution that is the modern university, defined by the separation and specialization of "disciplines," the constraint is in fact twofold: intramurally, it constrains the distinction, or even the opposition, of disciplinary domains, such as, for example, the domain of "humanities" or literary studies and the domain of the so-called technical disciplines; extramurally, however, the constraint operates between the academic institution and all others over against which it may be articulated as a cognizable entity. Taken together, these limiting and dividing functions work to absorb, as Weber puts it, the transformative potential of the practices they also permit and institute.

Here we would add that the point of setting the focus of theoretical inquiry on the relation between textual operations and the operations of institutions would be to formalize, *as far as possible,* the conditions in which the transformation—or deconstruction—of institutional constraints cannot itself be contained or "absorbed." That such theorization or formalization has found its greatest (although clearly limited) welcome in American university departments of literature has, to be sure, been interpreted in many fashions, including as a symptom of the conditions detected by Guillory. Such interpretations, however, risk misrepresenting their object if they do not also acknowledge that this formalization must repeatedly encounter and remark the limit of a certain nontheorizability. It is at this limit that what is called deconstruction happens or can happen. And because the limit in question takes shape necessarily as an instituted meaning, deconstructive thought has proceeded as the thinking of the limits of institutions, not only, but also the institutions in which it has itself assumed a certain currency or meaning: university departments or universities in general. It is entirely valid, of course, to acknowledge and even to underscore the ways in which deconstructive thought has been internalized by the institution of the university: courses are taught under that name, books are published on deconstruction by university presses that have been written by professors employed by universities, and so forth. Guillory, however, has mistakenly understood that deconstruction's critique of the institution *at its limits* had to mean that such thinking was somehow simply *against* institutions as such, therefore in a relation of disavowal to its own instituted status.[29] This serious (and contradictory) misapprehension betrays an unworkable concept of institution as a self-defined and self-limiting space of inclusion/exclusion. What it cannot account for is the transforming destabilization of such a structure, and what it leaves blank is the relation of institutionality to the trace of its difference from itself. This trace, however, continues to mark institutional space along its positioning limits as the divisibility of the outside/inside configuration. Unless one is willing to accept without question the tendency of the institution, in Samuel Weber's phrase once again, "to assimilate the practices it permits and to absorb their transformative potential," then one must acknowledge the possibility of a certain exteriority, or difference, within institutional space. Authorized or legitimated by the institution, deconstruction would be one of the names for a place from which such divisibility is indicated or thought. But it would also name a certain passage beyond the pertinence of assigning a location simply within or without legitimating structures to the thinking of their limits. To understand, therefore, something of the institutionalization of deconstruction in American universities, one cannot begin by discounting this deconstructive critique of institution. In particular, the appropriation of deconstruction by departments of literary studies must in part be explained by the unsettled relation literature maintains to its own institution, by the fact that the "object" of literary study does not take form only in a present relation or a relation to the present but in its historicality opens onto a future that cannot be made to stand before us.

In almost precise counterpoint to the principal arguments of *Cultural Capital,* Tony Bennett's *Outside Literature* is concerned, as the title of one chapter puts it, with "severing the aesthetic connection." It is a connection, Bennett insists, that has haunted Marxist literary analysis ever since Lukács tried to cement it in place using the sparse references found in the Marxian text. One of the aims of the (post-) Marxist thought to which Bennett subscribes is to tear down once and for all this flimsy construction of a Marxist aesthetic, so as to get on with the new tasks assigned to (post-) Marxist literary studies. We will say something in a moment about these new tasks. But already we may ask in what sense such a project can call itself "*post*-Marxist." To be sure, Bennett's thinking through of the necessary severance is carried forward by a running critique of the Lukácsian inheritance in such prominent Marxist thinkers as Althusser, Terry Eagleton, and Fredric Jameson, as well as other "progressive" critics like Frank Lentricchia or Edward Said. In the process, he offers a careful elucidation of the generally confused distinctions made by these critics and others among the three key notions of aesthetics (or literature), ideology, and science. But this generally meticulous critique can never overcome the essential ambiguity of what it is doing, for the step beyond Marxist analysis into the era of "post-Marxism" consistently resembles an operation to salvage the principles of that analysis from a contaminating influence. The contamination is traced to "aesthetics" and, especially, to—whom else?—Kant. Post-Marxism is finally indistinguishable from a better Marxism, one from which the ghost of Kant has been definitively expelled.

By "aesthetic discourse," Bennett understands an essentially narcissistic device, "a means for the individual's valuation of self as both subject of discernment and ultimate valued object."[30] The device relies on an intradiscursive circularity in order to posit the subject of aesthetic judgment as universal:

> an analysis of the constitution of the subject, whether this be conceived as self-wrought or culturally produced, provides the justification for the view that aesthetic judgment is, ought to be or one day will be universal just as this, in turn, supports the contention that there is a distinctive aesthetic mode of the subject's appropriation of reality. This circularity is an inherent property of aesthetic discourse. Susceptible to neither logical nor empirical demonstration, the existence of a distinctive aesthetic faculty is always ultimately sustained, but entirely intradiscursively, by the projection of a set of conditions in which the subject of value can be represented as universal. (150–51)[31]

Marxist aesthetic discourse would be no less guilty of this circular structure than other avatars, according to Bennett. As proof that the aesthetic connection has not yet been (but should be) severed in contemporary Marxist or para-Marxist discourse about literature in particular, Bennett cites the persistent manner in which that discourse appeals to the study of literature as a technique of subject formation. In a very general sense, the whole project of *Outside Literature* could be described as an attempt to survey the grounds on which one might affirm a study of literature and its history that would not be a subject formation technique. Because aesthetic discourse may well provide one of the most powerful and comprehensive justifications for the continued deployment of such techniques, Bennett, unlike Guillory, concludes that there is nothing to be gained and much to be lost by prolonging the search in that direction.

Perhaps, however, there is an unexamined *assumption* driving one to this conclusion. But to examine it, one needs to keep Kant's text open to the page where a warning is issued about, precisely, assuming too much when it comes to the subject of judgment. As we will see, the warning is sounded at the very point *before* a circle closes on that narcissistic "appropriation of reality" to which Bennett refers. When, therefore, this circular structure is traced back to Kant, as it is here or elsewhere, for example in Barbara Herrnstein Smith's analysis of the "axiological logic" of aesthetic judgment,[32] a collapse occurs that closes the subject up with a faulty assumption of its judgment *as* its own. This faulty assumption can also be described as a fiction, that is, as an act of referring to that which has never had any effective, real, or actual referent.[33] For that reason, at least, this moment suggests that the study of the kind of fictional practice called literature, if it would not be yet another technique of subject formation, still has a lot to learn from the Kantian analysis.

As Bennett rightly recalls, Kant's aim in the Third Critique is to establish the boundaries and operations of a faculty of judgment in general. Consequently, the interest shown there in the judgment of aesthetic objects is strictly limited and preliminary to staking out the possibility of the good exercise of judgment, particularly in the realm of what Kant calls practical reason, the realm of freedom, desire, duty, ethics, politics, and so forth. Aesthetic judgment would constitute a kind of test or limit case, where one may study the form of the pure judgment of taste, which is to say, where one may judge judgment itself in its purity. To judge judgment itself: this necessary pleonasm already introduces what is going to interest Kant in aesthetic judgment: a certain reflexivity or reflection of judgment upon itself, precisely what Kant himself is involved in doing in the Critique.

In the introduction Kant makes a famous distinction between two kinds of judgment: determinant and reflective judgment. They are distinguished as follows:

Judgment in general is the faculty of thinking the particular as contained under the universal. If the universal (the rule, the principle, the law) be given, the judgment which subsumes the particular under it . . . is *determinant*. But if only the particular be given for which the universal has to be found, the judgment is merely *reflective*.[34]

Now, in aesthetic judgment, that is, in the judgment of the beautiful, there is no universal rule, principle, or law given in advance. Such judgment, in other words, does not judge by means of a concept of the beautiful, but always in each case is given only the particular. It is therefore not determined (by a concept or a priori) but rather must reflect its own condition for judging the singular or particular object beautiful or not. It reflects its condition for judging when, in effect, it posits a transcendental position of understanding as a *pure fiction* so as to permit its own judgment through a kind of projected identification with this position.

As universal laws of nature have their ground in our understanding, which prescribes them to nature (although only according to the universal concept of it as nature), so particular empirical laws, in respect of what is in them left undetermined by these universal laws, must be considered in accordance with such a unity *as they would have if* an understanding (*although not our understanding*) had furnished them to our cognitive faculties, so as to make possible a system of experience according to particular laws of nature. *Not as if, in this way, such an understanding must be assumed as actual* [*Nicht als wenn auf diese Art wirklich ein solcher Verstand angenommen werden müsste*] (for it is only our reflective judgment to which this idea serves as a principle—for reflecting, not for determining); but this faculty thus gives a law only to itself, and not to nature. (16–17; emphases added)

The "as if" (*als wenn*) installs the transcendental position of understanding through which reflective judgment passes in its movement away from and back toward human understanding. This movement away and back, however, pivots in a mirrored reflection that, Kant insists, must not be assumed to be "actual" or *wirklich*, which could also be translated as effective, real, true, substantial. This warning about assuming the reality or substantiality of what is a mere reflection echoes back to the reminder inserted parenthetically in the preceding sentence: "such a unity as they would have if an understanding (although not our understanding) . . ." Kant is not saying exactly the same thing with each of these cautionary notes, but one may detect nevertheless a connection between them and a reason, therefore, to be doubly on guard in the proximity of reflective judgment. First, we must recall that it is not *our* understanding that is positioned as the furnishing source of a presumed unity. As Samuel Weber restates it: "In short, we treat the singularities *we* do not understand as though they were the products of *another* understanding, like our own and yet unlike it (for it has produced precisely what we do not understand)" (150). The risk here, which calls up Kant's parenthesis, is that the reflective operation will collapse the interval or the difference that holds apart "like" and "unlike," our understanding and "not our understanding." Second, this risk of collapse is then refigured as the risk of assuming the reality of this other understanding, which triggers Kant's second warning: "Not as if in this way, such an understanding must be assumed as actual." The actuality, reality, or substantiality one is being warned not to assume (*annehmen,* that is, take on) would be that of *our own* understanding, which only becomes fully *our own,* fully real or actual when it erases the interval of "not-our-understanding." To put it another way: The mistake of assuming the actuality of a transcendental understanding is realized or carried out in the form of the subject's appropriation of understanding to itself and no other.

It is certainly possible to show that this moment is in considerable tension or contradiction with other strands, perhaps even the dominant strands of Kant's analysis of judgment. But the fact remains that several current readings of the notion of the transcendental subject or of the subjective universal (Guillory's, Bennett's or Herrnstein Smith's), because they neglect altogether the problematic of reflective judgment, mistake what is opened up there through the fictional device of pure reflection. They tend therefore to read Kant as invoking a substantive understanding, *our own,* which would define a unified ground of historical action, even if they also insist that this is an ideological construct par excellence. Such a substantialization does what Kant explicitly warns we must not do: it assumes the reality or actuality of the unity of an understanding that is but the effect of the fold of reflection passing through the other's appearance. For that is indeed what is happening here: some unknown other appears, singular, without concept, undeterminable by the laws already given to *our* understanding. It is all a question then, as Jean-François Lyotard puts it, of *knowing* how to judge,[35] and therefore of knowing what one cannot know without concept. According to Kant, it is then that judgment must give itself a law, but it can do so only by passing through the other in a fiction of reflection.

Bennett quite explicitly disregards this fictional moment.

> Aesthetic discourse is ideological in the Althusserian sense that it func-
> tions as a discourse producing subjects. The universal valuing subject
> (man) it constructs interpellates the reader into the position of a valuing
> subject who is defined, in relation to the valued object (man), *within a*
> *mirror structure of self-recognition.* Yes, indeed, man is manifested in this
> object; yes, indeed, I recognise myself in it; isn't it/aren't I
> wonderful?—such is the effect of aesthetic discourse for the subject who
> takes up the position it offers. (165; emphasis added)

Such is the effect, however, only if and when one forgets to take
account of the "as if" by which the singular appearance of the other
is *assumed* to reflect the self, or the subject. There would be a different
effect, an effect of difference, if, instead, one drew all the possible
consequences from the suspension of that reflection between the
known and the unknown, the self and an other, the like and
the unlike, the determined concept of a unity and, in Kant's terms,
the "multiplicity of partial representations in its free employment,"
which is such "that for it no expression marking a definite concept
can be found" (160). This effect of difference in the suspended interval of the fiction would give another sense or would call differently
than that interpellation into the position of subject, which is all that
Bennett hears. Rather than a master technique of subject formation,
there is a deconstruction of precisely the pivot on which such techniques turn.

Here, then, is where we would situate the "object" taken up by a
study of "literature" that is not wholly assimilable to the ideological
constructs Bennett identifies with aesthetic discourse. That object is
a misnomer, a catachresis, "literature" as the name of the unnameable. As Samuel Weber has pointed out, in the passage just cited
Kant goes on to specify that those representations we call aesthetical
ideas engage the act of naming—or not—in language. And it is because the "ideas" remain rigorously "unnameable" (in the common,
denominative language of understanding) that the study of the unnameable (the catachresis "literature") "has also become an area in
which the question of institutionalization is increasingly discussed.
For that question is . . . another way of exploring the processes
and mechanisms by which a certain degree of unity—of names or
terms—is imparted to that 'multiplicity of partial representations'
which Kant described as characteristic of the aesthetic idea" (151).

Now, Bennett might very well point out that such "exploring
. . . of processes and mechanisms" appears to leave altogether open,

undetermined, the *political* direction or sense one gives to that activity. This is his principal reason for eliminating deconstructive practices from his search for a new grounds, other than subject formation, on which to affirm the study of literature. Responding not to Weber but to an essay by Derek Attridge, Bennett spells out his "differences" with the essay's argument:

> These concern, in the main, the exclusively oppositional, critical role Attridge envisages for the histories he favours—undermining existing truths but not establishing new ones in their places; resisting closures in the name of an indefinite openness. The disadvantage of this exclusively contestatory conception of history is that, while opening up new potential areas of practice, it does not offer the prospect of any positive knowledge which may be of service in relation to those practices. . . . Diachronised word-play is not a sufficient condition for the production of historical truths: that is, for the emergence of positive knowledges (which need not be thought of as absolute or transcendent) capable of serving as a basis for definite courses of action within the present. . . . Keeping the past open in the cause of keeping present political possibilities open and fluid serves every politics in principle but none in practice. (277–78; 281)

Bennett's call for the "production of historical truths" and for "positive knowledges" on which to base "definite courses of action within the present" takes this most unequivocal direction in the final pages of the book, although all that precedes has in fact been pulling in that sense. It is, without question, the sense of history, in both senses of the word sense. To make sense of history and to give history a sense of direction: that is the task Bennett assigns to literary studies, which is thereby made into a branch, a sub-station of the historian's discipline. This is, of course, anything but a new task, even if Bennett attempts to redraw the bounds of the historical literary object by figuring it as the set of institutions making up a specific form of sociality. In its principal gesture, however, Bennett's *turn* to "the procedures of historical scholarship" and to the historian's "regime of truth" is a *return* to what may be the oldest legitimating guise in which literary study assumed a position in the modern university.

But, in itself, the fact that it is not at all "new" is hardly the problem, although it does suggest that Bennett has opted for, in his own terms, "rules of formation" rather than "rules of *transformation*." This he does when he takes on Foucault's notion of being " 'in the truth'—not the truth in general, but particular truths, truths which exist not forever 'but only in time and *for* a time' " (279).[36] This is indeed, or should be, the historian's regime of truth, or rather, of "particular truths." The latter phrase echoes that "multiplicity of partial representations," which, as we saw, Kant assigned to "aesthetical ideas." The difference is that the partiality or particularity that concerns Bennett's historian is measured in terms of the general totality of time. Whereas the particularities that concern Kant's reflective judgment are not specified in terms of a *particular time*. This difference of particularities is the one that Bennett is working hardest to reduce. The reduction is carried out when he transfers to the literary object the particular time of the historian's object, which is always a past time. This transfer is meant to counter or reverse what he sees as the other, "post-structuralist" transfer, one that amounts to "a transference to the past of literature's own object and procedures. It is a literarisation of the past which must be judged as an attempt to extend the sway of literature's own regime of truth into that of history" (280). Rather than such a "literarisation of the past," then, Bennett would operate a reversal, as in a mirror: the historicization, or rather the *making-past* of the literary. The objects with which the literary scholar, like the historical scholar, should be concerned are those "particular truths" that exist only in a *particular* time and for a *particular* time, a time past.

The gesture we have just described would substitute reflective judgment for determinant judgment by subsuming the literary to a concept. This is the condition for the emergence of any positive knowledge. Kant would certainly have agreed, although he would have also pointed out that such a positive knowledge, determined by concepts, does not yet constitute what Bennett calls "a basis for definite courses of action within the present." The realm of knowledge and the realm of action are very precisely the realms Kant assigns, respectively, to pure reason and to practical reason, the objects of the First and the Second critiques. But pure reason, which discovers laws in the realm of understanding, cannot give the law to practical reason, which must discover the laws of moral action. This lack of a direct line of communication between understanding and freedom is the famous gulf Kant describes in the Introduction to the Third Critique, a gulf that judgment is supposed to bridge. For "we may also suppose that the judgment will bring about a transition from the pure faculty of knowledge, the realm of natural concepts, to the realm of the concept of freedom" (15). The transition is effected when the fiction of reflective judgment is no longer suspended or sustained but reduced and replaced by the concept (positive knowledge) that will allow a determinant judgment. This can happen only by determining as truth or concept the catachrestic name given to the other's singular appearance. In other words, it can only happen in the reduction of the space of that appearance, which is figured by a certain fiction. Bennett knows this, and that is why he determines "literature" as a particular historical truth. The alternative he glimpses in the mirror reflects what he calls "literary conceptions of literature," which are precisely not "conceptions" but the space in which something *appears to fold back* on itself. It is this fold of appearance that Bennett would arrest "in time and for a time" with the concept of historical truth, the truth of a *past* appearance. Little is to be gained, he writes, "from granting [literary conceptions of literature] an extended sphere of operation such that all documents fall within their compass. Textualising the past in such a way that it can be rendered permanently undecidable serves little purpose" (280–81).

That Bennett can be so confident of how to count up historical gains and losses, or how to measure great and little purposes, suggests at the very least that his post-Marxism retains a fairly firm foothold in a totalizing, teleologizing narrative of history. And it would be this narrative that he wants to protect by reversing, once again as if in a mirror, the extension of the "sphere of operation" granted "literary conceptions of literature." What does it mean to "reverse an extension" in this case? It means to limit the extension, by means of a certain concept of historical time, to the one time and place of the past in which the textual *document* appeared. It means, therefore as well, to disallow that extension, beyond the point of so-called historical appearance, whereby what has once appeared can continue to appear in its singular difference without concept. An undecidable past, writes Bennett, "serves little purpose," by which we understand: for the present, for the time of the present. But it would be precisely such an "extension" of past into present—and beyond—that is strictly contained by the decision to limit the "literary" to the past of its appearance.

That the "literary" remains a stage for the appearance of what does not present itself without difference from itself at any decidably present moment (past or present): this is the condition of any practice with literary texts, even the most "historicized" ones, but it is a condition that literary study, in the age of its institutionalization, does not easily acknowledge. It does not easily acknowledge, that is, a *historicality* of "literature," without which there could be no history of literature, but which is not reducible to a set of historical truths, however provisional. The difficulty is that, in its unpresentable difference from any present, historicality suspends the very possibility of the institutions of knowledge. Here "to suspend" does not mean simply to render "permanently undecidable," as Bennett warns. It also has the sense of suspending a disappearance, holding it in reserve, re-presenting that which is not altogether past and gone, repeating the traces of something that appears once more. The suspended possibility of institutions would also mean, therefore, that which presents their possibility, suspends them before our encounter—as if in a mirror.

This suspension comes to be figured here by what we called above a fictional threshold between "history" and "literature," which divides the pages that follow. Division One isolates a very limited number of moments from the vast store of texts written in the last century on the questions of the university, teaching, literature, and language difference. They are fragments less of a history of literary studies in the modern university than of a history of the modern university as seen across the division of literature. These texts are frequently marginal, both in the sense that they have not earned a place at the center of a literary, critical, or philosophical tradition and in the sense of their relation to the institutions they put in question. Perhaps they are marginal in a third sense as well, the sense that may appear when the preoccupation with a European (and predominantly French) past is juxtaposed with certain current concerns of literary studies in the United States. Despite this appearance, however, it is these latter concerns that have consistently determined or motivated the analyses undertaken here. If this is not already clear, then the concluding chapter of Division One will attempt to justify this claim further.

Division Two brings to the fore less an institutional formation, which may be the object of a possible history, than that unstabilized or noninstitutable excess of "literature" we called above a catachresis. The history of literature in the institution must not be mistaken for a history of this catachresis, whose time is always yet to come, which continues to arrive from an unknowable future. To illustrate: Melville's *Confidence-Man,* one of the most troubling works in the American canon. Academic criticism of this work has regularly avoided confronting the implications it bears that any possible meaning depends on the reader's act, which the text describes as the act of extending confidence or credit. And if this dynamic may be described as "properly" literary, then it is also the very property that prevents literature from assuming form as a stable object of study. For, beyond its historical reference and interest, the literary work engages the dimension of a future to which it applies for credit or meaning and as such it resituates every present, instituted meaning in the context of a possible transformation. Despite the fact, therefore, that academic literary studies has largely misrecognized this dimension of literature, the latter will nevertheless have been at work deconstructing its own institution.

This, then, is not an institutional history of literature, which is to say it is not a history of literature *in* the university. On the contrary, it is an attempt to glimpse how that history will have itself been inscribed within "literature" understood as a transformational relation to the future. Which is why the structuring threshold inscribed here is a fiction. Although that fiction is installed with the establishment of literature as discipline in the nineteenth century, which carves out a separate category within writing in general, it is also one that must be constantly repeated. Literature, in effect, is instituted as a division and as such its institutional status is never fully assured. This lack of assurance measures the risk of its possible disappearance, but also and at the same time the possibility that something else, a new catachresis, has always begun to divide its name into the future.

ONE | *THE UNIVERSITY FOUNDERS*

ALTHOUGH the institution of compulsory public education in the West was not in any simple or direct sense a prerequisite to literary studies in the modern university, it to a large extent established terms for that debate over the *public* aims of education, at whatever level, which is still with us. For this reason, it seems appropriate to begin with aspects of this debate in its inaugural form and to question the inheritance of this public space. Such questioning is fundamental, that is, it concerns the foundations and the founding of the institutions that frame the public discourse of education. In particular, the university is founded, and because it is founded, writes Jacques Derrida, "there can be no pure concept of the university . . . within the university, there can be no pure or purely rational concept of the university. An event of foundation can never be comprehended merely within the logic that it founds."[1] The ground of our interrogation cannot be delimited by a rational concept, which is precisely why it permits and requires a fundamental questioning. And a responsibility for our acts. "We are here," continues Derrida, "in that place where the founding responsibility occurs by means of acts or performances," acts and performances whose law is not simply that of reason. But there is nothing at all simple about this "not simply." It gives space to our interrogation, to that which "il s'agit ici d'interroger," it is a matter of interrogating here. Such an interrogation

> would be inseparable from novel acts of foundation. We live in a world where the foundation of new rights—in particular of new academic rights—is necessary. To call it *necessary* is to say in this case *at one and the same time* that one has to take responsibility for it, a new kind of responsibility, and that this foundation is already well on the way. . . . Such a foundation cannot simply break with the tradition of an inherited law or rights, or submit to the legality that it authorizes, even among

those conflicts and forms of violence that always prepare for the installation of a new law, a new age of rights.[2]

Of necessity, we are in that place—a space of interrogation—that requires from us new acts of foundation. A double constraint, a neither/nor stands at the gate of this foundation: neither a radical break with the law it inherits, but would disavow, nor a submission to a law it institutes but cannot cite. Between the two uprights of this gate, which support not a stable structure but an arena of conflict, a necessity makes its way beneath the arch connecting the two sides, pulling their opposed positions together. No revolution tears down the palace gates; a deconstruction of their opposition allows for a passage at the limit of what passed for a closed structure.

Besides, what would a revolution in the university today look like? Or a revolution in the educational apparatus in general? Who today speaks of revolution as the future of our educational institutions? No doubt many do, but they might be surprised to have to count among their number the former U.S. secretary of education, William Bennett. And yet, for a speech delivered to the Heritage Foundation in July 1986, the secretary chose the title: "Completing the Reagan Revolution: A Resumption of Responsibilities."[3] This ingenious title is working in two senses in Bennett's address, which we will consider very briefly before taking a step back—about two hundred years—to a predecessor discourse on educational revolution.

First of all, "the Reagan Revolution" (capital initials) is said to refer to "fundamental shifts in national policy" in two areas: economics ("historic tax reform") and foreign policy ("the rebuilding of our nation's defenses"). In this connection, the phrase "completing the revolution" has an additive sense: A fundamental shift in educational policy must supplement the Reagan Revolution in order to complete it and to cement it in place. And because at stake is the nation's future, our realization of "our potential as a people," this additive or complementary sense sketches a linear course. "National wealth and military strength are necessary means to national greatness; but they are not, of course, sufficient. . . . National greatness, in the end, depends on—is embodied in—the character of our people" (611). This "character" depends in turn on the well-being of institutions created to express the beliefs of a people, "and on the values according to which we shape the next generation of Americans." Here, "in the somewhat amorphous realm of beliefs and attitudes and values," the secretary proposes to "mount an effort of national recovery" "if we are to realize our potential as a people."

But the secretary is also aware that his title is working not only in this progressive, linear sense but in another sense as well.

It is worth pausing for a moment to ponder what a peculiar revolution the Reagan Revolution has been. True, we seem to have broken with the past, or at least the immediate past. And true, we look forward with fresh expectation to a future of our own shaping. [It might be recalled here that Bennett is speaking to the Heritage Foundation, whose role in "shaping" Reagan's foreign and economic policy he has cited as "indispensable" and "vital."] But this has been a revolution presided over and executed by conservatives—which means that it has been accomplished not by abandoning but, to the contrary, by recovering and conserving fundamental institutions, fundamental principles, and fundamental truths.

In this other, "peculiar" sense, "completing the revolution" describes not a linear progress but a circular return, the completion of a cycle of revolution. These two senses, however, are continually playing off against each other in this rhetorical performance, the one covering and serving as alibi for the other. Consequently, it would be equally possible to read the "progressive" sense as an alibi for the "conservative" sense and vice versa. That is, the vague appeal to the future's promise of "greatness" could be seen as a rhetorical mask laid over an unyielding rejection of the changes already in motion toward some future or, conversely, the equally vague appeal to "fundamental institutions, fundamental principles, and fundamental truths" could be heard as reassuring sounds that drown out the demolition of such institutions, principles, and truths. Bennett's discourse would not want to choose between these alternatives, because the two are dependent on each other for their effects. Which is not at all to say that this rhetorical construct somehow enjoys a status beyond the traditional political division of "conservative" from "progressive"; it is, rather, to remark that some of the standard rhetorical indicators have become—and no doubt for a long time now—uselessly imprecise tools with which to delineate political effects.

Although there would be much still to say about Bennett's speech, "Completing the Reagan Revolution," we will leave it aside for the moment and be content to draw some questions from this preliminary sketch. The questions are the following: Is there perhaps a connection to be sought between discourse on education—reforming, revolutionary, or conservative—and the tendency of these political codes (or their rhetorical indicators) to cover for each other? When "education" is taken as the object of a political program or a state policy, is discourse about that object thereby made vulnerable to a dissociation from its codes or a disruption of their pertinence? And finally, do such disruptions and dissociations have their source in a fictional topology according to which the thing called "education" can be comprehended as an "object" or objective *within* a state's purview?

In a rather simple sense, Bennett's speech, for example, could be taken as a singular demonstration of this fiction since its advocacy of any educational policy must remain within the strictly decentralized tradition of the American structure of compulsory education. Thus he must recognize that "the work to reinvigorate and renew and restore our common culture . . . is *not primarily the work of government.* But it is work that those of us in government must be attentive to and supportive of, work to which we can contribute in careful and limited ways" (612; emphasis added). As to what these "careful and limited ways" might be, one may fill in from memory how the federal Department of Education under Mr. Bennett's leadership intervened in the affairs of school desegregation, affirmative action, tuition waivers for sectarian schools, prayer in school, and so forth.[4] But it would be, at least for the imaginable future, out of the question for a U.S. secretary of education, whether in a "conservative" or "liberal" administration, to propose a centralized, national system of public education. One may still recall the resistance President Carter encountered when he created this department and added its secretary to his cabinet. And wasn't it Ronald Reagan who promised his conservative constituency, during his first campaign, that he would eliminate the department at the first opportunity?[5] Instead, the somewhat anomalous situation was created of a federal government department and its resources being used to *intervene* in favor of *nonintervention* of the federal government in those areas (segregation, affirmative action) which had been the only valid areas of intervention recognized previously.

Yet the idea of state-controlled, national public education has currency everywhere else in the West, and what we have called the fictional topology of this idea has been with us for at least two hundred years. Kant, in the second essay of the *Conflict of the Faculties,* is concerned with this idea and would even seem to have been making allusions to proposals for a national system of public instruction that were at the time—in 1795—preoccupying the legislators of the new French Republic.

Before inserting this essay into the *Conflict of the Faculties,* Kant gave it the title "An Old Question Raised Again: Is the Human Race Constantly Progressing?" The answer to this question is given in the affirmative by means of a complex and cautious reference to "the revolution of a gifted [geistreichen] people which we have seen unfolding in our day."[6] It is not, however, the French Revolution as event or series of acts that "demonstrates the moral tendency of the human race" but rather the "disinterested sympathy" that the spectator of these events experiences for the revolutionaries over against their Ancien Régime adversaries:

> It is simply the mode of thinking of the spectators which reveals itself publicly in this game of great revolutions, and manifests such a universal yet disinterested sympathy [Teilnehmung] for the players on one side against those on the other, even at the risk that this partiality [Parteilichkeit] could become very disadvantageous for them if discovered.

This sympathy [Teilnehmung] is also called "a wishful participation [again, Teilnehmung] that borders closely on enthusiasm, the very expression of which is fraught with danger."[7] As recent commentary has shown, the passage holds several key elements of the answer to the old question Kant is raising again.[8] But it is to a later passage in the essay, where Kant makes the first of only two allusions to educational institutions, that we will now turn.

Section 8 is titled: "Concerning the Difficulty of the Maxims Applying to World Progress with Regard to Their Publicity." It is under this heading of publicity or publication that Kant takes up the subject of public instruction in order, it seems, to denounce a disguise or concealment (Verheimlichung)[9] within the relations of a state to its people and to the instructors of the people, the philosophers, those whom the state deems dangerous and calls Aufklärer.

> Enlightenment of the masses is the public instruction of the people in its duties and rights vis-à-vis the state to which they belong. Since only natural rights and rights arising out of the common human understanding are concerned here, then the natural heralds and expositors of these among the people are not officially appointed by the state [nicht die vom Staat bestellte amtsmässige] but are free professors of law, that is philosophers who, precisely because this freedom is allowed to them, are objectionable to the state, which always desires to rule alone; and they are decried, under the name of enlighteners, as persons dangerous to the state. (161)

A first disguise is indicated here, the one that calls those responsible for "public instruction of the people in its duties and rights" appointees of the state rather than free professors of law, "*das ist die Philosophen.*" The point would seem to be not that free professors of law should necessarily remain free of any official tie rather than being appointed and supported by the state (which was one of the questions most hotly debated by the French legislators at the time), but rather that such appointment cannot preempt the freedom that must be allowed to them. Philosophers are appointed to teach *as* free professors of law; this freedom is "allowed to them" and indeed it is the condition of their appointment.[10] The deception is to refer to these instructors as "officially appointed by the state" and then to pretend that this appointment must entail a subservience to the will of the state, rather than a freedom from any will other than that expressing "natural rights and rights arising out of the common human understanding."

A second deception or concealment concerns the "danger" posed by such freedom, which puts at risk only the desire of the state to be the sole ruler of the people. What is concealed in the charge against the enlighteners is the far greater risk that would be posed were this voice of "natural right" to be silenced in obedience to the state's desire to rule absolutely. Kant spells this out as the passage continues:

> they are decried, under the name of enlighteners, as persons dangerous to the state, *although their voice is not addressed confidentially* [vertraulich] *to the people (as the people take scarcely any or no notice of it and of their writings) but is addressed respectfully to the state;* and they implore the state to take to heart that need which is felt to be legitimate. This can happen by no other means than that of publicity in the event that an entire people cares to bring forward its grievances [*gravamen*]. Thus the prohibition of publicity impedes the progress of a people toward improvement, even in that which applies to the least of its claims, namely its mere natural right. (Emphasis added)

The censorship or "prohibition of publicity" of the philosopher's voice conceals one danger beneath another, the danger to mere natural right beneath the danger to the state's absolute rule over a population ignorant of its rights. But Kant's particular formulation of the relation between the state and its educators needs to be heeded. The "free professors'" voice, he writes, "is not addressed confidentially [*vertraulich,* on a level of familiarity] to the people (as the people take scarcely any or no notice of it and of their writings) but is addressed respectfully to the state." There is, then, yet another form of deception or disguise: it holds that these official appointees of the state are appointed to address the people familiarly, in their own language, as one says, and to instruct them in how to be good citizens of the state according to the state's wishes. Instead, writes Kant, it is, in effect, a fiction that public instruction exists in an address to the people who pay little or no heed to the philosophers' voice and writings. In fact, public instructors respectfully address their teachings to the state. In speaking to the people of their "duties and rights vis-à-vis the state," these free instructors are really always addressing the state, instructing it in its duties and rights vis-à-vis the people. Far from serving the wishes and at the pleasure of the state, the free professors are appointed to instruct the state in the limits of its wishes.[11]

We could say that the fiction Kant exposes as such is that of a privately hired tutor instructing sons in the service of the father. This cannot be a model for *public* instruction, a lesson that Kant would have learned perhaps from *Emile* of all places. Rousseau's fiction of a tutor and his pupil is a model for *public* instruction only in the sense of its *making public* a teaching of rights and duties through, precisely, publication and publicity. The fact that *Emile* was officially censored by many of the states of Europe situates it within Kant's problematic of the philosopher's freedom to address the state as the state's teacher. And in this regard, we must ask how to read the novel's own confidential and familiar address to the mother: "C'est à toi que je m'adresse, tendre et prévoyante mère," "I address myself to you, affectionate and provident mother."[12] One could argue that this familiar address, inciting the people to subversion of state authority, constituted Rousseau's greatest offense. But was it also necessarily the work's greatest fiction? That is, in addressing itself to the mother, was *Emile* disguising its address to the state that had to go to great lengths to avoid heeding that address? Beyond that, we could ask: Is public instruction a mother that the father state must keep in check?

Kant, however, does not name Rousseau. The passage from the second essay of *The Conflict of the Faculties* we are reading never departs from the form of the general proposition, to wit: public instruction concerns the state and yet is not an object within its power. The state has the duty to maintain publicity "of the rights arising out of common human understanding" and to that end it supports "free professors of law, that is philosophers." The state, in other words, appoints its own teachers, the teachers of the *res publica,* overcoming what is objectionable to it in this limitation on its desire to rule without heeding any other voice. To better resist the lesson addressed to it, however, the state has several fictions at its disposal, for example: that teachers are the servants of the state, that their instruction is addressed in familiar terms to the people, that censorship of instruction preserves the people in their respect for the state.

These remain, in fact, formidable resources and not only for absolutist states, as the history of the debate over public instruction during the first French Republic can demonstrate. This situation—that of a newly constituted republic that proposes to institute a national system of public instruction in order, in Bennett's phrase, to complete the revolution—has no obvious precedent. The observations of Kant's sympathetic spectator on this scene will have, nonetheless, prepared us to see how certain of the conflicts were, if not wholly predictable, then at least liable to be explained by the force of the fictions Kant identifies.

The debate began in 1791 with the creation of the first Committee on Public Instruction of the Legislative Assembly, which was charged with presenting a proposal to fulfill the article of the Constitution promising a system of free public instruction common to all citizens at the elementary level. It continued over at least the next four years, during which time numerous proposals were presented, rejected, ignored, or accepted only to be thrown out in abrupt reversals of direction. In 1795—Year IV of the Republic—the law of 3 brumaire decreeing the organization of public instruction was adopted but remained in place for only three years before debate was opened again by the Directoire, which sponsored many reform proposals. The law of 3 brumaire, however, was not officially replaced until 1802.[13]

Of necessity, we can evoke only in passing some of the organizing questions in this debate, questions that persistently returned. Of the many proposals and projects, we will take the most well-known as a guide to these questions, that of the *philosophe* Condorcet, who was an eminent mathematician and disciple of d'Alembert, as well as an elected representative to both the Legislative Assembly and the National Convention. His "Report on the General Organization of Public Instruction," presented to the Assembly in April 1792, was the first project to come out of the Committee on Public Instruction, and although it received little debate before being summarily tabled, it remained a principal point of reference for all succeeding proposals. After the fall of the monarchy, Condorcet himself diverted his attention from education to the drafting of a new constitution. When this constitution was presented and rejected by the Robespierrists, Condorcet was one of the few who defended it publicly and denounced the makeshift proposal adopted in its place. His defiance of the Committee of Public Safety precipitated his arrest decree; he went into hiding but was eventually imprisoned and died there in 1794.[14] It was, then, not as a spectator nor with Kant's "wishful participation" that Condorcet beheld the revolution, but with the dangerous proximity of one of the principal actors in the spectacle. It was also, however, and as we shall see, precisely such a distinction of men of action from observant scholars or intellectuals that fueled the debate over public instruction.[15]

As the work of an exemplary *Aufklärer,* Condorcet's proposal relied on a boundless faith in the emancipatory power of science. Not only was elementary knowledge the means of guaranteeing the freedom of citizens from a dangerous dependence on more advantaged neighbors, but advanced knowledge—the perfection of the arts and sciences—promised a general benefit and prosperity even to those members of a society who did not or could not cultivate such knowledge themselves. Condorcet identifies this as the double point of view that any general system of instruction must embrace: on the one hand, in the name of justice and so as to "realize the political equality recognized by the law,"[16] that system must be universal and equally available to all; on the other hand, in the name of truth, that system must be "as complete as circumstances can permit" (182). The double exigencies of universality and completeness are, insists Condorcet, complementary rather than contradictory or mutually exclusive. He reasoned that all citizens had the right to as much instruction as they were willing or able to pursue. Any other reasoning would have to be ready to designate a limit to the knowledge necessary for citizens of a republic, and Condorcet understood that that gesture could only be equivalent to tracing limits on knowledge in general, which is to say submitting reason to an arbitrary tribunal.[17] It was thus the obligation of the people's government to maintain and support the development of every science to the highest degree possible. This support, however, could only be conceived as one with no strings attached. The principle of the autonomy and self-regulation of instructional institutions must be respected, he argued, *as far as possible.* "The first principle of any instruction being to teach only truths, the institutions that the government consecrates to this end must be as independent as possible from all political authority." Or in somewhat stronger terms: "Finally, no public agency ought to have either the authority or even the means to prevent the development of new truths or the teaching of theories that go counter to its particular political program or its interests of the moment" (183).

After this preamble, the Condorcet plan sets in place the five levels of a public education system (*primaire, secondaire, instituts, lycées*—the latter corresponding to what we would call today universities—and a Société Nationale des Sciences et des Arts) as well as the four "classes" that group, in the last three levels, the different disciplines (mathematical and physical sciences, moral and political sciences, applied sciences, and literature and beaux-arts). It was a meticulous plan and would serve as the groundwork for the legislation eventually adopted.

And yet, Condorcet and his proposal became a touchstone for many things the revolutionary republicans sought to eradicate or at least to contain. The principal fault found with the proposal was its virtual exclusion of "national education" in favor of "public instruction." The distinction of "éducation" from "instruction" became a commonplace in the debate;[18] it was formalized by a number of the proposals, for example that of Rabaut Saint-Etienne in his "Project for a National Education" presented some months after Condorcet's and in reaction to it:

> one must distinguish public instruction from national education; national education should instruct the heart, the former must impart enlightenment while the latter imparts virtue; the former will be the light of society, the latter will be its character and its force . . . national education is everyone's necessary sustenance; public instruction is the lot of the few. They are sisters, but national education is the eldest. What am I saying! It is the mother common to all citizens, who gives them all the same milk, who raises them and treats them as brothers and who, through the commonality of her maternal care, imparts to them that family resemblance that distinguishes a people raised in this manner from all the other peoples of the earth. (287–98)

This impassioned rhetoric, with its figure of tutorship in the Republic as *alma mater,* will suggest the seriousness of Condorcet's crime: by denying the priority of "éducation" over "instruction," of the "mother common to all citizens" over one of her daughters, he had proposed, in effect, a *lèse-maternité* and a severing of the Republic from its source. (We are also hearing, by the way, just one of the echoes from Rousseau's address to the mother. The debate might even be summed up as a struggle for the mother: is it *éducation* or *instruction?*) But the passage also suggests that the hierarchical distinction between education and instruction was still being thought in complementary terms rather than oppositional ones. Later projects, however, would go so far as to propose that the public space of the Republic—its festivals, meetings, and tribunals—was the only reliable educational institution, a kind of school without walls. The Montagnard Bouquier, for example, would write:

> What need have we to seek far and wide for what is right before our eyes? Citizens! the finest schools, the most useful, the simplest, there where our youth can find a truly republican education, are, without a doubt, the public meetings of departments, districts, municipalities, tribunals, and especially popular societies [. . .] the Revolution has, by itself so to speak, organized public education and distributed everywhere limitless sources of instruction.
>
> Let us not then substitute for this organization that is as simple and sublime as the people who created it a factitious organization which imitates the academic hierarchies that should no longer infect a regenerated nation. Let us carefully preserve what the people and the Revolution have done; let us be content to add to it the little that is lacking in order to complete public instruction. This complement should be as simple as the work created by the genius of the Revolution. (419–20)

In other proposals, public ceremonies and celebrations displaced almost entirely formal instruction. In the course of this considerable shift, Condorcet's proposal was increasingly seen as a masked elitism and an aristocratic throwback that would replace inherited titles with graduated academic degrees.[19] To Condorcet's vision of a future stretching out to perfection through the unhampered cultivation of all the sciences, of an education completing the revolution of an enlightened people, Bouquier and others evoked a revolution virtually complete in itself, needing only a minimal supplement, and indeed they saw a positive threat to this integrity coming from what Bouquier described as "a cast of speculative scholars [whose] speculative sciences detach [them] from society and become, in the long run, a poison that undermines, weakens, and destroys republics" (418).

Yet, despite their fierce opposition, these two sides of the ongoing debate can be seen as mirror images of each other if they are viewed through the role each foresaw for the state in the system of public instruction. Condorcet envisioned a complete educational system totally financed by the state from primary school up to a national society of eminent scholars in all disciplines. This system would be self-regulated and self-appointed, with no intervention by the state. Except for some fundamental training in nonreligious moral thinking and some public ceremonies, Condorcet's proposal made no provisions for civic education, which was thereby to be left to the family and religious institutions. The role of the state was thus severely circumscribed in every regard. By contrast and on each point, the other side reversed the state's role. Most plans provided for only primary schooling, state-financed in some cases and in others funded by parents directly. The principal concern would be civic education, and the state would have the major role in determining curricula and teaching staff. The Republic was thus both the model of the educator and the object of the education. This more active role aimed at forming men of action (as Bouquier put it, "the people who have conquered liberty need only vigorous, robust, hardworking men of action [*des hommes agissants*]"). As for formal instruction beyond the most basic level, it was to be left to private institutions and was not the concern of the state.

The point is not to argue that, despite such reversals, the two sides come down to "the same thing." Rather, it would be to remark the reversibility inscribed *at a certain beginning* in modern thought about public education as an object bounded by the *polis* and falling, therefore, within its purview. Whatever their views on the intervention of the state, neither Condorcet nor his opponents would have questioned this topology, or, to put it less subjectively, this topology supplies the metaphoric ground for one and the other construction of a national education, the education of citizens for the nation.

This reversibility has had time to act itself out through at least one full revolution, and no doubt more than that. If, for example, we circle back now to Secretary Bennett's speech, how will it sound against the background of these other discourses seeking to complete that other revolution? Consider just the following paragraph, whose sympathetic resonances with Montagnard preoccupations are most striking. Bennett is addressing "the failure of our institutions [to teach our children] about our nation—about our history, our heroes, our heritage, our national memories." He asks, "What is to be done?" and replies:

> Government has a role here—especially the localities and states that govern our public schools; and the national government has an important educational part to play as well—through *speeches, reports, recommendations, recognitions, and ceremonies,* through the dissemination of ideas and the setting of a national agenda, as well as funding for various enterprises. Individuals have an even more central role—at home, and in voluntary associations. But above all, we as a society, as a common culture, have to respond to the call of our national history, and to the responsibility it

imposes upon us of instilling in our children an informed appreciation of American principles and American practices. The variety of ways in which this can be done will become clearer once we rise above all the pseudo-sophisticated claims and counterclaims, all the educational cacophony and cultural confusion, and decide: yes, we need to know our national experience, so as to know our national purpose. (612; emphasis added)

When a U.S. secretary of education talks in 1986 about public ceremonies as a means for the state to intervene in the "education" of its citizenry, to inspire admiration and youthful enthusiasm by means of state spectacle, he is, of course, not saying "the same thing" as Robespierre in 1793.[20] While it is not perhaps tragedy being repeated as farce, a revolutionary rhetoric has clearly been emptied out so that it continues to turn on itself and on its own. At the very least, the repetition and the difference suggest that the options for this kind of discourse have remained more or less fixed even as the historical, cultural, and economic conditions for it are considerably changed. If we think the options seem less limited on the "left" than on the "right," then it may be largely because we are reluctant to relinquish our faith in coded political "road signs" to point the way to a changed social future. In this regard, one could cite the new old doxa that charges any attempt to dismantle this code as a disguised return to some unacceptable doctrine labeled reactionary, liberal, conservative, and so forth.

We have already implied that sexual difference had a more central role in the revolutionary debate about education than at first appears. "Éducation," rather than "instruction," was for "men of action" and was dispensed by the mother republic to all her citizen-sons equally. On the surface, the revolutionaries on both sides of this debate gave little thought to the education or instruction of their daughters. The exception was once again Condorcet, who, unlike almost all of his successors on the Committee for Public Instruction, unlike his predecessors or mentors Diderot and Rousseau, unlike Kant even, could think of no good reason to differentiate between the proposed education of girls and boys, young women and young men; he even went so far as to argue for complete coeducation, rather than any "separate but equal" principle.[21] In so doing, he counted on the "reunion of the two sexes" to foster a new principle for the advancement of science, a principle he named quite simply—or naively—"the desire to be loved." As he wrote in his "Première Mémoire sur l'Instruction publique,"

> The reunion of the two sexes in the same schools favors emulation, and brings forth a kind of emulation that has as its principle feelings of good will rather than personal sentiments . . . an emulation that will be inspired by the desire to earn the esteem of the beloved or to obtain that of one's family. . . . An emulation that would have as its principle the desire to be loved or to be considered for one's absolute qualities rather than for one's superiority over others could also become very powerful.[22]

It should be quickly acknowledged that no first principle is being uncovered here: even if one did not have to distinguish between a "good" and a "bad" emulation, there would still be the fact that emulation remains essentially a dual or specular structure and thus fundamentally related to the public spectacle that constituted, for Condorcet's opponents, the keystone and the touchstone of the best civic education, the education that Condorcet's proposal had neglected. As such, "good" emulation is a version of model formation and imitation.[23] And yet just as clearly, by situating this emulation in a proximity to the "reunion of the two sexes," it is not simply a matter here of the desire *to be like,* but rather "to be loved." In other words, only a different desire or a desire for the different could, in Condorcet's estimation, introduce something "powerful" within the institutional model.

Does this "powerful" something also propose another foundation for our academic contract, one that neither the state of reason nor reasons of state can, in themselves, supply? By "other foundation" one should hear an appeal to a foundation that, finally, *is not one* because it takes place only with or in the other, that is, from the place of an *address* whose singular demand has no model and gives no model to the response. It will have been perhaps this question of address—as Kant discerned in part by attending to Rousseau—that discourse about education or the university has mistaken for the question of the purpose and perfectibility of these institutions and that has kept it turning around in circles. While this discourse has been recently revived with much publicity, its appeal remains the very familiar one to the choice between a unifying model of national identity and what Bennett calls "cultural confusion." Some of our "free professors of law, that is the philosophers" have agreed that we have this choice and have made themselves into spokesmen urging it on the people just as if they had been "officially appointed by the state" to do so. They too would prefer to believe that *there is* still the choice between identity and confusion, the institution of the one and the address of the other.

With no regard for this choice, the question of the other address asks one to take responsibility for it. The grounds on which to found this new responsibility lie at the limits between the university's erected knowledge and its exclusions of what should not be known or make itself known, all that which has the potential of rearranging the space of our interrogation. While such grounds have only begun to be surveyed, we have long been receiving warnings that the university *founders* where it is *founded*. A warning, or perhaps rather just a question addressed from beyond the university's walls, interrogating its topology? Listen, for example and in conclusion, to the interrogation passed along by the poet of Amherst—by which one means of course the town rather than the college of that name, one of whose founders was Edward Dickinson, the poet's father, a man with severe ideas about the uselessness of educating one's daughters.

> I went to School
> But was not wiser
> Globe did not teach it
> Nor Logarithm Show
>
> "How to forget"!
> Say—some—Philosopher!
> Ah, to be erudite
> Enough to know!
>
> Is it in a Book?
> So, I could buy it—
> Is it like a Planet?
> Telescopes would know—
>
> If it be invention
> It must have a Patent.
> Rabbi of the Wise Book
> Dont you know?[24]

TWO | THE RHETORIC OF RUIN

THE struggle between public education and instruction during the French Revolution took place on the stage of what might be called a politics of memory. For the Montagnard camp, *éducation* should prevail over *instruction* just as the future of the Republic should erase the structures, habits, and memory of the past and the Ancien Régime. As the word says, education leads; it is directed toward a destination, here the Republic of citizens bound by their duty to protect this future against any return of the past. This bond is secured by memory, the memory of a promise made and a debt owed to the Republic. The calendar is reset from the date of the promise. The extraction of that promise is the principal affair of education and of the educators who are the representatives or delegates of the Republic. They are educators, then, almost in the sense Nietzsche elaborates in *The Genealogy of Morals:* they form men as animals who have the right to make promises. Instruction, on the other hand, has to do with the arrangement of those structures that form and inform pupils with the memory of a past. The instructor's duty is not only to the civil Republic but also to the Republic of sciences and letters, to that which, in other words, cannot be made to start from the *tabula rasa* of day one of the new calendar. Instead, the tablet from which he or she reads is so charged with writing and crossing out that the task is to decipher it and to select what should be retained, remembered. Instruction also requires a promise, and therefore a relation to the future, which is that of the enlightened Republic, freed from the scientific errors of the past. But the promise of instruction, unlike that of education, carries as well the duty to remember this past, and even to memorize it.

This politics or politicization of memory implies necessarily a struggle over language or inscription, over the marks in which memory preserves itself or loses itself, both preserves itself for a future remembering and loses itself as an immanent self-relation. When we say that a memory has been *preserved*—for example in a photo album or a public monument, on shiny black walls of granite—we do not consider this locution tautological, even though memory already has the sense of a preservation. Instead, the locution, no less than such acts of preservation, affirms that memory does not preserve *itself* but depends on exterior marks or signs. Wholly *within* the intangible faculty of memory, without any outside support or concrete surface, memories lose themselves, get erased. Monuments to memory are also reminders of what we tend most easily forget, namely, that the condition of remembering is an inscription that can never be wholly interiorized. It is not merely in a contingent or nonessential sense that memory needs external reminders or prompts; it is not, in other words, as an essentially self-contained or self-sufficient psychic faculty that memory exteriorizes itself in monuments and other inscriptions. Rather, what we call memory would be the space of an inscription in and by exteriority—difference or otherness. Proust called it involuntary, that is, not the function of a will affecting itself with its own past, but the impingement of a materiality on the surface of consciousness.[1] We say that at such moments memory is *awakened,* as if it had never really been lost to itself, merely asleep. And with that we forget everything that can inhabit or invade the sleep of memory as compulsively and involuntarily as we forget our dreams.

Memory cannot do without inscription, without exteriorization, but this necessity, which is the necessity of finitude, is also always the possibility of a perversion of memory, or simply a loss of that which was to be remembered. To return to the terms of the Revolutionary debate, we might say that for the educator inscription represented above all this danger of perversion or loss of the promise to remember, to preserve the Republic. It is thus only living, interior memory that can be entrusted with that promise; like Emile's preceptor, the educator of the Republic is suspicious of whatever can come between the pupil and his living memory. The pupil must become himself a tablet on which the indelible inscription is made, without recourse to the intervening and possibly perverting forms of exterior inscription. For the instructor, by contrast, it is the danger of a loss of memory, rather than the risk of its perversion, that dictates an instruction in the arts and techniques of inscription. To a certain extent, this distinction may once again be understood as a difference of *address* in the terms Kant defined. The educator would address himself to the people whom, despite the abstraction, he takes to be a living presence that is to be educated in its duty to the state of the Republic; "the people" is itself a kind of living surface on which to imprint the law of the promise. The instructor, on the other hand, addresses no finite presence and does not entrust memory to the finitude of the living. The instructor resembles, then, those whom Kant calls the *Aufklärer* or "free professors of law" who "implore the state to take to heart that need which is felt to be legitimate. This can happen by no other means than that of publicity."

With that publicity, however, these distinctions become blurred and their differentiating features are made to cross precisely there where they inscribe themselves for memory, that is, in those texts that can still be read two hundred years after their publication. To follow the revolutionary debate over education versus instruction into the domain of language reform or counterreform, which is to say the domain of an inscribed, literary legacy, we will consider two attempts to preserve this legacy from utter destruction, that of the Jacobin representative L'abbé Grégoire and the anti-Jacobin academician Jean-François La Harpe, figures of the educator and the instructor. The limit on the pertinence of these distinctions, as we shall see, is drawn by the ambivalent nature of the instituted sign, that is, of a possibility of repetition and thus preservation that is dependent on exterior, material inscription. Preservation will thus be figured repeatedly as a kind of ruin. And, to anticipate even further where this may lead, it is this possibility of figurative reversal that will consistently accompany efforts throughout the nineteenth century to define a literary sphere worthy of preservation and study. Needless to say, the possibility is still with us.

Henri Grégoire, more familiarly known as L'abbé Grégoire, was a member of the Convention and later constitutional bishop of Blois. Among his many and varied reports to the Convention, several dealt explicitly with language reform as a necessary component of total revolution. Michel de Certeau and a team of collaborators, in a study titled *Une politique de la langue,* have recalled one of the most ambitious of these reports: "Sur la nécessité et les moyens d'anéantir les patois et d'universaliser l'usage de la langue française [On the necessity and the means of annihilating patois and of universalizing the use of the French language]."[2] In this report, the product of both immense learning and an unfettered faith in the power of the reformer's will, Grégoire isolates certain persistent memory traces that survive in the language. These traces, he warns, act as so many chains riveting the speakers of patois to a pre-Revolutionary, even a feudal past: "The feudalism that later came to divide up this beautiful country carefully preserved this disparity of idioms as a means of recognizing and recapturing fugitive serfs and of riveting their chains. Still today the territorial space in which certain patois are used is determined by the frontiers of the former feudal domination."[3] Patois ties its speaker to a memory of the land divided and differentiated, rather than to the new undivided nation that has renamed the territory. "We no longer have provinces, and yet we still have almost thirty patois that *recall* the names of provinces" (230; emphasis added). Names that can no longer refer to any possible presence and that should therefore be discarded as useless persist all the same; when they are repeated, however mechanically, involuntarily, or unintentionally, they recall and refer back to what has been wiped off the map. Because they have the power to revive the memory of the thing named, are they not to be feared as one fears the thing "itself"? But then if the repetition of the name can repeat the thing, can bring it back, as it were, uninvited, was there ever such a thing to begin with as the "thing itself" unencumbered by a name? We will come back to this question.

The problem with names is particularly sharpened if one considers toponyms, those most effective locators of language-memory. Grégoire considered it serious enough to devote another entire report to a "Système de dénominations topographiques pour les places, rues, quais, etc. de toutes les communes de la République [System of topographic denominations for places, streets, quais, etc. in all localities of the Republic]." As in the report on the patois, it is a matter of erasing one memory, one language by another, of standardizing and of purifying language memory. Too many places, he observes, have borrowed their names from "monastic, judicial, or feudal establishments that have now been suppressed and *whose memory is nothing other than that of our misfortunes*" (158; emphasis added). To purge memory of its suffering, Grégoire proposes a rational system of renaming. In doing so, he cannot resist noting some of the other benefits to be anticipated from the adoption of his system, for example in communications that are currently so confused that "many letters, which do not show a precise address, have difficulty reaching their destination or never reach it all" (159). A rationalized topography is also a more efficient surveillance grid; hence this politics also always supposes, we must not forget, a police able to *locate* guilty memory lapses.[4]

It is, however, of other kinds of enforcement or persuasion that Grégoire dreams in this properly *utopian* text. The physical grid of the city, town, or village is but the sensible side of the sign; its intelligible face is a map to guide the citizen on a moral and internal itinerary of "the heart."

> It is possible that the appearance or the memory of a word that retraces, for example, generosity attenuates the desire for vengeance in an embittered heart. Perhaps one would sometimes see parents who, in the presence of the public, bring their guilty children to the squares and to the streets named for the opposite virtues of the crimes they had committed and, applying the accents of feeling and reason, instill remorse in their hearts. (170)

Grégoire recommends commemorating heroic events in the names given to public places because "names that are linked to great events, that retrace their memory, like the places that were the scenes of those events, have sometimes a magical force" (171). The word, the name is a theater for memory, a stage on which it replays its greatest scenes. The magical force is its power to replace or restage the thing "itself." But this is where the problem returns. The force of this commemorative theater is the same as the force at work recalling, repeating "our misfortunes" so that one cannot invoke the first without calling up the second. How, then, is memory ever to have done with its divided past? Must it not continue to inscribe itself under the sign, precisely, of the double sign that has its positive and negative faces? "One senses how useful it might be to perpetuate the memory [of heroic events], either with monuments, or with historic names that retrace the virtues of citizens and the crimes of despots so as to inspire love for the former and horror of the latter" (ibid.). But if one cannot perpetuate the memory of the one without the other, then the necessity arises to reinscribe yet again their difference.

The division of the sign in its literality, as literature, installs the necessity of a perpetual reinscription. That necessity dictates yet another report Grégoire prepared at about the same time he presented his system for toponymical revision. The "Rapport sur les inscriptions des monumens publics [Report on the inscriptions of public monuments]" recommended that from then on all public monument inscriptions be in French rather than Latin. We need not pose many questions to the manifest aim of this proposal, which is of a piece with the project to universalize and standardize a single French language by eradicating the patois. Grégoire has merely shifted targets from the people's idiom to that of the learned elite. But it is noteworthy that this reflection on the language of inscription (French or Latin) does not question the necessity of inscription as such, the necessity, that is, to write on monuments, to supplement memorial objects with writing. It is as if a monument—statue, place, ruin—were above all the support of the inscription it bears. We could take this as further confirmation that, for Grégoire, the thing to be recalled always remains bound up in its name. But his examples are by no means only names and the force in play here is not only that of reference or *renvoi*, that magical force possessed by names to call up again the things they name.

Several of the most memorable or striking examples cited by the report invoke as well a prescriptive or performative force. "What feelings," he writes, "flare up in the heart of a Frenchman who, on the debris of the Bastille, finds these words: *Here people dance!* [*Ici on danse!*]" (144). Such a prescriptive writing or graffiti on the ruins suspends the commemorated event in a signification or representation whereby it becomes in memory what it will have been. The commemorative inscription thereby projects a proleptic movement that aims to preserve not so much a past as a future. "Walls, marble, bronze must be made to speak the language of freedom to all *Sansculottes present and future*." (150; emphasis added). It is the prescriptive or performative force of the inscription that is vitiated when these talking walls speak a stranger's language.

Although this may be an obvious point,[5] Grégoire drives it home with the following most telling analogy. "A public monument is, so to speak, the abridged drama of a great event; to make it speak an unknown language would be as misplaced as, in *Macbeth*, having the ghost who comes on stage to frighten the assassin pronounce in a foreign tongue these terrible words: *you will sleep no more!*" (144). What, however, could be more misplaced in this context than the appearance on stage of the ghost of a murdered king? By some strange mechanism, the prescriptive inscription of a future liberty is illustrated by this *revenant* who promises, in all too understandable terms, a fearful future of no sleep or forgetting; it is illustrated, in other words, by precisely the memory such inscription is meant to exorcise and efface. Grégoire's example makes his point but also says something other than what he would have it say: It speaks the stranger's tongue *within* the common language. And thereby it inscribes the necessity of another inscription, another effacement.

Remember this ghost; it will come back.

In prescribing memorial inscription that would speak a language "intelligible for all" (ibid.), Grégoire envisions an immediate intelligibility of sense that would, in effect and paradoxically, do away with the need for what is being prescribed (translation, commentary, reinscription, interpretation). The gesture is therefore resolutely divided on itself—effacing what it inscribes and inscribing what it effaces. That is why it remains the site of an always possible return. Rather than indicating some kind of fatal naïveté in Grégoire's politics of memory, however, the prescribed reinscription submits to a necessity that many of his contemporaries in the Convention chose to ignore when they condoned the wholesale campaigns of destruction of public monuments and other artifacts. It was Grégoire who labeled this destruction *vandalism,* coining that word for the future's use. Less than three months after his report on the necessity and means of annihilating [*anéantir*] the *patois,* Grégoire presented the first of his three reports on this threat to the nation's artistic and scientific patrimony, titled "Sur les destructions opérées par le vandalisme et sur les moyens de le réprimer [On the destructions carried out by vandalism and on the means of repressing it]." This sequence does not simply mark, as it might appear, the shift from a politics of destruction to a politics of conservation—a politics of the museum;[6] rather, as we have seen, these forces remain indissociable, perhaps even indistinguishable, in a general movement of repeated and divided reinscription.

The consolidation of a national memory (through the preservation of a certain past) and the unification of a national language (through the destruction of regional idioms) are the two faces of a same coin or *médaille* whose emblem could be a certain medal Grégoire describes in his report. He cites it as an example of one of the many "monuments that despotism forced into hiding" and that the Republic, which has unearthed it, should preserve. The figure on the medal represents, he writes, "an armed hand cutting down lilies and breaking scepters" (271). For Grégoire and his contemporary readers, the image figures an act of regicide, the lily, or *fleur de lys,* being a heraldic emblem of the Bourbon dynasty. It is thus an image of destruction that itself should be saved from destruction. It also, in other words, serves as an emblem of the reversibility that is imprinted with each blow struck. To preserve *from* destruction, destruction itself must be preserved, furnishing thereby, as Grégoire puts it, "new arms to freedom" (ibid.). This graphics of reversibility or reinscription, preserving so as to destroy, destroying so as to preserve, leads Grégoire to envision in conclusion, and as closure, a totalizing inscription that would be, "if possible," engraved at once on both faces of memory's coin, its external and internal monuments. The final paragraph reads: "Let us therefore inscribe, if possible, on all monuments and let us engrave on all hearts this sentence: 'Barbarians and slaves detest the sciences, and destroy the monuments of the arts; free men love them and preserve them'" (278).

With that prescription, which draws on one of the oldest funds in the tradition of writing about writing,[7] we see something like the outline of this politics of language. The figure of a simultaneous inscription on the monument and on the heart, which would weld the written precept to the moment of its interpretation, is itself imprinted on the most common *commonplace* concerning the sign: it is a dual nature, at once sensible mark—what is inscribed on the monument—and intelligible meaning—what is or should be inscribed on the heart. Between that commonplace and the common place that is the promised object of Grégoire's reforms, the *res publica,* the difference or distance is *internal,* a distinction made only within what is held in common. The Republic is thought under the sign of the sign; its place is neither a territory nor the name of a territory, neither a sensible site nor an intelligible one but their "sole and indivisible" conjunction. As a memory promised to the future, the conjunction is projected out of a dual theory of the sign. That is to say, the revolutionary reforms we have just briefly reviewed must suppose both the detachability of signs or names, which is the condition of any possible renaming, and the opposite, the indivisibility of the republican sign, which is the condition of the promise, the sign, therefore, as a promise of its own disappearance as sign.

This is the double movement of reinscription we have just seen characterized in several ways. Reformers like Grégoire who drew on that movement were not, of course, in any sense "inventors" of what has always been and remains the very possibility of history, of change, but also of repetition and of continuity—of language-memory. If, nevertheless, theirs was a *revolutionary* reinscription, then it would have had the force of a certain break within that conditioning possibility. To put it differently: if the Revolutionary project cannot be divorced from a theory of signification, then this implies that its break with signs of the past may also be read in a certain breakdown or ruin of the sign. That idea is one we can pursue at least a few more steps, with a quite different set of texts concerned with Revolutionary language.

> *Revolution,* in the figurative sense signifies a change of state. History and politics call the remarkable changes that happen in the government of nations by the name *revolutions* . . . . There was one in France in 1789 . . . . There was another revolution in 1792, when the monarchy was overthrown and the republic was proclaimed. History will judge these

two successive revolutions, which as of the date of this writing [1793] constitute but one vast destruction, and which a third *revolution* will perhaps have replaced when this text appears. I make no decision yet here concerning the principal events, although one may already judge them at their worth. Whatever may be their result, I observe only their spirit. I want to show how things were effected principally by the power of words, and that things were absolutely without precedent because, for the first time, words were absolutely without reason.[8]

The passage is from an essay by Jean-François La Harpe. La Harpe made his reputation in the rhetorical competitions of the Académies, then went on to offer well-attended public courses on literature at the Lycée, an institution founded in 1785 for the liberal teaching of the arts and sciences. An open supporter of the Constitutional convention, he sympathized briefly with the Montagnards, but ended up going to prison for several months in 1794 for his anti-Jacobinism. Soon after his release, he became a virulent critic of the Revolution and an ardent defender of the Catholic church, all of which did not prevent his being named to the first chair of Letters at the newly formed Ecole Normale Supérieure.[9] His compiled lectures on classical and modern literature, *Lycée, ou Cours de littérature ancienne et moderne,* were reedited throughout most of the nineteenth century and, until the advent of Brunetière and Taine, set a certain standard for literary study in France.[10]

Although La Harpe is neither particularly cool-headed nor often astute in his several "commentaries" on the, as he sees it, negative course of the Revolution, his persistent will to understand what went wrong as a *linguistic* aberration is itself instructive. This will is announced both in the passage just cited and the title of the essay from which it is taken: "L'esprit de la Révolution, ou Commentaire historique sur la Langue révolutionnaire [The spirit of the Revolution, or historical commentary on revolutionary language]"; one of his later essays in a similar mode is titled "Le fanatisme dans la langue révolutionnaire, ou la persécution suscitée par les barbares du dix-huitième siècle, contre la religion chrétienne et ses ministres [Fanaticism in revolutionary language, or the persecution incited by the barbarians of the eighteenth century against the Christian religion and its ministers]." Despite his announced intention, however, La Harpe only rarely succeeds in thematically isolating his object—revolutionary language—from the surrounding phenomena. This is, of course, not all that surprising. All the same one may remark a curious effect on the discourse that would sustain the thesis that the Revolution went astray because "things were effected principally by *the power of words.*" According to La Harpe, the Revolution will have been first of all a reversal in the order of words and things, the former coming to usurp precedence over the latter, thereby overturning reason, which dictates the primacy of things and the derivation of words. Yet, in order to demonstrate the newly operative power of words to produce "things without precedent," La Harpe cannot consider words or language as such, but only as that which they produce: "things." The perversion (or the disaster) that La Harpe would analyze is precisely what must prevent him from isolating what he calls revolutionary language. The problem would seem to be that there is no longer language that is simply language and not also things. Rhetoric, which encodes a measured distance between language and its referents, lies in ruins. Once that distance has been collapsed, there is no longer a language in which to denounce the aberration that will not also produce the thing denounced. And indeed, La Harpe's language is in this sense, which is his own sense, revolutionary, even terroristic, in ways that need to be specified, but for reasons that are already in evidence. It is the evidence, for example, of a discourse that asserts "I observe only the *spirit* [of events]," and then calls this spirit "the power of words." The spirit and the letter have exchanged places, or rather they have become interchangeable, and not only in the hated discourse of the Revolutionary demagogue but as well in that of one of his fiercest adversaries. That is the disaster.

But before we accredit this version of disaster, let us look at another passage from the same text.

> In order to speak to one another, we must understand each other, we must have a language common to all [notice that this commonplace about the necessity for a commonplace is precisely the premise of Grégoire's reforms, the utopian commonplace of "a language common to all"]; and, as I have said elsewhere, all the essential words of the language are today inverted in their meaning, all basic ideas are robbed of their nature. We have a completely new dictionary in which *virtue* signifies *crime,* and *crime* signifies *virtue.* We have a completely new logic, which may be reduced to this form of argument: Two and two are four, therefore three and two are six, and whoever doubts this is a villain who deserves the worst punishment. This logic and this dictionary do not use good sense, but what I have just said is anything but an exaggeration. I could give excerpts from thousands of speeches in which that is exactly what is being said, and wherever one turns, one hears nothing else. (437)

Here the "power of words" in question is not, as in the first passage, a productive or performative power, so much as a power of inversion whereby a word can be detached from its "basic" or natural meaning and then attach itself to the opposite sense. It is a power of substitution, one word for another, and a power of definition, one word by another: "We have a completely new dictionary in which *virtue* signifies *crime*, and *crime* signifies *virtue*." With the figure of the dictionary, however, La Harpe concedes that the process of denaturalization he decries can be conceived as an *intralinguistic* phenomenon, although to be sure it is not as such that he wants to conceive it. He means to say that *acts* or *attitudes*—nonlinguistic "things"—which, formerly, would have been taken as examples of virtue are now called criminal, and vice versa. The problem is that this relation between words and nonwords, meanings and acts—the relation of representation in the sign—is itself so neatly *represented* by the figure of the dictionary, in which the same distinction no longer holds. This is a problem because, once again, La Harpe can only denounce this perversion by repeating it, by calling virtue a crime, and crimes virtue. "Virtue" and "crime" are still interchangeable *words,* rather than opposable acts to be called or represented by their appropriate names.

It would seem that this dilemma—let's call it getting stuck in the dictionary—is precisely the contrary of the one earlier identified. There we saw La Harpe producing things when he meant to speak of words, unable, therefore, to isolate language from that which it is supposed only to signify and forced to repeat the error of entangling letter and spirit. But, in fact, these two dilemmas are versions of a same condition that has been uncovered up to a point by the Revolution's ruinous reinscription of the rhetorical monument and that La Harpe obscurely identifies: namely, words *are* things before they are made to signify other things, other words. That is why one is unable to separate words from things, either in order to isolate words as such or things as such. The thingness of words and the wordness of things persist in distorting those "basic ideas" to which La Harpe refers and by which he seems to mean pure meanings, pre- or non-linguistic sense, virtue *itself* before and beyond the signifier "virtue," pure content, pure form, pure thing. The assailed distortions point to a shift within the signifying relation, which can no longer be seen as solely the heterogeneous relation of words to meaning, and which therefore is no longer thinkable wholly within the concept of the sign. And with that, the concept of language or rhetoric as a purely referential, representational instrument yields ground to something else, something monstrous.

"Monsters" is one of La Harpe's favorite epithets for the hated Montagnards.[11] And it is, in effect, a monstrosity that provokes his complaint about the apparently new state of linguistic affairs, as we can see in yet another essay titled, with characteristic emphasis, "De la Guerre déclarée par les tyrans Révolutionnaires à la Raison, à la Morale, aux Lettres, et aux Arts." This is the text of a speech delivered at the opening ceremony of the Lycée on the last day of 1794, which was La Harpe's first public statement after Thermidor and his own release from prison. He returns there to the thesis of "the power of words," combining the two motifs of the power over things and of inversion:

> The examination of words will necessarily lead me to the examination of things, which have all been made with words . . . . Do you not see that on this point, as on all the others, everything has been turned upside down? . . . By means that it will not be difficult to explain, sacramental words in any legal system, words that one was accustomed to respect when they were used in their true sense, had been progressively turned aside from this original and invariable meaning and finally led through daily application to an entirely opposite sense. . . . In the end, a language was formed that was the reverse of good sense; a language so strange and so monstrous that posterity will be unable to believe it except for the multitude of monuments that will remain. (18–19)

This strange and monstrous language appears here in the traits of a speech that has lost its memory of the "true sense . . . this original and invariable meaning." It is the monstrosity of the word as thing, cut loose from its past inheritance, its place in an order that, for having been consecrated by generations of use, constituted the word's very nature. A monstrous language goes against nature. As example, La Harpe takes the word *égalité,* which, he writes, "can never signify, for common sense, anything other than the equality of natural and civil rights." It is therefore monstrous to force the word to go against this common sense so as to proscribe "all species of moral and industrial superiority." The state that adopts the word in this sense as its motto violates the order of human nature since "everything that was on the bottom rung of human nature climbs to the top rung in the state. There in two words is the whole history of our tyrants" (ibid.).

This two-word history would be history as a splitting in two of *la parole publique,* of common sense, and, in the gap that is then opened appears a stage of conflict, struggle, and opposition, but also, as we shall see, of mimicry and imitation. For La Harpe, a word becomes monstrous when its two faces are no longer harmoniously joined, when the former unity of the sign is split and gives way to the most unholy combinations. Such words are to be compared to the monsters of classical myth, to the Harpies, for example, those half-women, half-bird-of-prey creatures that La Harpe invokes as the imaginary predecessors of the very real tyrants of the day.

> In a word, this irruption of our tyrants, when they arrived to terrify and wither our peaceful celebrations, can be represented only by one of those inventions of fable which, by creating fantastic monsters, aided imagination to depict real monsters . . . . I wish that our language, as flexible in every tone as that of Virgil when he describes the Harpies, could offer you these hideous, vile, and voracious animals, coming with their piercing cry, their filthy plumage, their hooked claws and their fetid breath, to swoop down on the feast of Aeneas, etc. (8–9)

The feast is that of an embellishing, aggrandizing rhetoric that, even when it invokes the most horrific monsters imagined by Homer and Virgil, elevates its objects and dignifies their memory. But it is precisely this sort of rhetoric that the irruption of the frightful beasts onto the harmonious scene has ruined. The feast of classical rhetoric, that commemoration whereby language repeats and recalls its commonplaces, is interrupted when this half-human beast begins to speak or rather to *mimic* the consecrated tongue of the celebration. And the ruinous effects of such mimicry would mark the very discourse with which one denounces it. I cite a last long polemical passage:

> when poetry, eloquence, history, those eternal depositories of the moral vengeance of humankind, speak of the famous villains who have oppressed it, they ordinarily show us these villains with several attributes of greatness and, as it were, elevated onto the theaters of crime. Here they will have to open the sewers, to descend into the mire along with our tyrants. . . . When reason, in astonishment, casts its eyes on these inconceivable speeches, repeated every hour and from every podium . . . when it observes this language unknown until now by human ears, this unheard-of mixture of monstrous depravation and juvenile rhetoric, of emphatic conceit and trivial vulgarity . . . which takes pleasure in horrors, mixing sarcasm with the dagger, and the most obvious irony with the most cowardly proscription . . . which finally puts on airs of a stupid hypocrisy and a theatrical charlatanism, proclaiming thousands of murders in the name of *humanity,* the code of armed banditry in the name of *Aristide,* consecrating the most execrable tyranny in the name of *Brutus;* does not reason then imagine that it is seeing highway robbers—who by chance would have opened a history book or attended a tragedy—parody

indistinctly in their tavern the heroes of virtue and crime, and act out in their orgies a bizarre farce . . . ? (15–16)

Forced to abandon eloquence and to open the sewers of expression by a "language unknown until now by human ears," La Harpe mimics the mimickers. But of course he also does nothing of the kind, the figure of a rhetoric abandoned and a descent into the mire remaining a most familiar trope—the trope, if you will, of the antitrope.[12] Rhetoric, rather, would be like the mire that sticks to a discourse the more vigorously one tries to shake it off. Nor can we think that La Harpe's refusal of an ennobling rhetoric is anything but a *feint*, since it is only the difference between noble and ignoble rhetoric, between true eloquence and its parody that can distinguish his own discourse from the monstrous travesty he means to represent and denounce. But is it not also precisely this difference that must be effaced or suspended when the "unknown language" is given the recognizable face of a rhetorical figure because, as he writes, poetry and eloquence elevate even the worst of history's villains? Once again, La Harpe is cornered by the dilemma of having to repeat the very aberration or monstrosity he wants to dispatch, of forging yet another Harpy that, in his own name and under his own signature, swoops down upon the feast in the form of "this unheard-of mixture of monstrous depravation and juvenile rhetoric." There will have been after all, and despite the feint, a mimicking effect. La Harpe's rhetoric cannot not enact its own ruin in order to preserve itself. And with that, the distinction is suspended between a noble rhetoric fit to speak the truth and its degraded imitation that imposes itself through the sheer power of words. In the struggle that pits the *ancien rhétoriqueur* against these *parvenus,* the commonplaces of rhetoric, of language memory, would have been both the prize at stake and the divided, divisive element of the struggle that defers any final declaration of a winner.

If one can all the same speak of a *common place* between Grégoire and La Harpe, it is because each turns his face toward the *same* idea of a common and undivided language (or sign), but they are facing in opposite directions: Grégoire looks to the future for realization of a promised unification, while La Harpe recalls with nostalgia a past before the irruption of disunity. Although this back-to-back figure signals the division between camps of political antagonists, we have also seen that, insofar as this is a politics of language, the division keeps redividing and producing effects of reinscription, repetition, or mimicry. The "power of words" or "magical force" that each antagonist cites, to exploit it, to repress it, would be at work tracing a silent collusion between the two parties. As if each were being secretly haunted by the other, by a ruined rhetoric that has yet to die off altogether or to be born again, *qui n'en finit pas de mourir ou de naître*.

Consider one last manifestation of this ghostliness in a text that, some 150 years later, is, we could say, still haunted by the ruin of rhetoric: Jean Paulhan's celebrated essay *Les fleurs de Tarbes, ou la Terreur dans les Lettres*. This extraordinary text examines from countless angles the thesis that words can desert thought and exert an independent power, the very power La Harpe could denounce only by repeating it. As a *political* theory of language, attributed to what Paulhan calls the Terror, this thesis does not divide antagonist discourses; on the contrary, it is shared by the Right and the Left, and by all manner of thinking about public speech, whether political or literary. The power of which everyone is speaking is despotic; it is a *usurpation*. The power of words is the power to take the place of the real, legitimate source of power—which is called variously sense, idea, thought, spirit, mind—and to enslave it. When, for example, literary critics charge a writer with repeating clichés or commonplaces, they are accusing "a thinking that is not so much lazy as it is submissive, not so much inert as it is pulled along and as it were *possessed*. In short, we take the cliché as a sign that language has suddenly outdistanced a mind whose freedom and natural play it constrains."[13] Wherever the power of words goes unchecked, there is a crime and it is always a violent crime, a murder. Language is entirely implicated in this murder: it is the scene of the crime, the weapon, the guilty party, but also the victim because the power of words kills the language of true expression. What Paulhan calls the Terror is the relentless attitude of suspicion in the face of this insidious power. Since its principal target is the cliché or the commonplace, the logic of the suspicion is finally always *misological* since "one after the other every word becomes suspect if it has already been used" (32). The Terrorist is repeatedly described as haunted by the ghost of a dead language that is also an innocent language, "this haunting by the innocent language that must have been in the past *also* thought" (248), "this haunting by any innocent and direct language, by a golden age in which words *would resemble* things, in which every term would be *called* . . ." (142). This ghostly language is constantly at risk of being forgotten, or rather progressively erased by the memory of words in themselves and by their sheer repetition. Terror would therefore be the practice of an exorcism or anamnesis, an unforgetting in the course of which a memory of innocence—pure memory, a memory of nothing but itself—would be called to replace a guilty and impure memory.

We will not try to reconstruct Paulhan's refutation of the misological Terror, which passes through a dizzying series of reversals before reaching an affirmation of the linguistic commonplace. In conclusion, let us merely superimpose two moments in this trajectory that clearly echo both each other and the motifs of haunting, ghosts, possession, crime, guilt—in short the motifs of a *disturbing* memory that, like Banquo's ghost, returns uninvited to the feast. Each occurs at a point where Paulhan is puzzling out the reasons for the success of the terroristic theory. What is, he asks in sum, the power of the "power-of-words" argument? If indeed the charge of "verbalism" is but a way of refusing to assent to the other's thought, to take it in as one's own thinking, then rather than a theory of language, is it not merely, asks Paulhan, a polemical, rhetorical tactic for imposing one way of thinking over another? The puzzling thing, however, is how this tactic could have imposed *itself* as a way of thinking about language over any other. How is it that this idea of language as an imposition upon thought imposes itself?

We cite first the second of the two echoing moments of response to this question. Paulhan has just conceded that the misological Terror poses the essential question to literature, namely: "whether literature favors or else ruins the only event that matters: the spirit and its free play" (67). But his complaint is that it approaches this essential question carelessly, and he fears it is in order to

> profit from the impatience and worry that its presence causes in me, so as to snatch a hasty agreement from me: who would not rush to the aid of a thinking that is being bullied?
>
> But who stops to wonder whether it is being *really* bullied? There are crimes so odious that, just by questioning the guilt of the accused party, one becomes right away suspect—as if the horror that the crime should inspire had to be opposed to any examination, and as if one were suspected of immorality for having kept one's mind free. So it is with the opinion I am examining here. It is surely without weight and proof, it condemns, haphazardly, thousands of innocents. *This is because, in order to impose itself, it threatens us with a sort of blackmail. As if we were in league with it, and it reminded us in a hushed voice of I-know-not-what cadaver among us.* We give into it before it has presented its proof. (80; all but first emphasis added)

Rather than push the investigation, rather than remember *whose* cadaver we are concealing, we assent to the thesis of a guilty language.
Our connivance is solicited by a kind of ghostly reminder of an
unassimilable remains. But, worries Paulhan, have we not surrend-
ered too quickly, conceded the argument before it has made its case?
Has there indeed been a crime that can be remembered or have we
not always *anticipated* it and therefore *precipitated* it? Perhaps, in other
words, the thesis of a crime and of guilt comes to fill in the place of
a gap in memory, to supply a cause for an excess, *I-know-not-what*
trace of affect or effect.

This would be the place to cite the other cadaver that has fallen
victim to a fatal anticipation, the one that Paulhan left lying in the
text some fifteen pages earlier:

> The power of words therefore would be quite exactly, in the microcosm
> of expression, the matter that oppresses spirit. Like a man who, in the
> face of a violent blow that is about to strike him, feels himself *already*
> turned into a cadaver, so thought enslaved to words keeps in vain its
> appearance: it is *already* dead, and reduced to nothing, a simple thing
> among others that falls when one pushes it and, once fallen, remains on
> the ground. (64; emphasis added)

If we superimpose these two moments of fatal anticipation, it appears
that the thesis of the power-of-words imposes itself through the same
mechanism as those unduly powerful words themselves: there is a
complicity of "spirit" or "thought" with a certain brutality when,
anticipating a coming blow, it turns itself into a cadaver. The result
is that the "living" entity would be already dead before being
killed off by words, already a simple thing among other things,
fallen, *tombée,* entombed. "Thought" is already a thing before being
struck by the word, or struck as a word: there are only things striking
against things, words against words. The thing itself, we said, is
already its name, and the name a thing, an irreducible thing.
"[Thought] is already dead, and reduced to nothing," writes
Paulhan.

But it is *not quite* nothing, of course: there remains the "I-know-
not-what cadaver among us" that persists as an unassimilable trace.
Language persists and with it the memory of an event, which was a
crime, *that never took place,* that was already past before it happened.
From this place, which is at once no place at all and the commonplace
of language, a memory insists and imposes itself as the ellipsis of the
deadly blow we know is coming because it has already struck.

We mentioned earlier a certain breakdown or ruin of the sign. In doing so, we were anticipating this cadaverous figure in Paulhan's text, this event that arrives as the memory of what never happened or has yet to happen, and that no sign can restore or name but only repeat. What could it mean to preserve the legacy of such an event in the name of "literature"? Does that invention in the wake of terror take the cadaver off our hands or simply banish it beyond the walls of our literary education? These are the kind of questions that will continue to haunt our attempt to describe how these walls came to be constructed.

THREE | *THE WALLS OF SCIENCE*

IN this chapter we will look briefly at three moments in the formation of literary study as a separate domain within educational institutions. These moments could be described as punctuating the history of that formation, between the emergence with the German romantics of the concept of literature and the overhauling modernization of the Western university under the aegis of science and principally historical science. It is not at all this history we will try to reconstruct, but merely certain conceptual negotiations with the distinctions that would define this new institution. At issue in each case is the *spacing* by means of which the distinctions (among different disciplines, but also between the institution and what it is not) are set out, that is, both held apart and held together. For the negotiations we describe are in fact always double, and the space they would define for literary study is at once that of resemblance and difference. In this sense, they supply three figures of what we are calling the division of literature.

In an essay of 1693, modestly titled *Some Thoughts Concerning Education*, it is precisely a certain "literary education" that John Locke sought to discredit as wasteful and useless. Usefulness or utility is virtually the only criterion invoked by Locke as the measure of an education's worth. His treatise is polemical, and in this it shares what seems to be an inevitable mark of the genre, a condition that will have remained more or less constant from Plato to his latter-day disciple, Allan Bloom. (To remark this is simply to recall that educational institutions are not founded on a homogeneous or unified ground, but one that is always traversed and fragmented by different forces or powers.) Locke's targets are, on the one hand, speculative philosophy and metaphysics, particularly Cartesianism, and, on the other, the teaching of classical languages principally through grammar. Neither of these well-ensconced practices contributed, in Locke's opinion, to a practical, useful knowledge, the benefit of which, he writes, can be noe other than the advantages & conveniencys of human life. All speculations in this respect, however curious or refined or seeming profound & solid, if they teach not their followers to doe something either better or in a shorter & easier way than otherwise they could, or else leade them to the discovery of some new & usefull invention, deserve not the name of knowledge.[1]

Useful inventions are clearly not those of a poetic sort, and Locke, who in fact was writing to advise a relative on how to educate his son, counsels this father to discourage any leanings in that direction. For example, he writes, if your son shows a propensity for poetry, you should try to stifle it rather than indulging it by exercises in the composition of Latin verse. "For it is very seldom seen," writes Locke, "that any one discovers Mines of Gold or Silver in *Parnassus*. 'Tis a pleasant Air but a barren Soil; and there are very few Instances of those who have added to their Patrimony by anything they have reaped from thence" (281).

The fact that Locke disparages the profitability or utility of poetic invention with a poetic figure that has become a cliché—" 'Tis a pleasant Air but a barren Soil"—is precisely the sort of divided gesture that turns up repeatedly in the vicinity of literature's or poetry's formation as an object of useful study. That gesture is not a simple suppression of the poetic or its simple exclusion from the institution of useful knowledge. Rather, poetic invention is being divided upon itself, here divided between a certain usefulness and uselessness. It remains useful as a conventional language within which to denounce its uselessness.

Utility, however, need not have the sense of financial gain, as it often does in Locke.[2] Moral utility can also be invoked to the same effect. Morelly, in his *Essai sur le coeur humain, ou principes naturels de l'Education* (1745), addresses the same dilemma as did Locke of a pupil who shows a talent or an inclination for poetry, but he does so armed with the criterion of moral utility.

In that case, as it often happens in the world, Poetry is more esteemed than Poets who often display certain failings; while one ought not to neglect absolutely such an admirable talent in a pupil, one must also take care that the unruliness or dissolution [*déreglement*] of the imagination, which is frequently to be found in such geniuses, not be allowed to pass over into the mind and the conduct. Often, this is a fervor that one must even repress.[3]

The well-ordered education would admit poetry only at a safe distance and on condition that it not "pass over" a certain demarcating line that sets an unruly imagination off from the heart of things. Better still to repress it.

Both of these texts, written before the era of literature's institution, prescribe an exclusion of poetry from the gentleman's useful education. Each nevertheless encounters a difficulty when it comes to either separating poetry out from "useful" knowledge or drawing the line on its unruliness. Exclusion tends to get written over as a species of inclusion. Before we turn to three nineteenth-century instances, we will form the hypothesis that this ambivalent marking of the poetic or literary is no less in evidence when it is a matter of including rather than excluding some kind of literary study from the space of legitimate education. That is, an ambivalent gesture of exclusion/ inclusion will be repeated in some form whenever it is a question of instituting the literary, of setting it up in some way that can be known, used, and repeated with certainty and without incurring too much risk. As a positive discipline, literature and literary studies will have been themselves invented through a series of delimiting demarcations within that other invention we call poetic. But that is not all. What we have perhaps just begun to glimpse is the pattern whereby a force of invention or making—a *poiesis*—divides and withdraws (or is excluded) from the institutions it installs. Such a pattern would also have left its imprint on the modern university in general with its internal division of scientific from humanistic disciplines. The localization (or, more precisely, marginalization, at least economically) of literature departments within that university would be one sign of a historical movement to efface, forget, or suppress the debt of technologically useful invention to this other invention—if indeed it is other—called *poiesis*. The discipline of literary studies, for most of its short history, would have collaborated significantly with this movement insofar as it has tried to understand its object according to models borrowed from history and science, indeed insofar as it has taken the literary as *object* that can be isolated from its instituting force.

THE WRITING ON THE WALL: HEGEL

Stated in such bald terms, without supporting documents, this hypothesis may be hard to swallow. Let us take, then, a kind of *digestif* in the form of one of the strongest defenses of "literary education" as formulated by Hegel right after the turn of the century. Hegel, it is well known, was always talking about digestion, for example: "The mechanical is that which is foreign to the spirit, which then has an interest in digesting the undigested material that has been introduced into it, in comprehending that which is lifeless in itself, and in making it its own property."[4]

The lines just quoted are taken from a speech dated September 29, 1809, which was delivered at the first commencement exercises of the Nuremberg classical *Gymnasium,* an institution that had just been revived under Hegel's direction. The foreign, undigested, mechanical material he is talking about is the grammar of Greek and Latin. Hegel is explaining to the well-to-do burghers of Nuremberg why they should consider themselves fortunate that the district school authority decided to close the popular modern school, the *Trivialschule,* where pupils were trained in the practical disciplines, and to replace it with a more scientifically, theoretically based *Realinstitut.* But it is especially the reopening of the classical *Gymnasium,* where the core of the curriculum is Greek and Latin language and literature, that draws Hegel's approval. Already in Hegel's day it was no easy task to convince practically minded citizens of the worthiness of this venture, and indeed despite his considerable powers as teacher, administrator, fund raiser, and public relations man for the enterprise, the *Gymnasium* would close again in 1816, finally succumbing to the pressures of counterrevolution allied with a demand for a less literary and less philosophical education. This was also the year Hegel was called to the newly founded University of Berlin to fill the chair of philosophy left vacant by the death of Schleiermacher.

We will examine briefly some features of the argument Hegel mobilizes in the circumstances just described. One of its most salient traits concerns specifically the principle of division between the classical and the modern curriculum. Having first deplored the state of education in which classical language training has been replaced by the study of "so-called Things and, among these, everyday sensible objects that are incapable of supplying any cultural material," Hegel applauds the "wise proportion that our most high government has established in this matter." It has decreed that there be two institutions: first, the *Realinstitut,* in which "the sciences and the acquisition of intellectual and useful skills" are taught as "*independent* from ancient literature" (Hegel stresses this independence with italics), and, second, the *Gymnasium,* where "the ancient languages are maintained." The benefit of this division as Hegel sees it is nothing other than the specific institution of what we are calling, with anticipatory anachronism, "literary education," its setting aside and apart from technical education. He writes: "Having thus set itself to one side, it has all the more right to demand that it be allowed to move freely in its separateness [*Abscheidung*] and to remain undisturbed even more at a remove from foreign admixtures or interferences [*Einmischungen*]. Through this separation [*Auscheidung*] and this restriction, it has obtained its true place and the possibility to develop itself more freely and completely."[5] The separate institution that sets the study of classical languages and their literatures apart, while conceding ground to technical training on the side, preserves the former from a disturbing mixture and institutes it in a purity. The school walls set up a kind of protective barrier to keep out foreigners. Hegel's description summarizes most succinctly the movement of institutionalization as one of *division* in the interest of purity. To be sure, there is a price to be paid, a certain sacrifice, but also a prize to be won.

Given this description of his institution's newly won right to expel the foreign from its midst, it is all the more striking that Hegel insists in the body of his speech on a cultural formation or *Bildung* that is essentially and necessarily an encounter with the foreign and the undigested. The freedom of this *Bildung* to move within the walls separating it from a certain technical foreignness is described as the formative possibility of coming up against another kind of wall, partition, or barrier [*Scheidewand*]. Hegel's whole theory of *Bildung*—culture, formation, education—depends on scaling this wall, or rather on taking it in—digesting it. I quote a long passage:

Cultural formation [*Bildung*] must have a prior material and object that it works on and reforms. We must acquire the world of antiquity so as to possess it but, even more important, so as to have something to work on. However, in order for it to become an *object* [Gegenstande], the substance of nature and of spirit must come to stand over against us, it must have received the form of something foreign. . . . This demand for separation [*Trennung*] is so necessary that it exteriorizes itself in us as a universal and well-known drive [*Trieb*]. The foreign, the distant carries with it an attractive interest that leads us to concern ourselves and to take pains with it; the desirable stands in an inverse relation to the proximity with which it is to us. . . . It is on this centrifugal drive of the soul that is founded, in sum, the necessity of offering to this soul the very separation [*Scheidung*] it seeks from its natural essence and situation, and of introducing into the young mind a distant, foreign world. But the wall [*Scheidewand*] by means of which is effected this separation in view of culture, which is what we are talking about here, is the world and the language of the ancients; and yet the wall, which separates us from ourselves, contains at the same time all the initial anchoring points and the threads of a return to ourselves, of a friendly reconciliation with ourselves, but with ourselves according to the true universal essence of spirit. (321–22)

It seems, then, that there are two kinds of walls, which we might call indigestible and digestible. The indigestible wall sets the study of classical languages and literatures off from foreign influences, in particular the demand for practical, technical formation. It is realized or materialized in the wall of brick and mortar—that is, a hard-to-digest, hard-to-infiltrate substance—that surrounds the *Gymnasium*. Once in place, it allows the activity programmed within to develop freely, which, as we've seen, does not mean without walls, but rather with a freedom to digest, to appropriate those other walls that are foreign languages and literatures. The dividing wall of *Bildung,* therefore, is itself divided between that which effectively separates or holds apart so as to prevent contamination, and that which poses itself as a separation only in order to be overcome. The question, of course, is whether this division between two kinds of walls—this wall within the wall—is itself digestible or indigestible.

If we look for a reply in the *Phenomenology of Spirit,* which had been published just two years earlier and which the commencement address freely adapts to the circumstance, there would seem to be little doubt that no wall can be left standing in the centrifugal / centripetal movement of Spirit always back to itself, comprehending in an always larger synthesis the foreign, the other into itself. The dialectic of Spirit, as Derrida puts it in *Glas,* is dialectophagic, consuming all natural languages and subsuming them to the universal language of the concept.[6] Thus Hegel, as we have seen, has no apparent difficulty in answering—in digesting or overcoming—the objection raised to a classical "literary education," the objection that it places a wall between the mind and the knowledge it acquires in a foreign tongue:

> A universal protest arose against such an apprenticeship of Latin in its unfortunate development; there arose chiefly the feeling that a people cannot be considered cultivated if it cannot express all the treasures of science in its own language nor move freely within it as concerns every content. This intimacy according to which our own language belongs to us is lacking from those forms of knowledge that we possess only in a foreign tongue; they are separated from us by a wall [*Scheidewand*] which does not permit them to be for the spirit such that it is truly at home. (315)

This objection is simply turned on its head when Hegel argues, as we have seen, that (1) the wall in question is merely an exteriorization of the drive that attracts us to the distant and the foreign so that, in effect, (2) the wall is but the means for spirit to appropriate foreignness in order to return to itself ("the wall, which separates us from ourselves, contains at the same time all the initial anchoring points and the threads of a return to ourselves"). With this reversal, it turns out that Spirit is never more at home than when it ventures into foreign lands.

The formation of Spirit, its education, is omniphagic, or rather it would be so if the wall in question here were only a concept, a linguistic concept, or a concept of language. But what about bricks and mortar, those decidedly heavy, unspiritual substances? What of Hegel's initial split gesture that consists of excluding a certain foreignness—the domain of the merely *practical* or *technical*—in order to free up the space for the all-inclusive drive of self-appropriation? What of the strange topology of an institution that is founded as a part in order better to englobe, include, comprehend the whole? Must it not thereby include what it sets out to exclude—mere Things, everyday sensible objects—that other part which would have to have a place *within* the space of that institution and not only, as Hegel describes it, alongside it, outside it? Is there not, therefore, another foreign material or wall planted within the domain of spiritual *Bildung,* one that it cannot simply transform and appropriate into its own substance, but that resists this work?

The speech of September 29, 1809, provokes such questions but gives little hint how Hegel might have confronted them, as surely he must have. When he gives a speech on the same occasion the following year, however, several themes of his address bring us into some kind of contact with the indigestible wall evoked above. It is not just the fact that Hegel marks an explicit transition in his speech from a treatment of the internal situation of the institution to its "external arrangement and means," its "material needs," and foremost among them the need to repair the building, which seems to have been ready to fall down. Nor is it the fact of his public acknowledgment of a gift to the school from a certain Frau Bauerreis of her complete rock collection: Her benevolence, he remarks, will allow the school to initiate students into that part of physical science "that considers the quiet birth of nature in stones, the mysterious process of formation that, like a language of silence, unpretentiously deposits in the depths of the earth its delicate forms that delight the eye, stir understanding to reach the concept, and give the mind an image of calm, regular, and self-contained beauty" (339). There would be much to say about this stony silence that is nevertheless *like* a language and that therefore presents no wall to understanding; on the contrary, it incites the mind to delight itself with the concept of beauty.

But there is still another allusion to a wall of sorts, one that Hegel allows, up to a point, to stand and to offer a certain resistance. Hegel reports to his audience that during the last school year, and on the order of His Majesty's government, military training exercises were made part of the regular curriculum for the senior class. This state of affairs requires a certain amount of explanatory comment, since it may not be immediately clear how the classical, "literary" education outlined the previous year can accommodate such a practice. Hegel writes:

> Just as the *nihil humani a me alienum puto* is a fine maxim from the viewpoint of morality, so too does it have a role in the technical domain, but its full meaning is in the domain of science. An otherwise cultivated man has not, in fact, limited his nature to something in particular; rather, he has made it apt for everything. To engage in a science or skill that is foreign to him, when that becomes necessary, there is literally nothing for him to do but to take the thing in hand and seize it, instead of remaining within the representation of the difficulties and the inability to surmount them. Thus, the practice of arms customarily seems to be something very heterogeneous to that which has study as its destination; but the young mind is not, in and for itself, so distant from this, and such a trial is what serves best to tear down the representation of the wall [*Scheidewande*] that we build around our destination. (331)

The practice of a certain technical skill, when it becomes necessary (when, for example, it is mandated by the state), tears down the *representation* of the wall behind which study is constructed as a pure science, a pure discipline without any technical admixture. This is to say that the separation of classical from technical study, upon which the institution is founded, is deconstructible *of and by* necessity.

But what is the difference between this deconstruction of the wall and the digestion of walls that goes on in the course of a classical *Bildung?* In other words, hasn't Hegel just given another demonstration of the omniphagic Spirit in relation to which nothing human can be alien? Yes, up to a point, but with the difference that the represented wall is attacked, so to speak, from a certain outside. It is the wall drawn *around* the destination of study and not a wall we present to ourselves within that destination only in order to scale them, not the silent language of stones or the foreign languages of ancient Greece and Rome. The rifles and swords are not said to speak any language comprehensible to mind, which is precisely why the latter risks immobilizing itself within its own "representation of the difficulties and the inability to surmount them." There is nothing to be done but to take the thing in hand and seize it, not as the mind seizes a concept, *ein Begriff,* not to grasp at the idea or representation of weapons, *begreifen,* but to clutch the thing in the hand, *zugreifen.* There is only force here, a grabbing or clutching from which mind is absent, or rather, as Hegel puts it, in which there is no time for reflection, no space for representation.

Although he will finally describe this practice as a training for the mind as well, an exercise in which one learns, precisely, a presence of mind, it is a presence that could just as well be described as an absence, the absence of reflection.

> Already as a means of cultural formation, this instruction is very impor-
> tant. To practice in this fashion to seize quickly, to have presence of
> mind, to execute right away what is ordered without first reflecting this
> way and that, is the most direct way of opposing the inertia and the
> distraction of mind which takes time to let what it has heard accede to
> meaning, and still more time to return to the outside and to execute
> partially what it has half understood (330).

The mind here is being trained to operate as reflex, rather than reflection; it would therefore be just another muscle attached to the hand. But in that case, is it still possible to assert that this is indeed *mind* seizing what is external to it and appropriating it to itself, or on the contrary, has there not been a prior erasure, an ellipsis of the only difference opposing mind to objects or bodies—the difference of a space/time for reflection within which there is at least the possibility to project certain consequences before executing the order to fire? In other words, is it not mind that has been seized by something external to it, and been given orders, canceling whatever walls of resistance it might want to set up, eliminating the differential interval that alone allows us to posit in the first place something like mind as opposed to anything else? Indeed, this prior erasure, as Hegel describes it here, is already the effect of a force—His Majesty's government—ordering the incorporation of military exercises into the curriculum, thereby tearing down a certain wall. Hegel, of course, had no choice but to comply freely, although he probably took time to reflect on his compliance.[7]

What this little episode might indicate is the precarious construction of the wall when it is taken up as the figure that would divide one kind of study or object from another. In its instituting moment, the discourse of literary studies would have relied on such a wall to set it off from technical or practical knowledge, the grasp of things themselves without the mediating, deferring, and differing interval of the letter of a language. Whether the wall is engineered from the side of utilitarian, antispeculative education or from the side of speculative, anti-empirical *Bildung,* and despite the fact that each is quite precisely what the other works to exclude, the construction of the wall between them is deconstructible. This suggests that the ambivalent gesture we began by describing with reference to Locke's division of poetry finds more than just an echo in Hegel's various divisive tactics in view of an institution that would incorporate, rather than expulse, the poetic imagination and its inventions. The point would be to see how the opposition of the one institutional program to the other is being overwritten, overridden by nonprogrammable forces of effraction that work at them at the edges, where instituting divisions are set down and immediately begin to redivide. In this regard, the episode may also have the value of a reminder that these forces at work opening the institution to some outside determine a process that is not necessarily to be evaluated only and always, according to some liberal, laissez-faire model, as a healthy thing, but which has also, now and then, here and there, to be resisted. But where and when and calling upon what force? If the literary is understood as nothing other and nothing less than the space of division wherein institutions are founded but also wherein they founder, can such an understanding provide, not a ground to be sure, but an always provisional strategy for the practical evaluation of the various forces at work shaping so-called literary education?

Hegel's walls do not yet delimit what we understand by a separate domain of literary study in the university. Indeed, in the distinction between the classical *Gymnasium* and the scientific *Realinstitut,* we may recognize the shift that was being negotiated toward the modern university. To assume a place in that latter institution, literary study would also have to shift in ways that Hegel would probably have deplored. Principal among these is the cognitive project that would be put in place to justify the establishment of a discipline of literature.

The notion that literature could be an object as well as an instrument of knowledge made its way under the general sponsorship, so to speak, of the positivistic model that, in the latter part of the nineteenth century, put its mark on the modern, scientific university.

The effects of this model on literary study were perhaps nowhere so evident as in France. Rather than try to defend that assertion, however, by comparing certain rhythms of the university's modernization in France, Germany, England, the United States, and so forth—a task that is quite beyond the scope of this chapter[8]—we will attempt to do no more than isolate some of those effects in the thought of two figures who played crucial roles in the institutionalization of literature in France: the philosopher Hippolyte Taine and the literary historian Gustave Lanson.

THE ANALOGY OF SCIENCE: TAINE

Nietzsche, who corresponded with him, referred to Hippolyte Taine as the greatest living historian.[9] But as a dead historian (he died in 1893), Taine has gone into an eclipse that began sometime before World War I, when most of his works were last edited. The recent reissue (1985) of his *Philosophie de l'art* by the respected series *Corpus des oeuvres de philosophie en langue française* seems unlikely to reverse this trend, which, moreover, few would argue is unjustified. But if a certain kind of oblivion may be merited, there is perhaps a way in which Taine's legacy has been all the more assured by the neglect accorded his writings. Precisely because Taine is so little read with the sort of attention demanded by work still considered important for us today, it has been possible to assume uncritically some significant features of Tainian thought about art and literature even as the principal tenets of his historical method have long been discredited.

Of these features, none has had quite the tenacity of the analogy, a pervasive and determining one for Taine, between natural science and the study of art. It is in the guise of this analogy that Taine, along with the generation of literary and art historians he trained, proposed in effect to justify the inclusion of their discipline within a university that, in France in the latter half of the nineteenth century, was being largely refashioned by historians and sociologists according to their own model of positive, scientific knowledge.[10] Now, a question one might ask after more than a century of experience and experiment is whether this analogy has exhausted its usefulness or, on the contrary, has remained, perhaps veiled in oblivion, a key element in the determination of a discipline of literary studies. The recent turn to a certain historicism by many who are nominally professors of literature might suggest that the analogy was never so dead that it could not be revived in some version. But in order to pose the question meaningfully—that is, with a clearer sense of what we are asking about—it will help to consider closely how the analogy functions in the site of its inauguration by Taine.

We call this site an inauguration, although of course that is somewhat arbitrary. Taine himself often pointed to the literary critic and journalist Sainte-Beuve as his predecessor, the one who had shown the path to be followed in the study of art. It is the path of the scientific historical method. Like Sainte-Beuve, Taine considers that his task is not to judge the work nor to establish rules for the artist nor to set standards of taste for the public. This repudiation of a former dogmatism is essential to what Taine calls modern aesthetics:

> Suppose that, as a result of all these discoveries, we managed to define the nature and delimit the conditions for the existence of each art: we would then have a complete explanation of the fine arts and of art in general; that is what is called an *aesthetics*. It is to this latter that we aspire, gentlemen, and not to any other. Ours is modern and differs from the old aesthetics in that it is historical and not dogmatic, that is, in that it does not impose precepts, but rather observes laws.[11]

Such laws are comparable to those observed by a natural science: physics, physiology, biology, or, in the version of the analogy to which Taine reverts most often, botany. Here is the first explicit formulation of the botanic comparison:

> [The modern method] proceeds like botany that studies, with an equal interest, now the orange tree and the laurel, now the pine and the birch; it is even a sort of applied botany, whose object is not plants but human works. As such, it follows the general movement that is bringing the moral sciences [*sciences morales;* today Taine would no doubt say *sciences humaines*] closer to the natural sciences and which, by endowing the former with the principles, precautions, and directions of the latter, is communicating to them the same solidity and assuring them of the same progress. (20)

We are reading from the text of lectures that Taine delivered at the Ecole des Beaux-Arts between 1864 and 1869. This pedagogical destination not only determines certain formal features, but as well informs the very method that is being taught. The *rapprochement* between the "moral" and the natural sciences to which Taine has just alluded is a movement that has as its principal stage the institution of the university. Or rather, it is with this movement that the reorganized scientific university can begin to emerge. Taine, who may be counted as a founder of the human sciences, would nevertheless remain throughout his career marginal to the institution of the university. This marginality confers on Taine's lessons a divided status: on the one hand, they have no legitimacy within the institution as defined by the dogmatic aesthetics or rhetoric to which Taine opposes his modern method; on the other hand, and as Taine puts it himself, they "aspire to" a new aesthetics and therefore to a new legitimating institution. What is important to grasp in this conjunction is the fading of the distinction between a method and an institution, between, if you will, the procedure *of* a discipline and its status *as* discipline for the university. With this fadeout, we can no longer be certain whether one studies art because it reveals certain laws or whether it reveals certain laws because one studies it.

Of course, even to entertain the question in its second form requires a certain twisting or distortion of "modern" thought, by which one generally means thought guaranteed by the very scientific method that is in question here. It requires, specifically, that one consider seriously some implications of the collapsed or faded distinction, for example, the implication that the scientific law is also, or perhaps one should say first of all, the law of an institution that constitutes objects for knowledge. That is, it is the law of an institution that *both* determines the object as having an essence or *nature propre,* which is therefore different from every other type of object so determined, *and* installs comparisons or analogies among the sciences or disciplines of these objects. How is this double and ambivalent project marked in Taine's method?

We can begin to look for an answer in the application of the method to the questions: "What is art and in what does its nature consist?" The first thing Taine does is to divide the possible field of this question: "Instead of imposing on you a formula, I am going to bring you into contact with facts. Because here, as elsewhere, there are facts, positive facts that can be observed: I mean the *works of art* classed by families in museums and libraries just as plants are in a herbarium or animals in a natural history museum" (20). In response, then, to the question *What is art?* Taine responds: it consists in the totality of the works of art, already collected, labeled, and classified as such. With that, however, he in effect answers a different question, not *What is art?* but rather *What was art?* The shift from art to historical artifact apparently follows directly from the other shift that is explicitly advocated here: from formula to fact, that is, from a prescriptive to a descriptive definition. This shift has already been identified as the basis of the modern discipline Taine is defining, but the distinction between prescription and description cannot be maintained without difficulty. By pointing to the art of our ancestors (descriptive definition), Taine cannot resist finally concluding what art is in its essence, which entails a prescription. We are therefore not very surprised when this modern, descriptive aesthetics leads Taine to repeat a classical definition of art in most of its details.

The essential character of art—its essence—is imitation. Like so many of his predecessors, however, Taine finds this formula to be insufficient. It must therefore be immediately refined or supplemented by another that is equally familiar and goes like this: Art does not imitate nature exactly; rather, it augments and brings out the natural essence that, in nature itself, remains hidden. With this, Taine echoes closely the moves of many eighteenth-century aesthetic thinkers, for example L'abbé Batteux and his idealist notion of *la belle nature* in *Les Beaux arts réduits à un même principe* (1741). At other moments, one is prompted to think more of Diderot and his *théorie des rapports*.[12] But the point is that Taine, like these earlier aestheticians, is unable to avoid the contradiction between formulaic or prescriptive definition (art as imitation) and a confrontation with the certain facts that contradict such formulas; or as Taine puts it, the fact that "the greatest schools of art are those that alter to the greatest degree real relations." And to this same bind he will bring a similar solution by finally assigning to art the function of supplementing a natural order that leaves essences insufficiently marked or visible:

> The goal of art is to bring out [this essential character] and, if art undertakes this task, it is that nature does not suffice. This is because, in nature, the character is only dominant; in art it is a matter of making it dominating. This character fashions real objects, but it does not fashion them fully. It is impeded in its action, hindered by the intervention of other causes. It has not been able to penetrate, with a strong enough or visible enough imprint, into the objects that bear its mark. Man senses this lacuna and it is in order to fill it that he invents art. (35)

We can summarize the pattern as we've seen it developing so far in Taine's definition of art. The descriptive definition—art as classified fact or artifact—quickly yields to prescription when Taine proposes to derive the essence of art from what can be observed of these artifacts. The essence of art—*son propre*—is imitation, but not exact imitation; it is imitation of relations, but once again not exact imitation; it is rather the imitation of the essential character of a thing that may be dissimulated or insufficiently marked in nature. At the end of this altogether classical development, Taine concludes that "*le propre* of the work of art is to render the essential character, or at least an important character of the object, as dominating and as visible as possible and, to do that, the artist eliminates traits that hide it, chooses those that manifest it, corrects those in which it is altered, redoes those in which it is annulled" (37).

Now, one will notice that this definition is affected by a kind of fold at its center. The proper nature or essential characteristic of art is to render the essential character of the thing represented. But this is to say in effect that the proper nature of art is to have no nature properly its own. Art is therefore not a thing *like* any other. Rather it must yield itself to rendering the character of the other thing; it thus gives itself the appearance of what it is not. This theory of imitation—and let us repeat one last time that it is anything but Taine's invention[13]—ought to prevent one from treating art as a thing like other things since it supposes necessarily that art is not comparable to anything it imitates, which is precisely why it can imitate or represent. Taine, however, does not draw this conclusion, and after having established in effect the fundamental, essential sense in which the art work is not like a plant or an animal or a landscape or a human being, he proceeds *as if it were* comparable to any of these natural phenomena. This then is the place of *analogy* with the natural sciences (especially botany and geography) in Taine's methodical description. But as analogy, it assures that this description will speak of everything but "art," which, precisely, is not a thing like any other.

Let us then look more closely at this analogy, which labors to make of art the object of a methodical science and thereby eligible for admission as a discipline in the university. As we do so, it will be good to recall the division that Taine performed at the outset when he designated the collected art works of the past as the entire field of such a methodical investigation. We have already seen how this division, which is meant to separate a descriptive from a prescriptive procedure by isolating what art was from what it should be or should become, does not hold up very well or for very long. A similar breakdown or confusion is going to affect the analogical mainstay of the scientific project. The fact is there is not one analogy here but two, and they tend to interfere with each other.

In the first version of the analogy, the art work is the object of a science, just as plants are the object of botany. In the second version, art is not the work produced but the *production* of works of art and in that it is like a science, for example, like botany. Taine explains in this fashion the importance of art, its place in the evolution of human knowledge. I quote from the final lines of the first chapter, titled "On the Nature of the Work of Art":

At this point, a higher life opens up, that of contemplation, in which man takes an interest in the permanent and generative causes upon which his life and that of his fellow men depend, in the dominating and essential characters that regulate every structure and imprint their mark on the least detail. To attain this higher life, he has two paths: the first is science by which, isolating these causes and these fundamental laws, he expresses them in exact formulas and abstract terms; the second is art by which he manifests these causes and these fundamental laws, no longer in arid definitions that are inaccessible to the mass of men and intelligible only for a few specialists, but in a sensible fashion, addressing itself not only to reason but also to the senses and to the heart of the most ordinary man.

In this passage, the two versions of the analogy are already crossing and interfering with each other according to a pattern that is going to become far more strained in the succeeding chapter, "The Production of the Work of Art." Once again, this strain should be read as, at least in part, an effect of the institutional marginality or rather the shifting of institutional margins out of which Taine writes. Indeed, given the frequent platitude and programmatic aspect of much of this writing, one would not be wrong to read the text as largely *dictated* by and from within the institution to which Taine aspires. For the dominant, even dominating trait of the passage is the insistence on the cognitive value of art, its worth as a necessary supplement to science.

Art is like science and as such deserves its place in the scientific university. But in this version, the analogy menaces the coherence of the comparison between the work of art and the natural object. Perhaps the best way to demonstrate this incoherence is semi-algebraically with the formula: work of art is to X as natural phenomenon is to natural science, for example, as plant is to botany. Taine, in effect, fills in the missing term of this analogical formula in two different ways. In one version of the analogy, X equals the *study* of works of art. And because of the relations expressed by the formula, such study may legitimately be conceived as scientific and methodical, which entails as well conceiving of the field of study as a de-limited and fixed one, as the field of catalogued, classified works of art. In the other version of the analogy, however, X equals the *making,* or as Taine will say, the *production* of art works and no longer the study of works that already exist and are labeled as such. But inserting this notion of a making or a *teknē* skews the formula out of its analogical symmetry. If art as the practice of art (and not the study of the art work as thing or phenomenon) can be said to be like a science, it is because it manifests a certain kind of knowledge of the world. But it also fashions the objects by which such knowledge is made manifest. At this point, the analogy is threatened by the uncertain value of the very term that, of the four, serves to anchor the others in a certain knowledge and delimit their meaning, the last term "science." Like all analogies, this one must be reversible, and here that reversibility upsets the very ground of scientific certainty to which the formula is meant to lead. For now it can be said that science, *like art,* makes or produces the object of its study.[14] It can be said, but for all the world Taine will not be induced to say it and give away the ground his text has been working to gain: the ground on which to establish a method's claim to produce only knowledge worthy of comparison to scientific knowledge. Instead, the dangerous reversibility that shows the scientist in the guise of an artist fashioning the very object he studies will be left to work its way through the text, like the corrosive acid in the paper on which most books are still printed. We know now that the pages of these books will soon disintegrate and become unreadable.

To return, then, to our point of departure: the double version of the analogy with science locates one particularly dense site of ambivalence in Taine's project. While this ambivalence undoubtedly has the unsettling effects we have seen on the cognitive claims of a discipline that Taine was laboring to justify, we should not be too quick to conclude from this that the demonstration has simply backfired when the analogy proves to be faulty. Rather, it has perhaps shown up a different relation of what is called art or literature to the cognitive, scientific institution, a relation of *invention,* or to use Taine's term, production.[15] In other words, the traces of this relation we have been able to read do more than disturb the logic of an analogy. Beyond that, they point to a fundamental instability in the scientific foundation of the modern university, a division or a fault line that is taken within that institution when it legitimates the study of art as a scientifically historical pursuit. Such an instability need not be seen as a danger, unless one adopts the attitude of a structural engineer whose job it is to retrofit old buildings to meet new earthquake resistance standards. And yet, the programs by which institutions attempt to contain divisional instabilities are also being overwritten, overridden by forces of effraction that are as nonprogrammed although less spectacular than earthquakes. As forces of transformation and not just destruction—the best word here is still deconstruction—they ally with that instability within (which is not, therefore, just within) that has characterized—some might want to say plagued—literary studies since their inception. This, however, is an assertion that still remains largely to be substantiated by following one or two threads of the history of literary studies in the university that Taine initiated.

THE DIVISION WITHIN: LANSON

Unlike his elder Taine, Gustave Lanson knew considerable success as a professor of literature in the French university during the period of that discipline's investiture. By championing the cause of literary history, Lanson succeeded in winning the chair of *éloquence française* at the Sorbonne in 1904, where he settled into his unofficial position as "the big boss of literary studies in France"[16] for at least the next twenty years. Many factors doubtless contributed to that success, but we will isolate the structuring logic that began to emerge in our consideration of Taine: the marked congruence between the *procedures* of a discipline and its *status* as discipline for the university. Lansonian theory and method, that is, would appear to be dictated less by some internal logic of the literary work than by a logic of the institution within which literature must take its place as the legitimate object of knowledge and study. In this regard, Lanson would be one of Taine's direct heirs (or beneficiaries) who brings this external, institutional logic to the surface and even cites it as a justification of the literary historical method he advocates:

> Even if the methods I have just defined were not the only method of literary history and the preliminary condition for the exercise of all other recommended methods, *it would at least be the one that was appropriate to the study of French literature in the university*. By means of this method, literature ceases to be a parasitical appendix there, an ornament as some say, an embarrassment say others; *it harmonizes with the general plan and with the essential goal of a university*.[17]

In other words, our method may not be the "right" one but at least it is teachable.

Lanson is writing here in 1901. The determination of, in Lanson's terms, "the general plan" and "essential goal" of the university had by that time been in the hands of historians since the reform of higher education was undertaken in the 1870s. It is they, trained in the new German historiography, who could be heard disparaging the ornamental, embarrassing "parasitical appendix" of literature, or rather "rhetoric," within that general plan. And it would be Lanson, more than any other in France at least, who fashioned the study of modern literature to fit the plan. Because Lanson's ambition in this regard is so baldly set out, his methodological writings often read like a programmatic brochure for the institutionalization of literary studies. And what show up there in sharpest relief are, once again, the divisions inscribed on a field by the institutional logic dictating them.

An essay from 1910 titled "The Method of Literary History" is one of Lanson's most complete programmatic outlines.[18] He is writing at the height of his influence in the university and on literate society in general. The fact that one can even distinguish these two spheres of influence was a rather recent development in the French republic of letters and it defines up to a point the rhetorical situation of Lanson's essay.[19] It would appear to divide the address of the essay between the university's watchdogs of methodological seriousness, on the one hand, and, on the other, those readers who, as Lanson puts it, "expect only a refined recreation from literature" and for whom, therefore, method is anathema. Lanson, in other words, is playing a rather difficult hand because the reassurances he offers to one side risk raising the suspicions of the other. Finally, however, we must read the principal concern of such a text to be the legitimation which by then it was increasingly the business of the university to provide, so that even when he addresses explicitly a general public as he does here, Lanson speaks with the authority that public now grants to the university. This "sociology" of the text, therefore, underscores the ways in which the process in question divides the literary into legitimate and illegitimate domains. And it is on the edges of this division that Lanson's essay displays an ambivalence that his method can neither absorb nor conjure away.

This ambivalence can be seen to cluster around the term "impressionism." With this term, Lanson designates literary criticism that merely records the reactions of the critic to what he is reading. From the standpoint of methodical, historical criticism, it is the repository of fantasies, the refuge of laziness and incompetence. Lanson, however, does not evict all impressionist criticism from the ranks of legitimate literary study. He attempts, rather, to insert a division between, in effect, a good, useful, "legitimate" impressionism and a dangerous kind. He writes:

> Impressionist criticism is unassailable and legitimate when it stays within the limits of its definition. The problem is that it never does. The man who describes what goes on within him as he reads a book, without

asserting anything beyond his internal reactions, furnishes literary history with valuable testimony of which there can never be enough. But it is rare that a critic abstains from slipping historical judgments in among his impressions or from taking his own particular make-up for the character of the object.

Already one begins to hear a certain hesitation in these assertions which slide from the initial categorical statement—impressionism *never* stays within its legitimate limits—to the more tempered assessment that the impressionist critic *rarely* respects the confines of his competence. Clearly, Lanson is not ready to require a strict expulsion of impression from method. He continues:

> As it is rarely pure, impressionism is rarely absent. It disguises itself as history and as impersonal logic; it inspires systems that exceed or deform knowledge.
> One of the principal uses of method is to hunt down this misguided and deluded impressionism and to purge it from our work. But we do accept straightforward impressionism, the measure of the reaction of a mind to a book; it serves our ends. (32)

One should take this language of purification and purge to be a significant symptom here. It occurs in the midst of observations that raise serious doubts about the feasibility of ever purging impure impressionism either from the pure variety or from strictly historical criticism.[20] The problem is that the division between pure impression and pure method is itself impure as long as impressionism can "disguise itself as history" and given that impressionist criticism never "stays within the limits of its definition.[21] Similar language recurs several pages later and will likewise be caught in a kind of logical crossfire: "Our whole method must therefore be disposed in such a way as to rectify knowledge, to purify it of subjective elements." This sentence concludes the first section of the essay. The next section begins by partially taking back what has just been put forward: "Still one must not push this purification [*épuration*] too far" (37). The section break introduced between the two propositions cannot attenuate the affront suffered here by the most elementary principle of clear thinking. How, you may well ask, is one meant to conceive a purification that is itself impure or incomplete? What, in other words, is a *partial* purification, one that goes only so far but not too far? And at what point does method become *too* pure of impression?

Lanson does not entertain these questions although he recognizes implicitly that the lack of answers to them is at the source of the kind of error into which the literary historian frequently falls. But that the scientific literary historian *knows* he may be in error will also be invoked as another criterion distinguishing him from the impressionist and the dilettante critic who is content to take his fancies for truths. For there *is* a truth of literature, by which Lanson necessarily understands an objective truth which alone can be the basis of knowledge: "Our whole method, as I have already said, is constituted so as to separate subjective impression from objective knowledge, to limit it, control it and interpret it to the benefit of objective knowledge" (47). We can see here again how Lanson's formulation is laboring to conjoin two incompatible operations: to separate out impression, that is, to purify objective method of an impure subjectivism, but also to limit and control impression, which is clearly not the same thing and recalls the mixed concept of limited or impure purification. Had he read Kant's *Critique of Judgment,* which seems unlikely, Lanson might have seen better the inevitable contradictions into which he is being led by a scientific positivism applied to aesthetic judgment, the contradiction that Kant seeks to avoid with the principle of subjective universalism as the basis of the judgment of taste. Although a certain Kantianism still exercised at the time a significant influence in French philosophy, literary historicism would seem to have evolved in relative isolation from that influence. Once again, it is necessary to see this development through the logic of the legitimating forces of the institution where the disciplines of history and sociology, rather than philosophy, were the arbiters of scientific rigor.

But the point is not to lament the philosophical naïveté of this literary scholar, in which he would certainly not have been alone then or now. Rather, one must try to read this troubled logic as symptomatic of the divisions installed by the institution for which or in view of which Lanson is writing. If impressionism must be somehow both purged and retained, separated out and included, it is because the institution of literary study is not a one-step but at least a two-step process and because the excluded term in the first step is the included term in the second step. This means that an instability in the divisional process cannot be worked out once and for all but must induce repetitions with a certain regularity.

We have so far considered only that version of the division whereby a method of literary study renounces impressionism so as to take its place within the scientific university. In this version the line of separation is drawn *around* the institution of knowledge and divides the two different ways of talking about literature that Lanson identifies as subjective and objective, impressionistic and scientific, illegitimate and legitimate, extra- and intra-institutional, journalistic and academic. But this gesture must be followed by another and seemingly opposite move that preserves literary study as a separate domain *within* the university, one that is unassimilable to the domains of history or sociology. In this case, the line of separation is drawn *through* the institution and can be seen to rejoin the discourse of impressionism to the discourse of method. We cite a passage from Lanson's essay that most explicitly aims to accomplish this second and no less necessary gesture.

> In the immense accumulation of printed texts, we are specially concerned with those that, by the character of their form, have the property of determining in the reader imaginative evocations, sentimental reactions, aesthetic emotions. It is in this way that our study cannot be confused with other historical studies and that literary history is something other than a minor science auxiliary to history. . . . This sensitive and aesthetic character of the works that are our "special domain" means that we cannot study them without a disturbance to our soul, our imagination, and our taste. . . . The historian, when faced with a document, undertakes to evaluate the personal elements in order to eliminate them. But it is precisely to these personal elements that the emotive and aesthetic power of a work are due; therefore we must keep them. The historian who would use the testimony of Saint-Simon takes pains to rectify it, that is to subtract from it Saint-Simon, whereas we subtract from it precisely whatever is not Saint-Simon. While the historian looks for general facts and concerns himself with individuals only to the extent that they represent groups or influence movements, we for our part consider individuals first because feeling, passion, taste, beauty are the things of individuals. (34–35)

From this one may clearly see how the first-step division installed between the scientific, historical study of literature in the university and the impressionism of an extra-institutional domain has to be reversed in a second step. But this second division is traced within that very institution where it sets off one discipline from another according to the destination each assigns to the texts it undertakes to study and to teach. And one should remark as well that this destination, which is first identified in formal terms, quickly comes to be characterized in terms of the individual and that notably singular but also representative individual called an author. By taking the individual author (e.g., Saint-Simon) as the distinguishing mark of disciplinary specificity, literary studies institutes its object as a consolidation of the subject, as that which works to represent subjectivity to itself.

But this passage also gives direct confirmation, if any were still needed, of the preeminence achieved by the historical discipline. When Lanson writes that "the historian looks for general facts and concerns himself with individuals only to the extent that they represent groups or influence movements," he summarizes succinctly the reversal that has long since occurred within Aristotelian distinctions, a reversal that makes possible, in effect, the scientific university. For Aristotle, one will recall, history is never concerned with the general or the universal; that is the domain of poetry, which is why it is "a more philosophical and a higher thing than history."

> The true difference [between the historian and the poet] is that one relates what has happened, the other what may happen. Poetry, therefore, is a more philosophical and a higher thing than history: for poetry tends to express the universal, history the particular. By the universal I mean how a person of a certain type will on occasion speak or act, according to the law of probability or necessity; and it is this universality at which poetry aims.[22]

Lansonian method would be but one effect of the highly complex displacement within this relation history-poetry, the particular and the general, empirical fact and universal truth. By means of the displacement, history assumes its ascendancy as the model of a general science, but it is now an objective, empirical generality, not at all the generality of the law, the idea, or the ideal.[23] We could say that this displacement occurs along the axis of the division subject-object, a division that is presupposed by that model of a technical or objective science. In fact, however, it is this division of subject from object that is being *produced* and *reproduced* by the institutional distinctions. As we saw in Taine's unstable analogy between science and art, a certain production of "its" object is the prerequisite of an auto-production of science itself. Literary science must likewise produce itself, but it can do so only impurely, by carrying over the impurity of an illegitimate "impressionism." It is this "impressionism" that falls to the literary historian, or, stated from another angle, it is to literature that falls the subject.

And yet Lanson, any more than Taine, cannot be content to stop there for that would mean renouncing all chance for historico-scientific legitimation. Therefore, after having established the difference between the domains of history and literature, he hastens to emphasize their resemblance:

But, all the same, what is finest and greatest about the individual genius is not the singularity that isolates it; it is, in this very singularity, to gather up in itself and symbolize the collective life of a period and a group, to be representative. We must seek to know, then, this whole humanity that has expressed itself in the great writers, all the fold lines of human or national thought and sensibility whose summits are indicated by the great writers.

Thus we must advance in two contradictory directions at the same time: bring out the individuality, express it in its unique, irreducible and unanalyzable aspect, and also replace the masterpiece in a series, make the man of genius appear as the product of a milieu and the representative of a group.

With the notion of the writer-representative-of-a-period-or-group, Lanson returns to the fold of history "properly speaking" as he has just defined it. When he recognizes therefore that literary history must "advance in two contradictory directions at the same time," he acknowledges that a fundamental, irreducible ambivalence will be its price of admission to the institutions of knowledge as a separate but also legitimate discipline.

One might be tempted to conclude that the hundred-year history of literary studies in the university was programmed by this contradiction, which has continued merely to work itself out. Although that conclusion would be suspiciously neat, there is still room to wonder to what extent literary scholars, in North America as well as in Europe, have remained heirs to the institutionalization that invented their discipline, a discipline that would, on this hypothesis, have continued to alternate between "impressionist" criticism and historical scholarship, the two poles of its ambivalence.[24] But such a history leaves out of account the way in which this ambivalence is working at the limit or the edge of the institution that is only partly able to contain it in some form or another. It leaves out of account, in other words, the transforming potential of such ambivalence, the dividing and redistributing effect of the division of literature, which is first of all a division of its own institution as a stable object for cognitive discourse. The division is traced in Lanson's own terms by the "impressionism" that literary historical method must neither do without nor surrender to. In a gesture that will become one of the mainstays of modern literary studies, Lanson attempts to recuperate this "unscientific" excess (or shortcoming) in the form of the individual genius of the author, who is also figured as a representative exemplar. If that gesture has been so often repeated and remains the core

even of apparently contestatory critical discourses, such as those challenging the "canon" of Western writers, it is perhaps because it retains the dual advantage Lanson and his contemporaries first uncovered: it meets the criteria for legitimation of a cognitive discipline,
as these continue to be arbitrated by the methods of social science,
while at the same time it reserves a specificity for the study of literature. This dual-purpose or double-duty discourse comes together, in
other words, in a logic of institutional legitimation of which the
token, for literary studies, is the exemplary or representative subject.
To represent representative subjectivity: that would be the task dictated by the institution to literary studies.

WE HAVE followed, in the preceding chapters, a selective course through late eighteenth- and nineteenth-century thought about literary education and its place especially in the university. Although some of the references may have been obscure (La Harpe is one of those figures honored by a Paris street named after him, but for reasons very few people can recall), the patterns we discerned there could be read as indicating a general condition, which we are calling the division of literature, that is not simply contingent on the particular circumstances of the texts we chose for the purpose. Indeed, we began by suggesting a certain repetition or continuity between a most unlikely pair of sites at the extremes of this two-hundred-year span: the Montagnard proposals for public education in France in the 1790s and proposals made in the United States in the 1980s by advocates of the "Reagan Revolution." What such a suggestion points to is, paradoxically, the substitutability of national and even nationalistic expressions when they turn their attention to the institutions of education as to a primary instrument for the reproduction of national sentiment. This is not to diminish the important and now widely recognized role played by the formation of national literary traditions during the nineteenth century in the consolidation of various modern Western nations, nor to dismiss the numerous tie-ins between this formation and the expanding imperialistic ambitions of these same nations (e.g., France) during the period. It is merely to underscore that, in placing the focus primarily on French texts from this vast storehouse, we have sought less to particularize the reference than to bring into view some general conditions of a thinking about literature and the institution of its study.

With this chapter, however, we will turn to a set of writings that, because they occupy such a singular place in French letters, may well appear to obscure rather than uncover these general conditions. If we nevertheless take the risk here of attending in some detail to this singularity, it is in order to bring out the most fundamental level at which the division of literature will have been at work across the history of its institutionalization: the division of, precisely, the singular, the doubling or repetition of that which has happened just once. In a sense that is more than superficially paradoxical, nothing would be more general—and generative—than this repetition of the singular. Nevertheless, the choice to read the repetition in the writings of Charles Péguy is anything but arbitrary. We mean thereby to mark the juncture with the institution of literary history in France, one whose installation was witnessed and vociferously decried by this author of highly idiosyncratic essays who resisted then and continues to resist classification by that very institution.

For the reasons to which we have just alluded, Péguy needs some introduction to the non-French reader. Even the briefest outline of his career cannot bypass the extent to which Péguy, by his own frequently reiterated admission, was a product of French republican education, something like the belated brain-child of Condorcet's aborted dream. A gifted pupil, Péguy was very early plucked out of his working class milieu by the newly reorganized public lay education system and sent on with numerous scholarships through the best schools of the Republic. This trajectory took him finally to the Ecole Normale Supérieure, which was then very much the main dispenser of what some today would call cultural capital. While a student at the Ecole, Péguy, like everyone he then found around him, became immersed first in the life and death struggles to organize labor and then in the Dreyfus affair. The latter was for him, as for so many of his generation, the experience of a political awakening that changed everything. For the rest of his life and although his political alliances would appear to shift dramatically from left to right, he remained an ardent Dreyfusard. When he failed to pass the *agrégation* in 1898, Péguy renounced a university career and set himself up as a bookseller-publisher. His *Cahiers de la quinzaine* in its early years was a Dreyfusard instrument and a clearinghouse for debates with and within the Parti Socialiste Unifié, under the charismatic leadership of its founder, Jean Jaurès. The *Cahiers* was a shoestring affair, totally dependent on subscriptions, which never fully covered expenses. The bimonthly issues were meticulously edited and proofed by Péguy, whose training as a typographer was always evident in his attention to printed detail. His own texts, with their often novel punctuation of excruciatingly long sentences, became something of an exacting test for the typesetter's craft.

Doubtless it is in part at least to this wholly idiosyncratic style that one must attribute the fact that Péguy remains untranslated and therefore virtually unknown to non-Francophone readers. And yet, when it is taken as a marker of literary distinction, which it frequently is, such apparent untranslatability is the reason more for attempting than for avoiding translation. An English translation of the no less daunting work by Péguy's contemporary, Proust's *Recherche*, for example, began to appear but a few years after the original. The fact that Péguy's texts have rarely passed into another language, therefore, has to be considered from an angle other than that of their stylistic "difficulty." We will have recourse, rather, to the notion of these texts' limited *appeal*, that is, of their appeal to a *single* nation, and above all to a single, national literary tradition.[1] Although such an appeal solely to France and to the France best represented by its literature is a grounding thematic in all of Péguy's writing, particularly after his nationalistic "turn" in 1905, it is less this thematic nationalism that we will consider than the shape conferred on this writing by the idea of the unrepeatable event of a single language, a single nation, a single literature. As we shall see, it is through this idea of the event that Péguy was led to oppose, in an unremitting and often ruthless fashion, the historicism of Lanson and the scientism of Taine, which had come to dominate the study of literature in France.

It would not be unfair to say that Péguy remained obsessed by the institutions of education throughout his life. Indeed, the more his own experience as pupil and student receded into the past, the more he wrote about that experience as having defined not only his identity, but that of every Frenchmen of every generation since. The will to emblazon the common experience of public education and introduction into the Republic as the locus of the promise of the past, one that has been betrayed by present modernism, is stamped on almost every page he signed after a certain date, the date on which, according to Péguy's own often obscure calculations, the mystical devotion to the Truth of Dreyfusism was betrayed by the temporal, political *obéisances* of his mentor and ally in socialism, Jean Jaurès. From that point on, Péguy's essays take on more and more the denunciatory tone for which he is best known. And among the preferred objects of this denunciation is the university, the institution of higher education, which for Péguy and many of his readers meant above all the Sorbonne and the Ecole Normale Supérieure.[2] It is in this manner that Lanson, among many others, got caught in Péguy's crosshairs. After having taught at the Ecole Normale, where Péguy was his student in 1895–96, Lanson had become the *patron* of French literary history from his chair at the Sorbonne.

To get a picture, which can only be a snapshot, of the highly complex political, institutional topography in which Péguy wrote and of which he wrote, it will be useful to adopt a somewhat imagistic language. Let us say then that we see Péguy in this picture as trying to occupy what looks sometimes like a surveillance post or a command post, if only because it stands outside if not above all the other housed institutions. But it is a surveillance post without any authority to punish the infractions it can discern from its vantage point. Péguy never belonged to any institution of authority but his own, which as he knew very well carried little weight beyond a dwindling circle of friends and subscribers.[3] Specifically, he had the support of no political party, no position in a state-run teaching institution, and no church affiliation, even after his return to Catholicism, which did not for Péguy mean a return to the church and which therefore the ecclesiastical hierarchy tended to view rather uncharitably. These three powerful institutions—parliamentary politics, state education, and the Catholic church—were in the foreground of Péguy's line of sight. A sociologist despite himself (for sociology ranked high on Péguy's list of the heresies of modernism), he described at characteristic length and with the typographer's eye for detail what he called the articulations of these three authoritarian and dogmatic institutions. And he read these articulations in the equally or perhaps even more powerful institution of the fourth estate, the press, pages of which he often submitted to his exacting scrutiny.

Péguy's position in relation to each of these four corners of solidly built legitimacy is at an angled intersection, at once a participation in and an exteriority to the enclosures they represent.[4] This is particularly apparent with regard to the institutions of education and especially the university. Péguy insisted repeatedly that the mission of the *Cahiers* was that of higher education, a kind of university without walls. In its second issue, he announces this intention of the publication:

> our *Cahiers* are doing higher education. Whether we succeed more or less, that will be decided by events [*il appartient à l'événement de le dire*]. But such are our intentions. . . . We believe it to be indispensable that this higher education happen somewhere. In the growing confusion of demagogic lies, it is indispensable that a periodical publish freely everything it can of free truth, without any concern for partiality, without any concern for base utilization—without any concern for primary education, for accessibility [*mise à portée*].[5]

Many of the essays published in the *Cahiers,* and not just those signed by Péguy, concerned pedagogical issues, the situation of public school teachers, the attempts by Socialist activists to institute free universities in working-class neighborhoods, and so forth. At the outset, the *Cahiers* pursued a kind of enlightened populism and allied itself closely with the anticlerical movement that would finally succeed, in 1901, in ridding the state-supported education system of many church-run schools. But Péguy's thinking about education was anything but a docile acceptance of the program that underwrote this reform.

In 1905, after a tense confrontation between France and Germany over colonial rights in Morocco, Péguy began to sound the patriotic note in marked dissent from other Socialists who sought on the contrary to defuse bellicist nationalism.[6] This rift with his Socialist comrades would continue to widen for the rest of Péguy's life, which he lost in combat at Charleroi during the battle of the Marne in September 1914. The force driving him to take his distance, in Péguy's analysis, was the complex formation he called *le monde moderne.* He understood the modern world as the third world, a temporal world succeeding the Christian world, which had succeeded the Hellenic. His complaint was that modernity had lost, or rather renounced the promise it had appeared to make that it would deliver a fourth world, a new world. It had, in other words, lost—or denied—the future of the world.

> It would have taken nothing [*Il s'en est fallu de rien*]. There is not the least exaggeration in asserting that in the last two thirds of the (last) nineteenth century and up to the dawn of this present twentieth century, communism or socialism or collectivism itself or anarchism or anarchy had what it took to bring forth (*avait dans le ventre de quoi faire venir*) into the world a world, anew, a fourth world, at least a temporal world, or perhaps infinitely more, I mean even, I want to go so far as to say a spiritual world, a new spiritual world, a fourth spiritual world, I mean a second second, a second Christian world, across this swathe of ashen snow of the modern world, a renaissance, literally a re-nativity, a second Noel, Christian, a return of the sap to the oldest trunk of Christianity, which would have pushed up a new trunk through all these ashes. (2:938–39)

"It would have taken nothing." The complaint is that this nothing turned out to be "everything." It swallowed the whole. The whole world fell into this little hole of nothingness, taking with it the chance for a future world, perhaps even an infinite world. For Péguy clearly, the infinite future that has been lost wears the features of a Christian rebirth even if the allusion to the "oldest trunk of Christianity" puts this figure in touch with its roots in Jewish thought. (We'll return below to this articulation in the dynamic of *prophecy* as Péguy tried to conceive it.) For the moment, and without commenting yet on any of the other traits of the passage (the organic motifs, spirit as that which can be reborn, and the hammered marks of Péguy's style of repetition), we will continue the quotation:

> But it so happened that this nothing was everything. For it happened that this nothing was this act of imagination, that it was nothing less than this—capital—error of the intellectual headquarters of the supposed socialist or communist parliamentary politics; anarchist politics, supposedly non-political and non-parliamentary; Dreyfusist politics, supposed non-political and non-parliamentary; revolutionary politics, supposed non-political and non-parliamentary; unionist politics, supposed non-political and non-parliamentary; and even collectivists; and even federalists; all of them intellectuals, in reality, all intellectual, parliamentary politicians, politically—or petty politically [*politicaillant*]—speaking, parlaying, parlying [*parlementaillant*], parliamentizing, all of them moderns in reality; all sons and successors, all pupils, on their own responsibility, of Renan. (2:939–40)

In a series of texts published in 1906, Péguy had begun to identify the historian Ernest Renan (1823–92) with what he called the metaphysics of modernism. He meant by that the claim and pretension of a temporal science to recover the infinitude of events in the world—in short, the belief in an infinite power and knowledge of science. This creed, however, was all the more totalizing of nothing and therefore of everything in that it denied that this belief formed a metaphysics and claimed that, as science rather than faith, it even put an end to metaphysics. The totalizing effect is tracked through Péguy's syntactic collapsing of a key difference: political/nonpolitical, before it lands on the figure of Renan as the father—and source—of modern intellectuals, the thinkers of modernity, those who profess its creed. "All of them intellectuals": not only do modern intellectuals run the political parties, not only have they, like Péguy, been trained in the universities by the successors of Renan, but intellectuals themselves form a party across the universities, the parliamentary structure, and the domain or institutions of publishing. What unites them, as Péguy sees it from his observation post on the margins of all these institutions, is an error that he writes to denounce as error, but that he cannot altogether avoid repeating. The passage continues:

It so happened that this nothing was everything, because it was successful, as nothing, as impediment, because the intellectual party has never succeeded at anything so well as at impediment, being expert and competent in everything that concerns sterility, failure, abortion; it so happened that this impediment, this nothing was everything, because it so happened that it was this construction, this imagination, this capital error, this intellectual construction: which was to imagine that the fourth world of Europe and of the Western world would come out of the third—like and because one had imagined, no less falsely—and this factual error . . . (2:940)

Here we will break into the passage because Péguy now opens up a series of subordinating clauses, one within the other. This long sentence will end only many lines later, on the next page. But before we lose too many threads in this densely compacted mass, we may pick out already the figure that is going to divide and be set spinning in two directions: the figure of organic, or rather mammalian reproduction, which is split between live birth or birth of the living and abortion or sterility. The error Péguy denounces here as the error of modernism is to imagine a direct, unbroken, and therefore organic relation between itself and the "fourth world" of the future. As we can already see, however, it is not the error of organicism per se that is denounced, but on the contrary the suppositon that sterile modernism had the capacity to bring forth a new world, what Péguy calls a new humanity. Yet, although according to Péguy there can be no continuity between the modern world and the world to come, although it is an error to suppose that the third world contains the seed of the fourth, nevertheless it is to a certain organic continuity that he appeals when evoking the new humanity to come. The question we have just begun to approach and that hovers over all of these texts is that of a history, or succession of "worlds," that is at once human, which for Péguy means organic, *and* discontinuous. It is the question of a discontinuity of successive worlds that nevertheless makes for a continuous, organic humanity, a "perpetually arborescent humanity" as Péguy writes in a passage we are coming to.

First, however, he will hammer away at the error he has just indicated. We interrupted the quotation at the point at which Péguy was about to identify the source or the cause of the error: "*like* and because one had imagined, no less falsely . . ." The cause of the error is a *reproduction* of error. In fact, this reproduction of error is the only reproduction Péguy discerns from one world to the next:

like and because one had imagined, no less falsely—and this factual error had brought about, prepared, ordered, introduced this error of expectation and anticipation; this error of judgment and knowledge of the past event had fathered [*enfanté*] this error of judgment and of knowledge of the future event, the former had been continued in the latter—for whereas worlds are not continued in each other, these errors did continue themselves in each other [*ces erreurs se continuaient*], it was natural, it was internally fitting [*convenable*], consistent, it was internally necessary that the errors of a world that believed falsely in the continuity of worlds, that committed this error, that worlds did continue themselves in each other, that these errors would continue themselves—like and because people had imagined, no less falsely, that the third Western world had come out of the second, and the second from the first; by a process of direct continuation or linear development . . .

Let us attempt to summarize the steps of the argument thus far: (1) up to the beginning of this century, socialism "avait dans le ventre de quoi faire venir au monde un monde, nouveau" literally, it had in its belly what was needed to bring into the world a new world; (2) but this promise of birth or rebirth was aborted by a mere nothing, which proved to be everything, a negligible gap that turned into an insuperable impediment; (3) the nothing became an impediment when the modern world began to believe, in error, that it could, "by a process of direct continuation or linear development," father a new world, that it was therefore, already, a realization of this new world at least in its anticipation, expectation, or promise; (4) such a belief, however, is nothing more than the repetition of the error whereby Western history has been falsely construed as a linear succession of continuous ages or worlds, rather than correctly as a repeated interruption of that continuity; (5) which means that the only continuity one can attribute to human history is the continuity of the erroneous belief that human history is continuous. Retracing these steps brings out the apparent reversal that has occurred between (1) and (5), between the lamented abortion of the birth of a new world directly from the belly of socialism and the observation of the error involved in supposing that any such "birth" was ever possible. It is as if Péguy had just diagnosed the error of his own disillusion with the socialist promise of a new world. But such self-diagnosis, if there is any, does not arrest the movement, the discontinuous continuity of this text, which is itself a discontinuous continuation of all the texts Péguy signed. Rather the figured interruption is reconfigured in a manner that will allow the whole cycle of a promised birth to begin again.

This occurs when the continuity of error is compared to a technical apparatus, which may then be more easily cast aside as an unfit metaphor for human history. A distinction will be dogmatically enforced between the human, which is organic and continuous, and the technical, which is discontinuous and disjointed. The former is unfolded nonlinearly as branches from a root, while the latter is laid down in a linear series of discrete segments without physical, material, or rather organic connection. Technical progress is measured as a plotted line between discontinuous points articulated in succession, whereas the events of human history, the several worlds of humanity only appear to succeed each other when submitted to a technical, arithmetical computation—first, second, third. This difference is the difference between a railroad and a tree:

> Humanity generally does not at all proceed, in this order and in this sense, by means of welds, sutures, seals, or mends. . . . It does not proceed by prolongations or shortenings. More or less arbitrary. It does not at all stretch out like the rails of a railroad, linear, parallel, that advance, that progress homogeneous: that begin again, *de plano, de nihilo,* every seven, or nine, or fifteen meters, or twenty-five or more, in step with the progress of industrial technique, that are joined together end to end each time, with, each time, an interval, an interruption, that is to say a rupture, a little interstice, to allow for heat expansion (this at least is what we are taught since grade school), that are thus broken and that cease each time they are broken. Humanity is not of mechanical fabrication or behavior [*tenue*].
>
> Natural, it proceeds naturally, according to a method, according to a rhythm that is natural. . . . An ulterior humanity, one truly worthy of this name, of making or of being one more of them, after so many others, of figuring, in its turn at the wheel, on that great calendar of names of humanities that have left a name; an ulterior nameable humanity is not born after and on an anterior humanity unless it appeals to a deeper sap, unless it appeals to a re-sourcing more profoundly sunk in the common sources of the sap of perpetually arborescent humanity. (2:942)

These lines attempt to force apart in an opposition the two figures of railroad and tree. They seek, in other words, to insert an ineffaceable, unbridgeable break or discontinuity between one realm and the other. Thematically, however, or in the allegory of this figural pattern, it is precisely this break that is taken as the mark of technical advance and progression. Without the principle of interval, interstice, or rupture, without this articulation across a measured spacing, the technical system would seize up, overheat, self-destruct. Not so, it is understood, humanity, which "is not of mechanical fabrication or behavior." The difference Péguy wants to enforce here is the difference between interval and noninterval; however, with each repetition of the pattern, with each invocation of a properly organic humanity, the interval or interruption which sets it off from inhuman technicity necessarily gets carried over or repeated. That is, it is only because the text repeatedly lays down an interval that something called "humanity" can be given a name, a sense, a destination, a past, a future: an identity. "Humanity," in other words, can emerge as a discrete name and therefore as the occasion of a repetition, "one more of them, after so many others," only by means of the repeated insertion of a gap, the space of articulation and disjuncture. Hence it cannot be simply opposed to the technical invention that illustrates this same spacing principle, but is itself articulated with and by technical devices. This is the affirmation that Péguy's text displays in its own spaced ruptures between the human and the nonhuman, what we might call its railroading of the distinction that can only repeat the interval holding the terms apart.

Although that affirmation is displayed, it is also denied or disavowed by the figurative thematics that would enforce the dogmatic belief in a humanity rooted in a natural soil and not a technical operation. To retrieve the affirmation, then, one must read against the thematics of root and race and nation and people and humanity. One must read the text in a noncontemporaneity with itself, watching for the discontinuities, the repetitions of an interval that holds its figured meanings in discrete patterns. Such a reading "against" a text's apparent self-presentation, in its manifest themes—above all against the theme of the commonly or properly *human*—would be a historical task, although not in the sense in which that task is largely understood still today, more than one hundred years after Renan began to publish his *Origins of Christianity*. It would be historical, rather, in a sense closer to the one that Péguy labored to retrieve from what he considered to be the ravages of scientific modernism, in particular of historical science. This sense, as we have seen, is in fact the possibility of a future sense, a future meaning of "humanity," the event or the coming into the world of a new world. It is a possibility that hangs on—nothing: a space, a gap, a discontinuity within the presentation of events so that they can continue to present themselves, so that they will not be seized up in a present without future. History as the possibility of future histories: this is the sense Péguy sought both to save but also, and with increasing fervor, to contain within the figure of an organic humanity, that is, of an essential continuity whose essence must deny its future.

Two gestures, two rails on which is set the engine of this writing: There seems to be little question that Péguy pushed his thought headlong in the direction of the catastrophic derailing that awaited French nationalism between the two European wars.[7] While many, including his eldest son Marcel, did not hesitate to enroll Péguy posthumously in the ranks of the rankest—profascist, anti-Semitic, antisocialist—as a martyred prophet, that undertaking cannot survive a serious encounter with the work it tries to characterize.[8] Our interest here is less to fend off these brutal appropriations (for that is the responsibility each reader must take for him- or herself), than to follow the broken trail or rail we have begun to remark, which is defined by an interstice or disjunction within the present of the event.

What Péguy calls the metaphysics of modernity consists in a certain closing of this gap. Although certainly he would not recognize it in the very gesture we just saw him execute, when he leaves behind the measured spacings of the railroad for the branching arborescence of humanity, the move is what he nicknames a "coup de pouce," a nudge of the thumb that fills in the space left between two phenomena or repetitions.[9] Taken as the characteristic move of the "modernes," especially historians and literary historians, it is denounced as a kind of scientific fraud, the fudging of data whereby the interstice between history as event and history as recovery or repetition of the event is filled in.

> This is where the *coup de pouce* comes in, which is a little *coup de force*, but so little, intercalated, set between and a go-between, between science and reality. . . . Given that there is a certain difficulty in joining, in operating the exact junction or joint, and even, just between us, a certain impossibility; so given that there is a certain space, a certain void, a certain hollow where you could insert your finger, but only your little finger, a certain solution of continuity, a certain opening, a certain angle, a certain fissure, a between-the-two between science and reality, a between-the-two between what one finds and what one would like to find . . . the *coup de pouce* is the most ordinary operation, the most innocent . . . . (2:834).

This nudge appears to close the gap between the reality of events, of all that which comes about only once in its time and place, and the recovery or repetition of these events through methodical, scientific, historicist procedures. The "coup de pouce" is the signature of modernity, that gesture by which it stamps its seal on history as its own history. It is thus an artifice, a technique, a mechanism that gives a mechanical repetition of unrepeatable events.

> Between these two experiences there is an incompatibility, a lack, a *lapsus,* a *hiatus,* an overhang, a between-the-two that is perhaps what one may imagine to be the most ineffaceable thing in the world, what one may suppose or imagine to be the most indelible and the most irreducible thing. . . . Between these two experiences, experience such as it is, all muddy, like it was when it came into the world [*comme elle est venue au monde*], and experience as it will be put down in dissertations and lab reports, theses and hypotheses, in sessions and conferences, there is but this very slight distance, which is so to speak the relation, or rather the nonrelation that is the most heterogeneous, the most impossible, even to imagine, the most halting that one can imagine, having one foot on and in the infinite, at least on and in an infinite, and the other neatly posed on a little footstool of finiteness, one foot in being and one in knowledge, one in matter and the material and one, and the other in the concept and the conceptual, in the intellect and the intellectual. It is this slight distance, infinite at one end, finite at the other, infinite thus throughout and definitively, it is this singular, this acrobatic, this mysterious, strange distance that our pal the *coup de pouce* will cause, neatly and silently, to disappear. (2:835).

The disparity or the *hiatus* between the two "experiences," between experience "like it was when it came into the world," the event of experience, on the one hand and, on the other, that same experience *repeated* as experiment or case study, can be made to disappear in two ways, or rather this disappearance can be seen from two angles. In its first, more pointedly aimed version, the critique would be directed at those for whom the "very slight distance" between an event and its repetition has been effaced or forgotten. This is the error, or rather the pretension of modern science, and above all those sciences of human experience, history and sociology, which have been taken as models of literary study. It is the pretension of the antimetaphysical scientist who does not acknowledge the metaphysical designs of science itself to be a repetition or second creation of the infinite: "what modern historians propose is this: to compose, one by one, to constitute a representation of the world, to constitute, piece by piece, morsel by morsel, a total representation of the event of the world, a second event, which therefore can be, if it is indeed total, only as infinite and as universal as the world itself" (2:848).

This charge of *lèse-infinité* against modern science is one of the most constantly sounded during these years (1906–9), when Péguy was working up to a doctoral thesis that he proposed, rather improbably, to present to the Sorbonne and to which he gave the provisional title "On the Situation of History in the General Philosophy of the Modern World."

But the fulminations against the disavowed or misrecognized metaphysics of modern science must also be read as almost an offshoot, a projection outward from what we would be tempted to place at the center of Péguy's thinking at this time: the unapproachable and unrepresentable singularity of the event. Seen in this way, the critique of science is the critique of but the most prevalent or dominant language of representation. Beyond that, however, it sketches an attempt to retrieve the singularity and originality of an event, also its unity and identity "such as it is," from the regime of repetition, which, however it represents the event, will have necessarily doubled the "such as it is" of experience, its singular presentation and thereby lost it or hidden it. In part of the passage we elided, this operation of doubling or representing is itself represented, with an allusion to *Tartuffe,* as "the operation by which an intelligent operator hides the breast that one should not see," that is, naked, material reality. For this experience "as it is, as it presents itself," Péguy reaches for names of what can have no name: "imperfect, unformed, vulgar, suspicious, itself suspect, dirty, real, totally unwashed and still covered with scraps and mud" (2:834).[10] It is this messy event that will be cleaned up and dressed up by a representation simply by virtue of the repetition whereby the sudden, one-time appearance is made to reappear. But of course, a repetition is no less at work in these attempts to retrieve the original event "as it is, as it presents itself" in its unformed aspect. That attempt no less comes up against what Péguy calls "the non-relation that is the most heterogeneous, the most impossible, even to imagine" between the singular event and its repetition. The very slight distance between the one and the other, between the one and the double is unbridgeable, indelible *and* it is bridged or effaced in the very naming of the event as it presents itself. This closing of the gap is impossible *and* inevitable with the result that the error can be denounced only by being repeated. And in this regard, Péguy's operation here must include itself as example in the very operation it is calling the *coup de pouce.*

The *coup de pouce,* we said, is modernity's signature, that by which it marks and signs, at a certain date, its event as third world in the history of humanity. But if event as such, "as it presents itself," can never present itself as such, as singularity before and beyond representation or repetition, before and beyond its signature in a language, then that signature is also improper or fraudulent. It is suspect and dirty. Péguy's denunciations of the fraud and the dirt clinging to the event of modernity are the negative face given to the unformed reality that has appeared in his lifetime; but for them to achieve their effect *as* denunciations, as negative judgments on the value of that event, a *coup de pouce* and a *coup de force* will have been necessary: another signature, that of Péguy. This latter signature would be that of an event that is dirty, not in the negative sense of fraudulent, but only in the sense that it is covered with the scraps and mud of its emergence, autochthonously, from the soil of material reality. Reality, which is to say, the singularity of time and place. But this dirty, singular event immediately doubles itself and thus dirties itself with fraudulent representations. How is one to keep a signature clean in these circumstances?

We could follow that question in several directions irradiating across Péguy's writings. There would be, for example, the *typographical* direction, the careful attention to the presentation of a printed text and spatial relations on a page. All work should be done cleanly, with respect for the instruments of one's labor. As an intellectual from the working class, Péguy abhorred the carelessness of bourgeois habits of disrespect toward work, and first of all their own work.[11] We could also follow an intersecting direction from there toward the confusion or messiness Péguy analyzed so relentlessly in the institutions of power: politics, the university, the press. An interesting instance of this analysis for our purposes comes in one of Péguy's most direct attacks on Lanson in *L'argent suite*.

Lanson had a regular bimonthly column of theater reviews in *La Grande Revue*, a journal that, like the *Cahiers*, was born out of the Dreyfus affair. Péguy had also published in its pages. In June 1912, however, Lanson began in addition to publish a regular weekly column in the large circulation daily newspaper *Le Matin*. These were literary reviews and appeared under the heading "Mouvement littéraire, Les Idées d'hier et de demain" [Literary Movement: Ideas of Yesterday and Tomorrow]. Péguy judged this event to be significant and above all regrettable, for a number of reasons. Essentially he saw the appearance it was given on the enormous public stage of the newspaper's pages as a humiliating affront to all intellectuals, including himself. This appearance is characterized first by the placement of the column at the bottom of one of the last pages, lost among the advertisements for dressmakers and publishers: "How to describe our surprise when we found . . . these species of rubbish piles [*crottes de bique,* literally, witch's turds] lost among the *communiqués* of caba-rets and among the dressmaker's ads and among the paid announce-ments from publishers" (3:870). It is *as if,* by a *coup de pouce,* the noble signature of the professor of literature at the Sorbonne had been reduced to and dirtied by these *crottes de bique.* Péguy writes that he is wounded by this vilification of the delegated signatory of literature and the university. "With this figure, with this signature we are shown too little respect" (3:871). Lanson is being treated, and thus we are all being treated like a little boy. Even when, later, Lanson's column is given a more respectable place in the newspaper, at the bottom of page five with a separate heading and typography, Péguy reads only a refinement of the insult.

> But this ground floor full of art nouveau typographical flourishes, full of *modern style* embellishments, at the bottom of the big Saturday women's page, or something similar, is itself the object, and something like the residence, of a perpetual typographic insult. There is about the whole thing an insufferable derision, a contempt for the spiritual. And typo-graphical contempt, which is the worst kind of contempt, of what it is to be a professor, and a critic, and even what a newspaper article is. And what creates an especially bad effect is the fact that beneath his article and continuing the same columns they have put the paid advertisements of publishers. (3:872)

If we were to read this as the description of a certain modern event, then Péguy is clearly working here to name that event as the humiliation of literature and of the university, their emergence in an association with commercial ventures and promotions in a market. But the analysis does not stop with this characterization, which would seem to cast journalism and commercialism as simply the unworthy associates of a higher "spiritual" reality. There will be in fact a kind of reversal of this hierarchy when Péguy remarks that, to become a literary chronicler, Lanson has had to abandon his own professed method for the scientific study of literature, the method of "unlimited exhaustion of historical detail" (3:878). On the whole, Péguy judges this to be a good development, a public demonstration that even a staunch proponent of "the method" must concede its limits. But that demonstration would be complete only if the author-ity of this putative scientific method were not also being used to legitimate or underwrite Lanson's nonscientific journalism. And Péguy sees that, on the contrary, it is "with his title, solemnly, an-nounced as such, going into this newspaper, under cover of all his titles, [that Lanson] has officially constituted himself there as the representative of letters and the University."[12] Once again, a certain kind of fraud or *coup de pouce* is perpetrated by this transfer of titles between institutions. The cumulative effect that Péguy decries is less the debasement of the institution of "letters and the University" than the extension of the legitimating power of scientific method to the larger stage of public discourse about literature, at the very point at which in fact that method has been summarily abandoned: "All we ask, and it is rather simple . . . since, in order to become a writer, he was forced to renounce the scientific method, like everyone, all we ask is that at the same time no one tries to make us believe that he became a writer by maintaining the scientific method and by means of the scientific method." (3:875).

Once again, therefore, modern science, the reigning doctrine of the university, is the principal target of Péguy's denunciation. In particular, it is the scientific method as applied or transferred to the study of literature that Péguy qualifies interminably as a usurpation, a summary brutality, an act of violence. Recalling Lanson's lectures from his days at the Ecole, he ironizes about this literary history "that unwound itself like a string" or that rolled smoothly, far too smoothly over the rails of its reconstructed event.[13] Instead of a jolting appearance, the literary event "had both of its arms strapped to its sides and its legs straightened out and its two wrists well tied and its ankles tightly bound" (3:860). Some of his most vehement pages are devoted to this lamentable state of affairs, to this "superstitious idea" that

> there is allegedly no certainty other than scientific certainty, and that in order to certify what is not properly science, what is naturally outside of science proper, outside of the domain and the domination of science proper, like literature, without mentioning here all the rest, it is necessary to transport brutally and it suffices perhaps to transport brutally to this other domain the methods, procedures, assurances, theories, manias of the sciences proper. (2:589)

This objection, of course, is grounded in the no less dogmatic belief or superstition that a domain can be determined as "naturally outside of science proper," that science and nonscience, therefore, each have a proper and limited extension. The notion that the properness of literature is brutalized or negated when it is taken as the object of some more properly scientific inquiry has by now become a familiar, well-worn complaint. In this regard, Péguy stands in a direct line of succession that would include certain antistructuralists, for example, who in the 1960s began warning about the barbarous treatment being inflicted on the literary legacy when it fell into the hands of linguists or anthropologists. Likewise, the opprobrium he reserves for systematic thinking anywhere in the vicinity of literature finds clear echoes in many forms of the suspicion aroused within and outside the academy by so-called poststructuralist literary theory. All of these rightful successors to Péguy's alarmed mistrust share some version of the romantic humanist belief in the *genius* of literature, that essential mark of its demiurgic generation which is, finally, inaccessible to all the techniques of science. The defense of the properness of literature against the incursions of science, theory, method, systematicity, or technique is always a defense of the properly human against what is taken as inhuman: inorganic, inanimate, mechanical, technical.

That Péguy placed an unlimited faith in the grounds of this distinction, and thus in the notion of the properly separate domains of science and literature, is not in question. But neither is it what should continue to interest us in this exasperated scorn for the trespasses of scientific method across the poorly defended perimeter of literature's domain. If these protests cannot be consigned altogether to the past of an organic humanism, it would be once again because of the place they *reserve* for what is called, in a text we are approaching slowly, the *sovereignty of the event*. To get ahead of ourselves somewhat by anticipating one of the consequences of this reserve, we will say that it shelters whatever may remain still to come about this text, whatever has not already exhausted itself with the figure of the human as genius, subject, incarnation of the divine, autochthonous heir to its own history. Countering the *coup de pouce* by which modernity covers over that slight distance between past or future events and the present of its own representation, Péguy sets aside the space for the event of the absolutely other than the present.

It is a small space, however, a mere interval that is nearly buried beneath an overgrowth that proliferates whenever Péguy touches on certain crucial articulations. We can take an example from a text written in 1906 but, like much of his writing, left unpublished by the author. The central concern is again the transgressive usurpations of academic scientific historicism against literature, this time at the hands of Lanson's predecessor as the dean of French literary scholars, Ferdinand Brunetière. The latter had by then suffered the disgrace of being turned out of his position at the Ecole Normale and refused a chair at the Collège de France in 1904. The decision to pass over Brunetière for this prestigious position in favor of a relatively unknown literary historian (a certain Abel Lefranc, a name Péguy claims, to cruelly comic effect, he is unable to remember) became a political football in the fight over religion in the public schools. Brunetière had long championed his "theory" of the evolution of literary genres, modeled only very loosely, and opportunistically, on Darwin, and for this reason he could be associated with Renan and Taine as a frontline advocate of historical literary science. But this association did not sit very well on him, despite the appearance he tried to assume as one of the new gang of literary scientists.[14] When finally in 1895, he published his essay "Après une visite du Vatican" the game seemed to be more or less up because Brunetière declared there the failure of science and his renewed Catholic faith. Two years after the election at the Collège de France of the properly anticlerical Lefranc over Brunetière, who had rendered himself politically unacceptable, Péguy rather improbably declared that the case of Brunetière had been misjudged all along. Those who concluded that Brunetière deserved to be drummed out of the corps for his scientific apostasy had simply failed to read beyond a superficial appearance. In fact, he will argue for many pages, there is no doubt that "not only is M. Brunetière, historian of literature, an adherent of the modern world and of its supposedly scientific methods, but he is one of the most deliberate and perhaps the firmest adherent" (2:594). For proof, Péguy asks one to read carefully no more than a single sentence from M. Brunetière's latest book.

The sentence is lifted from the first page of *Honoré de Balzac (1799–1850)*, which Brunetière had published some months earlier. An announcement of the book's purpose, the sentence reads in Péguy's quoted version as follows: "uniquely a Study of the work in which we have sought above all to define, to explain, and to characterize this work such as it would still be if Balzac, instead of being born in Tours, had been born for example in Castelnaudary, and if, instead of studying law, he had studied medicine" (2:603). Péguy's initial blast at this posed hypothesis of the "as if," which like the *coup de pouce,* will be taken later in the same essay as an identifying mark of scientific modernity, is typically hyperbolic:

> this rigid arrogance toward reality, this insolence of the military upstart [*parvenu*], toward any kind of reality, this presumption, this pride, this haughty disdain of all life, of all reality, of all race, of all genius, of all originality, of all origin, of all beginning, of all source, of everything that grows, of all that is, of all that emerges, of all that has a source, of all that comes or is coming [*de tout ce qui vient*], finally this claim to

classify, this universal distribution of prizes, this scientific disdain of all traditional, usual, familiar, memorial reality. . . . Who among us will not be wounded in the deepest part of himself, in what he has that is most secret, most dear, breached, wounded, in the very source of his life? Penetrated. Someone has entered his home. . . . By such words, by such propositions, who among us will not be wounded to the very quick of his interior life, at the deepest point of that religion that has remained within us and for us the great religion, the supreme religion and the point of departure of the mother religion: the absolute respect of reality, of its mysteries, the piety and the religious respect of sovereign and master, absolute reality, of the real such as it is given to us, of the event, as it comes [*comme il vient*]. (2:603–4)

The tangled mass of the sentences winds around the point called variously: life, reality, genius, beginning, origin, source, the real, and finally event. A shower of words rains onto the page at the point of a wound, there where a breach has occurred in life's most secret interiority. A source, an origin, an originality, a genius: their secret and their mystery is the effect of their absolute singularity, which ought to be respected, that is, beheld only from the unbreachable distance of an absolute respect. This interval of respect seems to hold apart two moments, two positions: an original moment or beginning position and a second moment that comes after, that is defined and positioned with respect to the first as an afterward. It is this pattern of measured interval that should be respected.

Why? The answer is both obvious, right on and as the articulated surface of the text, *and* it is made to disappear, in a kind of sleight of hand or *coup de pouce,* beneath the branching profusion of organic figures of origin: the interval must be respected so that the "first" moment can continue to return, so that its event can come back, be repeated as the event that it is/was. The interval of respect is laid down as the *possibility* of repetition, which is to say also the lack of respect for the original event in its absolute singularity.

This condition of the coming of an event as a coming back, a repetition, situates another interval beneath or behind the one that Péguy can only respect in the breach, with the repeated *coups de pouce* of his figures of the origin: it is an interval in the event itself, or rather that by which the event "itself" cannot be or become itself, come into its own, so to speak, except by coming back and re-peating.[15] The event comes only to come/by coming again, a phrase that we could render more succinctly, if we were writing in Péguy's language, as: "l'événement ne *parvient* qu'à venir encore." In a sense, everything is being played out here in the difference or the distance between *venir* and *parvenir,* two intransitive verbs distinguished only by the intensive prefix *par-*. To *parvenir* means to arrive at a destination, to reach or attain a goal, to propagate through space or time to a given point, to succeed in some endeavor, to arrive at a stage of development. Compared to *venir,* its use intensifies the sense of movement toward a given and known destination, indeed, it is reserved less as a verb of movement than arrival and arrest. Doubtless that is the reason for which its nominal or adjectival form, *parvenu,* has the sole and pejorative meaning of upstart, social climber: a *paysan* or a bourgeois *parvenu.* It is in this form that it occurs in Péguy's invective, but in a somewhat unusual association: the *parvenu militaire,* the martial appearance having been dictated no doubt by the connotations of brutality and violence, of inflicted assault and forced entry into civil interiors. The *parvenu* is the figure of a certain repetition, a bad repetition because it attempts to halt or capture the event it repeats: "this eminently modern thesis that the stuff or life of literature can be seized by modern, supposedly scientific methods . . . that it can be enclosed, claustrated" (2:596). It is repetition as a kind of house arrest, with the suggestion of an empty imitation, since a *parvenu* is someone who "has elevated himself to a superior condition without acquiring the manners, the tone, the *savoir-vivre* of that condition" (*Robert*): Balzac, who is the pretext or the origin of Péguy's rage, certainly knew something about that, which he passed on to Rastignac and to so many others; but perhaps Péguy, the *parvenu militaire,* did as well, and that knowledge may have added vehemence to the denunciation.

In any case, the portrait of the *parvenu* usurping the place of the event is itself standing in for another picture that this text seems reluctant or unable to bring into focus. Or rather, the other picture is the very movement of the event's repetition in the text, a *venir* or coming that is precipitated out as the difference between original and *parvenu,* as a figure, therefore, of arrested movement. But if this arrest must be denounced as a wound inflicted to the very quick of life, it is so that the original, the source, the beginning can begin *again,* so that the event "of all that comes or is coming" will be respected and welcomed. There is thus affirmation of the event as first time *and* immediately another time, but it is sounded in and drowned out by the negative tones denouncing everything that acts to arrest the movement of this affirmation.

In this regard we could say that Péguy's texts are above all a demonstration of the founding gesture of writing, of literature in the broadest sense: an affirmation of their own event, which bids or begs for the future of a repetition. Because this bid is submitted by Péguy over against all the institutions to which he pointedly does not apply for legitimation of this gesture, above all the university and established organs of publication, the latter are cast as the instruments of arrest and their power as the brutal capture of both past and future events in their own present form. One may therefore hear Péguy's protests against the institution of literary history and academic literary studies as also raging against the forces of his own delegitimation, against all that attempts to appropriate the acts of writing and publishing to present institutions, against, therefore, the arrest of writing's event. This might, moreover, begin to account for the seeming inexhaustibility of Péguy's phrase, the sentences that come to an end only to begin again at nearly the same point, having covered only a slight distance from one repetition to the next, laboring and belaboring their sense: as if there could be no end.

What we are saying, then, is that Péguy *supposes* the event's repetition even as he *poses* the unrepeatability of the origin, the beginning, the source. The latter position rests on, depends on the former supposition. In many, indeed almost all of the texts where he writes of the event, the affirmative supposition is never examined as the support of the position taken up against modernity. A significant exception, to which we will turn now, is found in the text from 1907, the same one in which Péguy poses the argument of the *coup de pouce*.

It is a passage that follows on and from the essay's central proposition, or rather its opposition to what is identified as the central proposition of modernity:

> Our first proposition, our central proposition was thus and could only be a recognition of the position, of the central proposition of the enemy . . . it was thus and will necessarily be to recognize that the central proposition of the domination attributed to the intellectual party in the modern world is that the modern historian, in the first degree, and the modern sociologist, in the second degree, can constitute, set up a total, exact repertory of the infinite, universal event. (2:840–41)

After several syntactic relays, Péguy is led to comment on a text of the revered Pascal, whom he never approaches without enormous respect and numerous precautions, careful to preserve the event of Pascal's text with lengthy quotations and deferential commentary, if any. Pascal is one of those writers who, whenever they are convoked to come into Péguy's text, always precipitates distaste at the idea of accompanying it with commentary:

I am constrained to become the commentator of this text. It is a nasty occupation, not at all to be recommended, a shady occupation, a double occupation, a false occupation, a crooked and a low-born occupation. . . . I go at it cowering and against my will all the more so in that it is a rebel text and a powerful one and it will defend itself and I don't like blows, as everyone knows, especially I don't like to receive blows, not that I will attack it or want to attack it or have any intention of attacking it. But finally I will have to attack it at least in the sense chemists give to the word attack. And it is a marble that defies attack. (2:861)

The text in question, cited *in extenso,* is the *Fragment of a "Treatise on the Void"* in which Pascal compares the history of the progress of human reason and science to the ages of a sole man who, as he passes from childhood to maturity to old age, learns to reject his own earlier errors; likewise humanity as a whole has learned to correct the scientific errors of the "ancients," which in this regard should be compared to the ignorance of childhood. "All men together make a continual progress in science as the universe grows older, because the same thing happens in the succession of men's generations that happens in the different ages of an individual. With the result that the whole succession of men, over the course of so many centuries, must be considered like a same man who still lives on and learns continuously . . ." (2:858). Péguy will "attack" this proposition of "indefinite linear progress, continuous or discontinuous, perpetually pushed onward, perpetually obtained and acquired, perpetually consolidated" (2:868–69) with a counterproposition that he announces under the title "the resonances of voices."

It is, he writes, a proposition he had begun to formulate some months earlier, in a text prefacing the issue of the *Cahiers* dated February 3, 1907, where he advanced the distinction between the linear progress of techniques and sciences, on the one hand and, on the other, the nonlinearity of what he calls voices, which resonate only once, are irreplaceable, and thus cannot be superseded the way one technological invention replaces another. By "voices" Péguy intends a variety of phenomena: "a metaphysics, a philosophy, an art, a race, a people, a work," all of which he subsumes once again to the name event. "An event comes or it does not come. No metaphysics, no philosophy—no religion—can have its time served [*faire faire son service*] by another. And none can serve the time of another" (2:666). Now, it is in particular this discrete temporality of events to which Péguy will return in the later text, taking issue with Pascal's, but especially with modernity's version of the linearity of historical succession.

It is a curious argument that seems to get detoured about halfway through. It begins with the proposition we have just evoked:

If in fact each man—I mean each man worthy of the name—if each people—in the same sense and on the same condition—if each nation, each race, every culture gives its voice at its date [*donne à sa date sa voix*] in the universal concert . . . in the concert of humanity, in this concert that is not eternal, but so to speak temporally eternal, temporally figured like a first image, like an imperfect image of eternity, if each speaks in his turn and at his date . . . (2:870)

This odd proposition is not ventured as a hypothesis; it is rather asserted as the empirical knowledge of an observed condition: "and it is rather remarkable that since the beginning of the world we know, there has been no example of two creatures speaking at the same time, two races, in the same time, two nations, two peoples, two cultures, two men . . ." What is most remarkable here, of course, is the structure of such an assertion in which the "world we know" is being defined or limited as precisely the world of a single voice speaking one at a time, in which the time of the world "since the beginning" is marked out by the dates of single "voices." The least we can say about this definitional circle is that it solipsistically casts out and beyond the order of knowledge a "world" of more than one voice, more than one time, or more generally still, more than one world. It is, one might say, the proposition of uniculturalism, of the world as a single world differentiated only over time by the "voices" each of which resonates "at its hour, makes itself heard at its date and at its turn."[16]

Now, we must recall that this proposition, which Péguy himself calls "very odd [*singulière*], very mysterious, and very important," is the opening gambit of what has been announced as a refutation of Pascal's "ages of man" analogy, particularly in its modern extension by the theory of historical, scientific succession or "progress." However, the principal of temporal succession, that is, of nonsimultaneity, is accepted at the outset as the defining condition of "the world we know." From this position, the question Péguy will open up, although only briefly before getting detoured back onto the preferred ground of organic history, is that of a nonsimultaneity that is also not a temporal succession, but indeed the very limit on this temporality of events. For Péguy this limit is traced *between* the temporal, which is the finite order of succession, and the extratemporal, which is the infinite order of a transcendent, timeless, or eternal "voice," the voice of God. And yet between the temporal and the extratemporal, the limit is nevertheless inscribed *in* the temporal as the event of a certain dislocation of historical succession. It is also, therefore, a dislocation of the event of history, its displacement out of the cumulative, linear, or organic mold by which human reason attempts to account for itself and to count only on itself. The question opened up, therefore, is that of the event of *another* time that arrives at its time: out of time, in time.

We will try to paraphrase the steps leading up to this dislocation. The argument proceeds at first through an apparently normal succession of temporal, logical propositions: obviously, writes Péguy, it is necessary and sufficient that a man, a race, a people, a culture, another, appear at a given point in the flow of duration, "at a given point of what we have named and will continue to name the event," for this man, "this other man, this new man, newly appearing," to have the possibility of either knowing or not knowing "another man, another people, another race, another culture," of either hearing or not hearing "at least an echo, however weakened it may be, of another voice" (2:871). This is not to say, of course, that it is sufficient that a man, a people, etc., come after another for him to have a determined knowledge of that other, or even any knowledge of it at all. But, on the other hand, it does suffice that one be born *before* the other for it be irrevocably the case that one can have no knowledge of the ulterior other, the one who comes after. Each of these propositions seems to rely simply on the principal of succession: if one comes entirely before another in the order of successive duration, then there is no possibility that one can know or hear even a weakened echo of the other's voice. This is because posteriority is a necessary, although not a sufficient, condition for such knowledge.

We will have already remarked, however, that there is another condition, other than sheer temporal succession, being assumed here. This condition is never acknowledged as such even when Péguy turns to two examples that foreground it. It is the fact and the condition of writing, the possibility of a "voice" that is not the voice of anyone living, a "voice" that survives itself in writing. Péguy's first example is that of the *Timaeus*. The most cultivated and advanced Egyptian of ancient Egypt did not know the *Timaeus*, he could not but have no knowledge of it, he did not hear it because "this unique voice had not yet spoken" (2:872). On the other hand, even the most foolish Greek who lived after Plato (and, adds Péguy in a humorous aside—for there are regular humorous intervals in Péguy that keep the rails from overheating—"there must have been all the same one of them who was the most foolish") could know it, could have heard it "because it had spoken, because this voice had resonated once, had temporally resonated once for all time eternally in and among the peoples of the voice." This condition of prior resonance is necessary, but is it not also, wonders Péguy, sufficient? Is it not sufficient in the sense in which "we will have to ask ourselves whether once a voice has resonated, does that not suffice, whether thereafter temporally every man in a certain sense and very profoundly has not heard it"? This is a question about the event of a "voice," which resonates at its date but also beyond its date and beyond therefore the limits of any living voice. By event of a "voice," we understand that Péguy means the event of a world, for it is only in this sense that every man from then on could "hear" it, the "voice" of the *Timaeus,* which is to say, the other's voice and the voice of the dead. Everything is at stake, of course, in the elided assumption of writing, which is the possibility of all these possibilities, the condition of all these conditions. The event of the world is, first of all, the event of a certain writing, a certain spacing between this time and another, this culture and another, this nation and another, one born after or before the other. This is what Péguy's text affirms—the spacing or writing of the world's event—but also elides in the metaphor of voice. Everything is at stake in that elision, in how we read it, which is to say in how we *remark* once again the space it occupies in this writing.

There is a second example, besides the *Timaeus.* Besides the (elided) space between the Egyptians and Greeks, there is the (elided) space between the Greeks and the Christians. After the resonance of Egypt in Greece (about which resonance, moreover, Péguy has little to say: he is manifestly uninterested in the pre-Hellenic and especially non-Hellenic "voice"), which is a temporal resonance, there is the resonance, called "intemporelle," in Greece of the Gospels, which were to be spoken only several centuries later "on the borders of a temporal lake" in Galilee. But before Péguy has adduced this second example, he has already approached the question of prophecy in the part of this passage we have elided. We named this point above the dislocation of the event of history. Here is the elision now without further paraphrase:

> Except for the case, unless there be a case of prophecy and revelation. But exactly this is a particular case, perhaps exceptional, a case which precisely exits from the temporal, at least from the pure and simple temporal. The set of all these propositions, principal and subsidiary, which form a set, a family of propositions, will also probably make up a whole *cahier,* perhaps several, which no doubt we will entitle: *On the Sovereignty*

of the Event, because such will be in fact the central internal mark and preoccupation. What is the event. Since it is sovereign. Temporally sovereign. This sovereignty, the sovereignty of the date and the event has only one limit, it admits only one family, one class of limits, it receives only timeless limits [*limites intemporelles*], either absolute or at least in a certain sense, limits such as, such as might be prophecy and if not revelation, which is in a certain sense temporal, then at least certain installments, certain anticipations, certain advances of revelation. (2:871)

The question or the statement (for Péguy does not punctuate it with a question mark) "What is the event" must be thought at its limits, in function of its limits, of which there is only one kind (only one "family" or "class"), what Péguy calls in general the "intemporel," timeless time or time without time, time *before* time and before the inscription of the event in time. An out-of-time that nevertheless inscribes itself in time. But where "in time?" And when "in time"? Péguy has the answer:

> If a Greek had known the voice of Jesus, before it had spoken temporally in the world, before it had spoken by similes on the borders of a temporal lake, this Greek could only have known it by a timeless ear [*oreille intemporelle*], a timeless voice itself and speaking a timeless language. In other words and to speak a proper language, there would have been properly and formally a prophecy, and anticipation of the revelation. (2:872)

This passage remains in the conditional, even the past conditional. It could have happened but it didn't. The past conditional, the tense of regret, as the French say. For, he adds, "you know, my dear Lévy, that we do not know that there has been a single prophet outside of a certain people whom we love very much."

As he often did, Péguy turns and apostrophizes his reader, here his fellow Dreyfusard friend since 1898, Edmond-Maurice Lévy. This particularization of the address occurs at the precise point at which Péguy singularizes the voice of prophecy as that of the Hebrew prophet foretelling the event of Christ. At this point of maximal dislocation in time, at this limit between time and not-time, what happens, what is the event? On the one hand, Péguy executes one of his most spectacular, most violent *coups de pouce* when he writes "we do not know that there has been a single prophet outside a certain people." With this categorical enclosure of prophecy within a single historical people, a single "race," the enormous dislocation that has opened up seems to be just as quickly contained and ordered by the voice of the *logos* itself, which is Christian revelation. But on the other hand and *first of all,* there is address, apostrophe, the figure of the other's name: "Or vous savez, mon cher Lévy," "Now, you know, my dear Lévy . . ." The other is called by name, his dear name, to come, to affirm, to confirm what "we" know, you and I, Jew and Christian, lovers of a certain people, a people of the book, lovers of the book.[17] Or, more precisely, the other is called on to confirm what we do not know, "we do not know that here has been a single prophet outside of a certain people." If there is a *coup de pouce,* a violent signature that repeats the other as the same, the past's future as the present, then where and when does it happen? "You know . . . we know": the space of the dislocation, of the prophecy, of an "intemporel" that precedes and limits the temporal, is marked or held open by an address and, *at the same time,* the "intemporel" of this precedent is appropriated to the time of the present, to the temporal order of historical succession. *Post hoc ergo propter hoc.*

At the same time: this is the mysterious sovereignty of the event. At the same time as it comes out of time, that is, for an absolute first and only time, it begins to repeat, to beat time to the time of the world. At the same time, then, it is at or on the same time *and* it "is" not time but out of time, out of the temporal order. This is the event of the dislocation of the order or regime of the event. What is the event: the arrival of the first time or its repetition? And if there is a violent *coup de pouce,* is it the violence of the arrival of the absolutely other or the violence of the other's appropriation by present time, by modernity, by all that which comes after? Which does violence to which and to whom?

At the same time, in the space of this dislocation of the "same time," there is address. "You know, my dear Lévy . . ." What does Lévy know? What happens in this apostrophe, by which Péguy addresses himself *to* Lévy? But in which, at the same time, he hears Lévy's address to himself? What does Péguy say to himself *as* Lévy, as if he were speaking to himself but from the other's place? *As if* therefore, he and Lévy were the same (and remember that the "as if" is another name for the *coup de pouce*)? To Lévy, whose dear name is *also and at the same time* taken for the name of a "certain people"? We must listen to the rest of the address:

> Now, you know, my dear Lévy, that we do not know that there has been a single prophet outside of a certain people whom we love very much, you and I, especially when it does not get the unfortunate idea of trying to renounce itself (which is also in vain, for it fortunately does not succeed in the least). It is even a singular fact, my dear Lévy, and you,

my dear Marix,[18] a unique fact and if not mysterious at least singular and striking [*éclatant*] on the contrary, a fact of ancient history so striking that our history professors were out of luck, it is striking to the point that finally everyone ends up noticing it, it is a singular fact, unique in the history of the world, that we do not know that there has been in the whole history of the world a single example that there was a single prophet who emerged from another race, except for the race of prophets, except for the race that is the only one to have given prophets, the only one to have been a race of prophets, except from the race of that people which has since fortunately come to reside among us, from the anxious, eternally anxious people, from the restless people, from the race of that people whom we love, you and I, especially when it does not try, thereby renouncing its greatness, to pass itself off for another, for other than it is, to pass itself off for anyone whatsoever [*n'importe qui*] (fortunately a vain enterprise), for anyone else whatsoever, people and race to whom once again very recently and in this modern century and this century of domination by the modern and by the intellectual party we owe it to have known and loved, and to have been loved by him, by their enemy, their master, their greatest enemy, the great Bernard-Lazare, the man who spoke to them with the greatest severity in the world, with the greatest exactitude, who judges them with the most severity, with the most justice, the most sadness, for he had been the comrade of many of them, with the most exactitude. (2:872–73)

The necessary, and perhaps as well sufficient, condition for reading such an address is that we come after its event. But the question we are still asking is what it can mean to come *after* an event that begins by repeating itself, by postdating itself in a sense, or simply by *posting* itself to an unknown future address. In the dislocation of time that thereby happens, before and after are no longer simply determinable in their historical, temporal relation. If there is an event of address, then it will have begun immediately to carry beyond the date and place of its issuance. This is the condition for our being able to read it at all. But how far will it have to carry before reaching its destination? And has it already reached destination and exhausted its trajectory in a past? Is it, in other words, *parvenu* or, on the contrary, is it yet to come, *venir,* does it still have a way to go? A future? Is it to be given a future? Does it give a future?

These questions are all bound up with what we are saying about the dislocation of the event, the condition of our reading *after* what is already a disordering of temporal succession. Dislocated, the address resonates out of temporal order, like a prophecy of that which has not yet happened, but *at the same time* there is the event, the happening of the prophecy. Or rather, there is not prophecy, but a command, an injunction, an order given. Péguy addresses a commandment to the Jews of Europe: Do not renounce yourself, do not try to pass yourself off as anyone else. How far does this address carry? Does it not resonate most loudly in the command transmitted to all European Jews barely twenty-five years later? Is this then its destination or the evidence, on the contrary, that it went disastrously astray? Perhaps the one in the other?

The condition of not being able rigorously to tell the destination from the disaster of destination is precisely our situation of coming after. But no text simply plots its own disaster. There will have been an attempt to keep a straight course. Péguy's is no different; indeed, keeping a straight course of address is the principal preoccupation of these lines. This is how we must understand the insistence, to the point of numbing redundance, on a sole race of prophets in the history of the world. It is, above all else, to this assertion that Péguy confides the function of keeping the address on course. The course of the address is stamped and restamped as going from the Jew to the Christian, prophecy to revelation, divine inspiration to earthly incarnation. This has happened only once in the history of the world; this is the history of the world we know. The destination that Péguy determines for his address is the endpoint of this sole and unique speech, in the whole history of the world, whereby the European Christian addresses himself, destines himself to himself, in the words of a Jewish prophet. For the address to stay on the right course, there must be only one addressor and only one addressee. This identification of a sole people of prophets is accompanied by the command to this people to identify itself, to identify with itself, to uphold, therefore, the order and the direction of the address. But as we have seen, it is precisely this command that, by trying to safeguard the arrival or revelation of the address, sends it on the way to disaster. More than by anything else, then, this disaster is sealed when the dislocation of the event called prophecy is arrested in a sole figure, a sole people, a sole culture, a sole world.

This seal, however, also marks or guards a secret, to which the questions we are asking about the event are confided. There is a secret command of the event, that which cannot be repeated. Or, at least, it ought not to be repeated. It ought, that is, never abrogate in a repetition the absolute singularity of the address to/from the other's difference. Péguy obeys this command of the secret, but in a highly ambiguous way. The great Bernard-Lazare has just been cited. This name never appears in Péguy's text unless accompanied by an infinite respect for the man who, before anyone else and years before Zola caught the public's attention, demanded justice for Alfred Dreyfus. In 1907 Péguy is writing four years after the death of Bernard-Lazare, and it is to this event that he is recalled as the passage continues:

> And when he died and during all the years that, in the beginning of the decomposition of *his* Dreyfus affair, preceded, prepared, obtained his death, we were the work to which he brought everything that he still had of friendship, faith, *prophecy,* force and action and vital strength, everything he still had of *temporal* activity, for he was a Jew, this great Jew: up until the perfectly serene fading away of a death which for him was no longer purely and simply, ordinarily, commonly the death of the moderns, the temporal death of the moderns, the death of the modern intellectual party, for I will relate the words, his words, which he said to me one on one [*seul à seul*] on the bed that was to become his death bed, that was already becoming his death bed, words that have been kept carefully guarded [*que l'on s'est bien gardé de rapporter*], that he himself perhaps kept guarded, instinctively, out of modesty, from others, old comrades, friends from the early days, words that will be recovered when I publish, if ever I publish this *Portrait of Bernard-Lazare* that I began to write almost right after his death, that I have not continued, that I have not finished writing—does one ever know if one finishes, to write, a portrait—because I was not old enough, that I will publish if I get old enough . . . (2:873–74)

The secret is repeated here but as unrepeatable. Which of these warring gestures gives the most violent *coup de pouce* to Péguy's hand as he writes? Without repeating Bernard-Lazare's own words, without attributing them through quotation, without evoking the voice that lodged in his own ear a death that he heard as "no longer the temporal death of the moderns," but infinitely more, Péguy nevertheless repeats: he repeats the scene, he sets the scene of the unrepeatable, singular death of the friend, mentor, father, the infinite spirit and origin of a world other than the modern. There is at once, at the same time, respect of this infinite other world that is always already dying and whose portrait one can never finish writing or knowing, and an always possible (necessary and sufficient condition) betrayal of it, repetition of its singular event. Bernard-Lazare dies, Péguy lives on, the (re)incarnation, the repetition. The Jew, this great Jew, the prophet, (re)born as the Christian, the spirit (re)born as temporal work. Alone on a bed with Bernard-Lazare, Péguy (re)conceived *another death,* which is to say another life.

That this gift of life should be an originary violence takes the passage further: "He brought to us also this unique force of disillusion, with others, this force of disillusion that more than the unique force of anger and indignation is, still more, the indelible mark, the infallible sign of impregnation . . ." A force of disillusion that is the infallible sign of impregnation? Although the term in French does not ordinarily denote pregnancy (*imprégner* means to permeate, to imbue), it is used here in a very curious formula that seems to point to some secret, utterly idiomatic coupling of the two ideas. The lines force a link, close a logical gap following some secret necessity. And if we reinsert this forced linkage into the larger scene recounted here, then it can be seen to articulate the legitimacy-illegitimacy of a certain succession.

Once again, two violent *coups* seem to face off across the divide of their articulating, coupling interval: the *coup de pouce* of this impregnation, in anger and indignation, and the *coup d'état* or usurpation of the legitimate name of the father. Péguy continues the sentence in his preferred manner, which is to repeat and reformulate; the syntax becomes more and more untranslatable:

> he brought us a serene but bitter bitterness, that force of bitterness and disappointment that, still more than holy wrath or vehement indignation and just as the spirit, the force of justice and revolt mark the prophet, *signs the passage,* the descent, the violent imperious seizure, the only mastering domination, the head that no longer belongs to itself [*la tête qui ne s'appartient plus*], that has another job, from now on another destination, another election than to be the (individual) head of the spirit and the body of this man, the incarnation, the *incapitation,* the taking possession, the installation, the sovereign, masterful, imperious installation in the head of a prophetic spirit. Hebrew. And to me he deigned to give his last friendship. (Emphasis added)

The threads of the event we have been following are here all knotted together in this scene of a certain *passage.* The passage is signed, marked but not by Péguy, or not simply by Péguy: for the passage in question is precisely that of a violent seizure of an (individual) head that at that moment no longer belongs to itself. It is, rather, what Péguy names with the invention of the word "incapitation," a word that is itself a graft with which to name the grafting of another's head onto the body of the same. A monstrous birth must follow and it is this, finally, that Péguy calls the sovereign installation of "a prophetic spirit." This installation or institution is what Péguy called above an "impregnation," that is, a monstrous act of grafting and a violent imperious seizure.

At the same time, nothing is seized, nothing properly speaking, nothing that is proper to, belongs to "this man." The head in question never belonged to anyone properly speaking, for it is a figure. But it is the commanding figure of the army of metaphoric repetitions that march in strict order through the passage or across the bridge Péguy remarks here. The successive Western armies of all its wars, coming and past, of (self-)domination march with them. This head is at the head, dominating from its sovereign position, its command post, the violent event that is Europe's coming revelation, the apocalypse of its history. Péguy claims to see it, or rather to foresee it, when he places himself at the head of this installation, the last witness of the prophet's will for the future. The event he claims to witness from this position can be described as the violent impregnation of one man by the spiritual force of another, creating another line of descent, another destination. Another heading, perhaps another beheading.

Four years after Bernard-Lazare's death, Péguy remembers, repeats, and repeats that he cannot repeat. A blank, a passage is left open. He does not fill it in, the incapitating words will not be repeated. Eleven years after that event, almost to the day, the incapitation is sealed by a decapitation.

> They take cover a moment behind the embankment of the road between Iverny and Chacouin. On the other side, a tall and dense beet field. Captain Guérin gives the order to cross it. Hardly had the assault begun when he falls, killed on the spot. "I am taking command," shouts Péguy drawing his sabre. The men slip on the beet leaves. Faced with violent enemy fire, he orders a halt and commands the men to fire at will from the prone position. As for him, he remains standing, in front, his spyglass in his hand, directing the fire, pointing out the enemy, running from one man to the next, stopping at times to catch his breath. Lieutenant La Cornillière also falls. Going to his aid, Roussel is wounded grievously in the chest. Irritated by the ravages inflicted on his company by an enemy which he can see is in retreat, Péguy yells furiously: "Fire! Fire! for God's sake! . . ." He refuses to get down. A bullet hits him in the forehead. He crumbles. The man next to him hears him whisper: "Oh, my God! . . . my children! . . ."[19]

A blank, a passage is left open, sealed open by a singular passing. This open seal is the possibility of our coming after an event and yet still being able to hear its resonant echo, which may be already something like its prophecy. What is the prophecy of an echo? A literary history, perhaps, the disaster of an address.

FIVE | *THE UNIVERSITY IN*
DECONSTRUCTION

IN WHAT sense is the university and the intellectual work that is
supposed to go on there public? Who or what is the public addressed
by the work of the university? Is there or can there be a sense in
which that work is not addressed to any public that can be identified?
On a first level, one could say that the research and teaching activity
of the university is public because it is evidenced by publication. This
apparent tautology merely points to the fact that the work of the
university, unlike that of other institutions one might think of, includes the generation, support, gathering, storage, evaluation, study,
preservation, and publishing of publications. In this sense the university is perhaps the most public of all public institutions. But of course,
in another sense very little of this activity can be expected to find
its way to a mass public, the undifferentiated audience sought by a
commercial mass medium like television or daily newspapers. By
comparison with the publicity of these institutions, the university
might as well be a secret society shrouded in obscurity. One thing
the Great PC Scandal of the 1990s will have made clear, however, is
that this appearance of obscurity is itself to a considerable extent
maintained and promulgated by the institutions of the mass media
themselves. The latter, in other words, have made it their job to
inform their public that it is not addressed by the work of the university, that that work is too obscure, too technical, or too specialized
for it. (When it is a matter of scientific research, these are terms of
respect, but in the case of the humanities, they are marks of disdain.)
This kind of reporting, with which we have now become so familiar,
determines public interest in the limited sense of common sense,
immediate self-evidence, and so forth—the interest, in other words,
of the largely ignorant and intellectually unadventurous. Imagining
that they address themselves to this public, while in fact fashioning
it by means of their address, the mass media seek in effect to disbar
the question: what other kinds of address might there be?

There is a difficulty in approaching this question when it has become commonplace to dismiss the noncommonplace as either incomprehensible or dangerous or both. In such an atmosphere, certain academics in the fields of the humanities have started worrying about their own academic elitism, but for reasons apparently quite different from those one may find in the mass circulation press. Although it is tempting to understand this difference as an opposition between two ideas of the public that the university is supposed to serve and represent, there is in fact something more complex or more duplicitous going on. Elements of the press, for their part, would appear to have set themselves up as guardians of an elite tradition—the Western canon of Great Works—that the academics they attack have put in question in so many ways. This attack, however, also takes aim at what is portrayed as the intellectual elitism of academic discourse, so that the logic of its address is populist, even demagogic. That is a first complication or duplicity. On the other side, the academics in question have taken aim justifiably at the ideological target provided by the defense of a cultural tradition in the popular press that masks its anti-intellectualism, but then they turn their weapons on themselves when they condemn their own theoretical discourse as elitist. That is the second complication or duplicity. We will come back to these complications in a moment when we consider how they inscribe the institution of the university within public space.

First, however, we might bring out one more sense of publicity as it pertains to the work of the university. In his "Answer to the Question: 'What Is Enlightenment?'" Kant distinguishes between the public and the private use of reason. "By the public use of one's own reason I mean that use which anyone may make of it *as a man of learning* addressing the entire *reading public*. What I term the private use of reason is that which a person may make of it in a particular *civil* post or office with which he is entrusted."[1] The public use of reason must never be restricted, whereas the private use of reason can "quite often be very narrowly restricted without undue hindrance to the progress of enlightenment."[2] Kant gives several examples: a military officer must not argue with an order even if, privately, he believes it to be ill-advised. But the same officer, speaking as a man of learning, may quite justifiably criticize military policy publicly. Likewise, a clergyman may disagree privately with points of doctrine that he nevertheless must teach to his congregation as prescribed by the church. "Conversely," Kant adds, "as a scholar addressing the real public (i.e., the world at large) through his writings, the clergyman making *public use* of his reason enjoys unlimited freedom to use his own reason and to speak in his own person" (57). It should be noted that Kant does not speak here either of that other civil servant that is the university professor or of the civil institution that is the university. Instead, all his examples assume that the "man of learning" or the "scholar" is simply the name given any educated citizen who exercises his public reason. The "man of learning," the "scholar" is the public man, who reasons with no limiting obligation to any particular institution.[3]

Now, perhaps Kant does not mention the university because that civil institution would impose no such obligation. In other words, unlike the military officer or the cleric, professional men or (*pace* Kant) women of learning, that is, members of a university faculty, would be under no constraint to suppress even in a limited manner the exercise of their private reason in order to carry out conscientiously the duties of their office. Indeed, the professional scholar as scholar would, in theory, have no such thing as private reason, or perhaps one should say that his or her private reason is indistinguishable from public reason, from reason in the service of the "real public (i.e., the world at large)." Thus, whereas every other civil institution installs a division within the faculty of reason of those appointed to uphold it, the institution of reason in principle would be upheld only to the extent that no gap between public and private reason is allowed to occur.[4]

If that is the case, then the institution of the university would be the institution of publicness itself, which means an institution in which internal (private or intra-institutional) interest cannot or should not be disjoined from external (public or extra-institutional) interest. Rather, the two are or should be the same, which is to say that there should be no difference between the institution of the university and all that is not that institution: the public. The university would thus be an institution without division between its inside and its outside even as it divides itself off from or within the society. The instituted division ought not to exist, although it does; and it certainly ought not to enclose or define an interest that is separate from any larger public interest. Rather, the mark of instituted difference should be a kind of empty or effaced mark, a redundant trait of public reason without reason.

The short essay, "What Is Enlightenment?" was published in 1784. When, more than ten years later in *The Conflict of the Faculties,* Kant returned to the subject of publicness and publicity as regards the activity of the scholar, circumstances had changed for this philosopher of public reason. First, in the interval Kant had experienced the strictures of a state censorship put in place in Prussia in 1788, which had refused to grant permission for the publication of *Religion within the Limits of Reason Alone*. He had thus become considerably more wary in his formulations concerning the possibility of an entirely free exercise of reason. In addition, the "public reason" that Kant had figured in the earlier essay as that of the "man of learning," the "scholar" is presented in the later text as that of the professor, appointed by the state to the faculties of its university. What has thus intervened from one text to the other is the institution of censorship and the institution of the university. These are made to coincide when Kant holds up the image of the state "which always desires to rule alone."[5] This desire, however, encounters a stumbling-block in the freedom of the *freie Rechtslehrer,* the free professors of right, i.e., adds Kant, the philosophers; the latter are not, he insists, "officially appointed by the state." Now, it may at first appear unclear how one is supposed to read this latter distinction. By "freie Rechtslehrer" who are not officially appointed by the state, one may understand independent men of learning "unaffiliated," as we say today, with the university, on the model of the French *philosophes*. The fact that Kant remarks that these free professors are "decried, under the name of enlighteners [*Aufklärer*], as persons dangerous to the state" would tend to support this reading. But that would be to overlook the more interesting and important point being underscored here. The distinction Kant is making is not one between appointed professors and unaffiliated enlighteners, but a distinction *within* those who are officially appointed to the university's faculty of philosophy. Officially appointed, the latter are nevertheless free professors of right. Notice, however, that if Kant must insist on this distinction, it is because one risks neglecting to grant the freedom from institutional, official constraint that appointment to an institution abrogates, as it does, for example, in the case of the institution of the church or the army, to recall the earlier examples, or in this text, as it does in the case of appointment to the "higher" faculties of both law and theology within the university. In other words, one risks instating for the professor of philosophy the very division between private reason and public reason that should not obtain in that case. And yet, Kant must acknowledge that division even as he insists that it does not affect the free professor's freedom to profess publicly the rights of the public. Once again, we come across the figure of the university (at least insofar as it concerns the faculty of philosophy) instituted by a division that does not divide, a division that is or is supposed to be a purely formal mark, one that does not set anything apart from the space of public reason.

The institution formally demarcated or divided in this way is not restricted by the very division instituting it: this is made clear by Kant at another point in the same passage we have begun to read for a second time (see chapter 1, pp. 44–48). This passage occurs, as we recall, in the second part of *The Conflict of the Faculties,* in a section titled "Concerning the Difficulty of Maxims Applying to World Progress with Regard to Their Publicity." The section concerns "popular enlightenment" [*Volksaufklärung*], the public instruction of the people. Now, as we have already seen when we first encountered this passage, Kant gives a most interesting analysis of the philosopher's popular instruction, which turns on a differentiation in the *address* of that instruction. The philosopher does not, Kant insists, address his teaching to the people directly, but rather to the state. He writes: "Their voice is not addressed confidentially to the people (as the people take scarcely any or no notice at all of it and of their writings), but is addressed respectfully to the state; and they implore the state to take to heart that need which is felt to be legitimate." That is, the public discourse of the philosophers is not addressed to the public as such, but over the heads of the people, so to speak, to their rulers. At this point, someone might want to say that Kant's free professor of right is elitist, or more precisely paternalistic. That is, he is an *Aufklärer* in the quite specific sense that Kant understands enlightenment: a passage from childhood to adulthood. But the paternalism here defines an opposition to the wishes of the state to rule absolutely over a population that can easily be kept ignorant of its rights. If one restores the context of this passage, it becomes clear that Kant is in fact placing a severe limit on the expectation that state-appointed professors will instruct the people in familiar terms about their duties and obligations to the patriarchal state. But it is less the matter of Kant's paternalism that should interest us here than the effect of an address that is directed elsewhere than to its apparent addressee, which is the people, and that is addressed rather to the state, which for Kant meant to a king who was able to order, but also to suspend state censorship.

Censorship divides public reason from private reason; it activates, in other words, the very division that, in the case of that institution of public reason which is the university, should remain without effect, without divisive or censoring effect. But how is that possible from the very moment reason institutes itself *as* reason, that is, by a mark of difference? What is the difference, finally, between reason and censorship? Or between censorship and public instruction? And where is this public instruction supposed to occur if not within the walls constructed by reason?

Kant has been brought into the discussion of the university's publicness for several reasons. First, because enlightenment, as understood by Kant, remains the legacy of the modern, scientific university and this is perhaps most evident in our own heightened concern with diversified representation in all aspects of university activity. That this legacy is also a certain suspicion of legacy, of all that by which the past passes itself down to a future and works to determine that future, indicates the historical and not only demographic sense in which nothing perhaps is more American than the multicultural challenge to the notion of a unified, determinant past. But that is only a first and more or less superficial reason to recall Kant's analysis of public instruction in an age of enlightenment (which he distinguishes from an enlightened age; we have a long way to go, wrote Kant in 1784, before mankind will have entered an enlightened age). The second and more important reason is that we are asking with ever more urgency the question Kant addressed in the passage just read: What or who is the public of the university? The question recurs, it insists, because it is ever more the case that the people in general "take scarcely any or no notice at all" of professors and their writings, and because it is still the case that, practically or empirically speaking, "public instruction" designates a system of selection or election that effectively closes the classroom door on the vast majority of a population. The enlightened age is still postponed. And in that postponement, the modern, scientific university comes to share a responsibility for having delayed its promise for so long. Yet, even as we indict the university for its failure, we reiterate the demand that the promise be renewed, that the long-overdue letter of public instruction be finally delivered. Perhaps that letter has been misaddressed, or perhaps it has simply been kept circulating within a narrow compass? In asking about the public to whom the university addresses itself, we ask the question of the destination to be reached and to what end. The concept of the university in the age of enlightenment, the modern university, is inseparable from the concept of an end, a destination, a finality.

One need not demonstrate at any length that, in certain recent debates, it is the ends of the university that are at issue, explicitly or more often implicitly. As a minimal indication of this, we can select statements from each of the declared adversaries in one of the first battles of the PC wars to be projected on the large screen of the national media: the University of Texas freshman composition initiative and the editorial response it prompted in *Newsweek*, signed by George Will.

In their "Statement of the Black Faculty Caucus," the authors, Ted Gordon and Wahneema Lubiano, conclude their argument for a multicultural curriculum in these terms: "What we are talking about here is no less than transforming the University into a center of multicultural learning: anything less continues a system of education that ultimately reproduces racism and racists."[6] Here destination is very broadly figured in general terms: the university once it has been transformed "into a center of multicultural learning." While it is doubtful that George Will read this "Statement" and its conclusion, his own editorial concludes by warning explicitly of the destination toward which Gordon, Lubiano, and their allies are leading the university: "So it goes on many campuses. The troubles at Texas are, as yet, mild. But the trajectory is visible: down. So is the destination: political indoctrination supplanting education."[7]

Will and the authors of the "Statement" appear to be firmly locked in mirrored dissent from each other's understanding: for both sides, it is a matter of "political indoctrination" versus "education." Allowing for a two-hundred-year delay in translation, we can see that these are essentially the same terms debated by the Convention when Condorcet submitted his "Report on the General Organization of Public Instruction" in 1792. At issue is still a certain elitism versus a certain populism. What holds this distinction in place is a notion of destination, an endpoint that can either be attained or missed, an addressee in the future. This is not to equate the very different sets of references that distinguish Will's position from his chosen adversaries and that make this polemic a struggle for legitimacy (retaining it or gaining it). It is merely to observe that, for both sides, legitimation of the references passes by way of the prior figuration of their legitimate destination, one toward which these references are said to address or destine themselves. If this sounds circular, it is; nonetheless, this circle of destined reference is what we generally understand by legitimacy: it is, in other words, the legitimated mode of legitimacy.

One may also remark something else at work within the scene we've briefly evoked. What we have just called the circle of destined reference, the form of legitimate meaning or value, describes a figure of auto- or self-legitimation. The legitimated figure of legitimacy, in other words, is a circle of auto-destination, a kind of self-addressed envelope. What is missing from this circle of self-address is an addressee who is not already a figure of the addressor, an addressee, that is, who is other than the addressor. So, it is here, within this circle, that the question of a destination *not already comprised* by the space of legitimated knowledge arises. But how can that question arise *within* the circle? Unless an opening has been left, a space wherein the auto- or the self- of destination *dis-closes* itself? Unless the dis-closure of the circle opens up a space that is neither within the legitimated domain nor simply outside it, but along the edge where the two divide? To call it a space, of course, is to have recourse to a figure and to the very figure of a bordered extension that is being dis-closed. This is not just a problem of nomination or figuration, but also of legitimation because to the extent that this dis-closure of the circle along its unfigurable edge lets one challenge the legitimacy that is conferred by circular destination, it can be seen to arise as an illegitimate question, as falling outside the realm of legitimate reason. And this despite the fact that, as we've already suggested, the question can only be posed because that realm itself in effect produces the question of its limit at its limit. If the circle had effectively realized or completed its closure, there would be nothing to dis-close, nothing to discuss, nothing to say—nothing. And manifestly that is not the case. The legitimacy that concerns us most—the legitimacy of the very figure of legitimacy—is open to question and to challenge only in a space opened *within* the circle, but which is therefore not part of that figure. It is within without being a part of the circle and as such it is the very possibility of the figure's reconfiguration. Within without being within, and vice versa: like Kant's division of reason that is without reason and without, therefore, a determinable destination.

We have been using the term "dis-closure," spaced with a hyphen, in order to bring out the pairing of two effects at work here: on the one hand, the effect of a certain repetition or retracing that discloses, i.e., brings into view, the circular outline; on the other, the effect of this dis-closed or un-closed figure, that is, of a figure that does not complete itself, that does not completely return to itself. Perhaps, however, it is already clear that the term "dis-closure" has been standing in for another, apparently more familiar term: deconstruction. Before the latter word was introduced, we have begun to survey the ground on which the current debate over legitimacy has been waged. This deferral was a strategic attempt to keep a critical space open that, in the context we are discussing, risks being closed down as soon as we invoke deconstruction by name. The risk of closure is an institutional effect, the effect of an instituted name that works to dispel a referential uncertainty. Concerning the institution that is the university put in question by the PC debate, the term "deconstruction" is most often presumed to refer to a theory, a method, a school, perhaps even a doctrine, in any case, some identifiable or localizable "thing" that can be positioned—posed and opposed—within that institution, but also that can be excluded from this defined enclosure. What is interesting, however, is less the imaginable reasons for this kind of positioning and opposing of names, than the disclosed movement in an unfigurable space between names and between positions, the space for different kinds of effects.

We will take a brief example here. In its issue of July 18, 1991, the *New York Review of Books* published a review by the well-known American historian C. Vann Woodward of Dinesh D'Souza's *Illiberal Education,* the book that, along with Roger Kimball's *Tenured Radicals,* called neoconservatives to arms against, in D'Souza's phrase, "the politics of sex and race on campus." Woodward's review was in the main sympathetic to D'Souza's argument while making numerous assertions that other university historians and scholars found inaccurate or objectionable. Two months later, the *NYRB* published some of these objections, along with a long response to them by Woodward. One of the letters-to-the-editor was signed by Clyde de L. Ryals, who identified himself as a professor of English at Duke University. As the letter is short, we will quote it *in extenso:*

> In his review of Dinesh D'Souza's *Illiberal Education,* Professor Vann Woodward refers to Duke University's recruitment of "superstars leading the then fashionable school of critics of the humanities who were known as deconstructionists." Since a number of observers of the current academic scene seem to share Professor Woodward's belief that the humanities departments here are filled with deconstructionists, I hope that you will allow me to correct this misapprehension.
>
> So far as I know, there is not one deconstructionist in the Duke English Department or in the Program in Literature. There are persons interested in gender, sexuality, Marxism, reader-reception, new-historicism, canonicity, popular culture, and many other types of criticism and theory, but to my knowledge there is no one here who identifies him/herself as a practitioner of the kind of deconstructionist criticism associated with Jacques Derrida.[8]

This objection will be answered by Professor Woodward, but before quoting that reply, just a few remarks about Professor Ryals's letter. Its point is to underscore Woodward's confusion or conflation of the many sorts of critical activities actually espoused and represented by name within Duke's English department or its Program in Literature with the single name, "deconstructionism," which Professor Ryals reports, perhaps not without some pride, is totally absent from their ranks. But for whatever reason Ryals may be riled up over that confusion, his rhetorical demeanor remains quite careful, although insistent: "So far as I know," he writes, "there is not one deconstructionist . . ."; "to my knowledge, there is no one here who identifies him/herself . . ." This repetition of a similar limiting construction within one two-sentence paragraph carries an implication that Ryals no doubt did not intend: it is as if he were admitting that there may be some authentic deconstructionists among his colleagues, but their association has not been revealed to him, as if, at Duke at least, the "deconstructionist criticism associated with Jacques Derrida" had become a kind of secret society in which only initiated members can be sure to recognize one another.

This implication, which may remind one of other, more sinister contexts, doubtless does not correspond to Professor Ryals's own notion of his own intention. It nevertheless appears as soon as that intention is published, a fact that Professor Woodward in his reply does not fail to remark. He writes:

> Professor Ryals assures us that "there is not one deconstructionist in the Duke English Department or in the Program in Literature." This comes as no surprise. In fact the term deconstruction has, for various reasons, become to some at least something of an embarrassment. That is not, however, to retract my suggestion that its one-time rhetoric helped smooth the path for multicultural innovations, some of which are of doubtful value. (76)

Woodward easily flushes out the problem with Ryals's assertion, although as a historian and a professed liberal, he ought to have been more on guard against echoing a certain question that once upon a time began, "Are you now or have you ever been . . . ?" But it is not this echo that should interest us as much as the fact that these two academics, each for apparently quite different reasons, question the legitimacy of understanding the work of the university in terms of deconstruction. For Woodward, as well as for the neoconservatives whose assessments he relies on, deconstruction is simply an umbrella name for "multicultural innovations . . . of doubtful value," when they are not downright harmful. This denomination is justified in Woodward's view because deconstruction's rhetoric "helped smooth the path" for these innovations (which, let it be said in passing, is hardly a discriminating criterion since one could say the same thing for many, vastly heterogeneous factors). For Ryals, on the other hand, who speaks for colleagues "interested in gender, sexuality, Marxism, reader-reception, new-historicism, canonicity, popular culture, and many other types of criticism and theory," it is important to discriminate and to call a new historicist a new historicist and so forth, to use, that is, a plurality of names (for it is less the names as such than their virtually endless plurality—the list concludes with "many other types of criticism and theory"—that provides the legitimating function here). Ryals's unintentional parody offers itself as proof that the historian is incorrect since it *just so happens* this list does not include the designation "deconstructionist."

Beneath this dispute, however, there is a profound agreement: deconstruction is the name of something that *has no place* in the university, either in Woodward's prescriptive sense that it should have no place or in Ryals's empirical sense that in fact it does not. To reach that agreement, the parties to the dispute (whom we are treating here, no doubt unfairly, as typical of sides opposed in some larger debate) must be able to invoke with a degree of assurance, explicitly or implicitly, an idea of what the university is or should be, in other words, its destination. Even Ryals's brief *mise au point* must intimate such an idea: it is a plurality of coexisting "interests" that complement one another within the larger, overriding interest of *universitas*. The problem with this harmonious picture of pluralism is that it is invoked in order to establish somewhat triumphantly the absence of one of "many other types of criticism and theory." Pluralism, at Duke at least, has a limit, the name "deconstructionism," which functions to bring the different elements together within a kind of unity. A limited plurality is always, finally, a unity.

For Woodward, a version of this same idea is made explicit in the concluding paragraph of his reply, which we quote for its appeal to the "mission" and "purpose" of the university as well as for its exceptional incoherence:

> We desperately need to go beyond the defensive to the positive, to what we have in common. We must seek agreement on the ideals, mission, purpose, and character of the academy—what the university means. One way to say what we are is to agree on what we are not. I do not think the university is or should attempt to be a political or a philanthropic or a paternalistic or a therapeutic institution. It is not a club or a fellowship

to promote harmony and civility, important as those values are. It is a place where the unthinkable can be thought, the unmentionable can be discussed, and the unchallengeable can be challenged.

The incoherence of this exhortation surfaces, for example, in the abrupt shift from a definition by means of exclusion ("One way to say what we are is to agree on what we are not") to a definition that would have to include what has just been excluded ("It is a place where the unthinkable can be thought, the unmentionable can be discussed, and the unchallengeable can be challenged"). This last rhetorical flourish sounds admirable until one realizes that Professor Woodward has in mind an already limited definition of the unthinkable, unmentionable, and unchallengeable, which definition "we" would agree not to think about, mention, or challenge. Or one could also wonder how the appeal to "what we have in common" and the imperative to "seek agreement" could be followed by the assertion that the university "is not a club or fellowship to promote harmony."

What this series of disjunctive sentences discloses, besides the historian's evident disregard for his own language, is the difficulty that gets in the way of the project to pose "what the university means" or "to say what we are," a difficulty that arises because prescriptive definition slips from under its ontological mask in the very process of its articulation. To say what we are as institution, that is, as a non-natural, cultural invention or artifact, is to say what we should be, what we are *meant* to be, or what we *will have been* in a future past from which the deferred moment of arrival at destination is seen as already included in the present of the definition. It is to attempt to circle back from this already comprised destination in order to pose a presence-to-itself that includes an always deferred *meaning* ("what the university means") in *being* ("what we are"). Woodward's incoherence is but the marker left by this circle's failure to close completely on itself, or, in this case, even to come close.

We have attempted to make several points with this example. Let us reiterate what they are and then try to take each one a little further.

1. When Woodward takes "deconstructionism" to be the generic name of the brand of thinking that has, as he put it, smoothed the path for multicultural innovations of doubtful value, he is merely repeating the gesture of so many other journalists who have, deliberately or not, made themselves the spokespersons of an old political reflex to seek a clearly identifiable enemy. What is rather remarkable in this identification, however, and what can be gauged in Ryals symptomatic response, is that almost none of those singled out as

suspect of "political correctness" would accept to be called a "deconstructionist"; they are even rather hostile to those of us for whom this
label is not problematic, at least not for the reasons alleged here.
Although the press, of course, cannot be concerned with this kind
of distinction, which is deemed by them to be too subtle, its identification of "deconstruction" as the enemy nevertheless allows a crack
to appear that traverses the whole field of academic political discourse, from left to right and from the interior to the exterior of
the university institution. Between the two sides is this thing called
"deconstruction," which one side wants to get rid of as much as the
other. This rejection thus forms a kind of secret and unavowable
liaison between them, even as it destabilizes the terms of their opposition. It is, in other words, a deconstructive effect that will have
occurred and that will have indicated the limit, by exceeding it, of
the most recognizable political and analytical discourses.

2. By "deconstructive effect" is meant a shifting of apparent divisions, in this case, the dividing lines that are supposed to set off an
institution like the university and its defining discourses from, to use
Woodward's phrase, "what we are not." The fact that this effect
shows up around the use of the term "deconstruction" to name a
referentially stable unit that can be either inside or outside that institution is not incidental, although it does complicate the analysis. The
exchange between Woodward and Ryals (but here we could have
taken other examples as well) can be read on one level as a dispute
about referential value, which is possible only because each assumes
the indisputably referential value of his own use of a term. Beyond
this level of initial paradox, however, which could be illustrated just
as well with any other term, "deconstruction" here is both the name
in dispute and a name—more or less conventional, more or less
instituted—for what happens when instituted, referential boundaries
shift. Which means that what we earlier called the profound agreement between the parties to this dispute—deconstruction is the name
of something that *has no place* in the university—is reached by
reinscribing a deconstructive shift in the very space of a proscription
of that name.

3. This implies that, regardless of what some may want to think
about the place of deconstruction *in* the university, the university is
in deconstruction. Such an affirmation is not an announcement of
something that has overtaken this institution recently and from without, as various accounts would have it, something that would have
come either from the radicals whose 1960s ideology has taken refuge
in tenure or from the imported writing of a few European thinkers,

mostly French.[9] Such pseudo-historical fables cannot dis-close how it is that, already in its Kantian form, the university divides itself, not only into internal divisions, departments, or faculties, or within these into warring schools of thought, but divides the very division by which it is set apart and instituted over against all that "we are not." If we recall the brief reading of the two texts of Kant, it led us to pose an apparently paradoxical figure, that of an institution without instituted difference, without division between its inside and its outside but which nevertheless divides itself off from or within the general social space. This means it is possible that a division be not a division, or the other way around, that the nondivision be nevertheless a division. It is possible, in other words, for division to divide itself in its very mark. This possibility, indeed, is the general possibility of the mark as institution, as instituted sign. And by the same token, the instituted mark, institution in general cannot exclude the essential demark-ing or division that structures it. An instituted difference cannot, in other words, exclude what it is meant to exclude.

4. If, like any institution, the university is in deconstruction, it has also been a place, particularly in the United States, in which that deconstruction comes to be at least partially formalized and theorized. This work of formalization or theorization is only partial because, for the same reasons just mentioned, it cannot formally exclude non-formalizable, nontheorizable—i.e., practical, pragmatic, or sheer "accidental"—elements. What this means in practice is that, as theory, deconstruction will have had effects that do not in any simple sense belong to or return to its formal structure. Woodward and other journalists implicitly recognize this when they see deconstruction as responsible for a vast array of institutional realignments, most of which, of course, they deplore. Despite this tendentious and hopelessly misinformed account, one may be tempted to find it closer to some truth than an opposing account of deconstruction's effect in or on the institution, or rather its lack of effect because it is, to quote no one in particular, "too theoretical," "not political." The fact that deconstruction can be positioned as at once too political and not political at all, as both PC and not PC, signals that the terms in which the political is posed in this debate are inadequate to account for all the effects being produced.

To call these other effects deconstructive is not to imply that they return to the theoretical formation called deconstruction as to their cause. Rather, they are so-called because they mobilize the division within the trait whereby something called deconstruction can be identified. Which leads us to one more point, which is capital: it concerns a public address that is always necessarily divided, not in the sense that Kant set out when he spoke of the "free professor of right" who speaks to the king even as he appears to address the people. No, it is an address divided precisely by the absence of any king, real or symbolic, which is to say by the absence of any figure who can stand in for the final destination of public discourse.

In this absence and because of this absence it is possible to reflect on the relation of academic, disciplinary discourse to a "public." We can ask, for example, about the prevalent presumption that such discourse is unintelligible or simply without pertinence for the "public." When the discourse in question concerns literature or literary theory, then this presumption is most often accompanied by a denunciation of this presumed unintelligibility. Once again, it would be possible to cite examples of critics from both the "right" and the "left" in broad agreement that literary theory really *ought* to be intelligible to "the public" and who are ready to denounce it by this criterion.

According to Bruce Robbins, what we are witnessing in this appeal to public understanding or approval is a struggle within the pre-set conditions for the legitimation of discourse.[10] Robbins aims his own critique not at those who seek this legitimation for theoretical discourse; on the contrary, he insists that an address or an appeal to "the public" is always implied in professional, academic discourse, even when an argument is being mounted against such appeals. Moreover, Robbins makes clear that, for him, whatever "moves scholarship in the direction of the public" is "*as such* . . . politically desirable" (96; emphasis added). A few pages before the end of the essay, he will be careful to differentiate this monolithic "public" toward which we are urged to "move": he advises reconceiving "the contemporary public sphere . . . as a plural, provisional, and multi-layered concept, a concept that includes rather than excludes the disciplines and that disperses its debts and obligations rather than concentrating them in a single totalizing instance" (114–15). Thus reconceived, "the public could no longer serve as a potent because non-specific abstraction, always at a convenient distance from where one already is."

If, however, "the public" is where one already is, how does one "move in the direction of" it? What, exactly, are "theorists" being urged to accomplish in this move "in the direction of the public" that is *as such* politically desirable? "The public," we are assured, need no longer be an abstraction, but can be concretized in the localizable instance of wherever one already is. Although doubtless this is not intended as an apology of solipsism, quite the reverse, nevertheless the argument here seems to place an unwarranted faith in the power of good intentions, in a collective will to recall that, from now on, whenever we appeal to "the public" we actually mean a pluralized or detotalized concept that includes rather than excludes the site of academic discourse. If this "move in the direction of the public" remains enigmatic, it may be because it is understood principally as a discursive, rhetorical move the aim of which is not necessarily to make that scholarship more "accessible" to a nonacademic public. It thus remains unclear how the appeal of its "political desirability" can work other than as a promised reappropriation for academic discourse of a defensible *figure* of "the public." In other words, this move projects its primary political appeal to an *academic* "public."

Things are not quite so simple, however, for Robbins also manifestly wants to advance the recognition of the public status of professional discourse, and to effect a greater consciousness of the intellectual's public, political responsibility.[11] This is without doubt a necessary task to which Robbins brings an impressive set of tools. There is one tool, however, that seems to have been refashioned almost beyond recognition, which is the notion of access by a nonacademic public to the intellectual debates of the university. Robbins seems to want to stay on the fence on this question, reluctant to judge political desirability by the criterion of public access (which as he very well knows is one of the oldest and most dangerous of rhetorical ploys) and at the same time unwilling to renounce the figure of the move "in the direction of the public." The resulting position may look uncomfortably twisted, and indeed Robbins explicitly claims in his final sentences a certain paradox that is, he writes, "not to be avoided" (117).

But not everyone has shown the same restraint, if that is indeed what it is. In his *Public Access: Literary Theory and American Cultural Politics,* Michael Bérubé makes an often forceful argument for understanding the public, political responsibility of the intellectual in terms that he wishes at least to be themselves more recognizable to the nonacademic readership for whom he is also writing: it is the responsibility to translate the stakes of literary theory into the more general idiom of a literate but untrained reader perplexed by what has been going on in literature departments of our universities for the last decade or more (which is, one may safely conclude, a still minuscule section of the general public).[12] Having neglected this task for too long, Bérubé observes, academic literary theorists have allowed public debate to be framed by a reactionary crew of journalists, politicians, and their professor allies who are decidedly unsympathetic to literary theory. Bérubé, however, is writing to demonstrate that this abdication of a certain public forum and of advocacy need not necessarily follow from the reputed difficulty of the discourses in question. And indeed his witty, pop-culturally with-it style could almost convince all but the most ascetically inclined "theorists" that he's right.

Almost. Why the hesitation? It is not because there is a major fault to be found with Bérubé's analysis of the effects of the reactionary takeover of the press in its "reporting" on literary studies. Nor even that one must judge his efforts in a contrary direction to be fruitless. But there are two ways in which Bérubé, differently but perhaps no less finally than Robbins, seems to avoid the really difficult points of the argument he is trying to make concerning a public sphere of politico-intellectual responsibility. Actually, the two points meet and are fused in the same difficulty. It is, precisely, the criterion of *difficulty* as measured by the media's norms of publication or public discourse. Robbins's analysis of the legitimation of professional discourse makes little mention of the very material conditions in which such discourse is allowed to find a readership or prevented from reaching any but an almost private audience.[13] One result of this omission is that the figure of the "public" he claims to find in the most politically desirable professional discourse is not directly interrogated for its restriction by the codes, frames, meanings, and general fashioning of public media, both academic and nonacademic. Bérubé is, by the very nature of his project, more attentive to these questions, but even here a kind of distraction affects his observations, as if he were not willing to look too hard at the very processes he describes.

For example, he recounts in considerable detail how, in the course of his research for his first article in the *VLS,* which was titled "Public Image Limited: Political Correctness and the Media's Big Lie," he turned up some rather nasty information about Dinesh D'Souza's activities as editor of the *Dartmouth Review.* Because this essay is not one of those included in *Public Access,* Bérubé cites from it the paragraph in which he documents this shameful behavior. He then comments: "Because of the *Voice*'s strict space limitations, I could not go on to say that . . . nor could I explain that . . ."[14] This remark about "space limitations" is made as if in passing, but he then relates with a little more energy how the same essay came to be reprinted in Paul Berman's collection *Debating P.C.,* but minus the paragraph he has just quoted (and, needless to say, minus its already deleted expansion). "When it became clear that Berman would not consider reprinting the piece unless the 'questionable' allegation was dropped, I dropped it. Only to include it here, of course, with suitable commentary" (18–19).

One could well imagine several reasons that would justify Bérubé's decision to compromise with editors in each case; nonetheless, doesn't this episode call for some additional reflection after the fact? Was Bérubé not even tempted to hypothesize about what it reveals perhaps of differential editorial constraints, about the "reader" being fashioned or "addressed" according to whether he or she was likely to buy the mass circulated Berman book (a Dell paperback, sold at many chain bookstore checkout counters), the *VLS,* or Bérubé's own book? How does one plot the correlation between a descending size of the print run and a diminishing constraint on the freedom to print what an author in fact wrote? What assumptions are holding in place this apparently direct correlation? Are they invulnerable to critique? Likewise, what determines the "strict space limitations" of a given publication? Clearly, these are not naturally given limits and they are applied differently to different subjects and different authors. And finally and most important, is the "public intellectual"'s overriding responsibility to *submit* without question to these restrictions in order thereby at least to get into print with some version, however curtailed or reframed, of a contestory argument or analysis? Is there not another, equally imperative responsibility that requires not just the critique of these structures, but active efforts to transform them whenever possible?

This objection should sound familiar. It was made more than sixty years ago by Walter Benjamin in "The Author as Producer," which already cites a number of precedents for it, the most important for Benjamin coming from Brecht. Benjamin's own version of the argument has also been a continuous reference since for Marxist (or "post-Marxist") and non-Marxist thinkers alike.[15] In it, he insisted on what he called a "decisive difference between the mere supplying of a productive apparatus and its transformation" and offered the following proposition: "that to supply a productive apparatus without—to the utmost extent possible—changing it would still be a highly censurable course even if the material with which it is supplied seemed to be of a revolutionary nature" for it is well known that this apparatus "can assimilate astonishing quantities of revolutionary themes, indeed, can propagate them without calling its own existence, and the existence of the class that owns it, seriously into question."[16] The conditions that dictated this proposition in 1934, in an address to the Institute for the Study of Fascism, and the accompanying analysis of journalistic, literary, and artistic practices have doubtless changed in very significant ways in sixty years. But the expansion, technical diversification, and generalization of public media have, if anything, dramatically increased their capacity to assimilate or propagate "revolutionary themes" and discourses without the conditions of a certain intellectual or artistic "mediatization"—production and consumption—thereby being necessarily transformed. Why then does so much recent reflection on the role of the public intellectual or on the political responsibilities of literary theorists generally leave out of account the "decisive difference" to which Benjamin refers?

If we had to hypothesize a reply to that question, we would draw from the other major proposition of Benjamin's essay. It concerns the debate over the place of literature and literary criticism in political struggles. He addresses his audience as follows:

> For I hope to be able to show you that the concept of political tendency, in the summary form in which it usually occurs in the debate just mentioned, is a perfectly useless instrument of political literary criticism. I should like to show you that the tendency of a literary work can only be politically correct if it is also literarily correct. That is to say, the politically correct tendency includes a literary tendency. And, I would add straightaway, this literary tendency, which is implicitly or explicitly contained in every *correct* political tendency of a work—this and nothing else makes for the literary quality of the work. *Therefore* the political tendency of a work includes its literary quality *because* it includes its literary tendency. (221, trans. modified; German edition, 102)

It would no doubt be hasty and historically careless to suggest a simple parallel here between the debates agitating communist circles in Western Europe in the 1930s, to which Benjamin refers, and the debate about the political responsibility of literary theorists or critics in the U.S. in the 1980s and 1990s. Nevertheless, the occurrence here of the phrase "politically correct" (*politisch richtige*) stands out when the passage is read some sixty years later, rather like a sore thumb waving in the direction of what has become in recent years one of the most successful crossover gadgets to appear on the public stage of debate about the intellectual's political role. Whatever resemblance we might wish to discern here would have to acknowledge, however, that Benjamin is writing in order to sound an unexpected note, one which he anticipates his comrades in the audience will not hear without impatience: "This is, you will perhaps object, a very specialized, out-of-the-way theme [*Das ist, werden Sie vielleicht einwenden, ein recht spezielles, ja ein entlegenes Thema*]."

The unfamiliar or unwelcome note is the direct link asserted between the "politically correct" and the "literarily correct." And what is more, adds Benjamin straightaway and thereby seeming to go even more out-of-the-way of direct, immediate political "tendency," the "literarily correct" will necessarily include what he calls "literary quality." Benjamin then explains that with the pair quality/tendency he intends to displace that other pair form/content whose undialectical relation has given rise to so much fruitless debate. It is not, then, *formal* quality that must be taken into account but the quality of a transformation of forms and instruments of literary production, what Benjamin refers to, with a term borrowed from Brecht, as *Umfunktionierung,* functional transformation.

There are many ironies here, of course. As the editor of *Reflections* is quick to point out, Benjamin "demands a new, open, and experimental Marxist art in the manner of Tretiakov and Brecht exactly at the moment when, in the Soviet Union, Karl Radek is attacking James Joyce, and eager Party functionaries are declaring that nineteenth-century traditions are the best way to the future."[17] To the aberrations of Soviet Realism we could add the irony that much postcommunist or post-Marxist literary thought in the United States, if it wants to mark its solidarity with the Left, continues to seem constrained by the suspicion that Benjamin encountered, the suspicion that talk of literary transformation is too specialized, too "out-of-the-way," or, to use current vocabulary, "elitist."

This brings us finally to the second point as regards the related efforts to publicize literary theory and to theorize the literary public. It is the point of the difficulty involved when one seeks to do more than "talk of literary transformation," that is, thematize it and adduce examples, as Benjamin does for the most part in "The Author as Producer." The transformation in question, or rather the deconstruction, of the institutional apparatuses (educational, critical, political, mediatic, literary, and so forth) can occur necessarily only at a certain limit of the comprehensibility supplied by these institutions. A theorization of deconstruction at these limits will also, just as necessarily, produce the effect of a difficulty for comprehension, especially where this theoretical effort takes up Benjamin's challenge not just "to supply a productive apparatus without—to the utmost extent possible—changing it."

For the writer, the literary critic, or the cultural theorist, the "productive apparatus" is most often the medium of a written discourse or some kind of publication, localized, at least in its production (for reception remains far more difficult to locate or even to describe and this is a major question to which we will have to return below), in technical media of reproduction of some sort, which are also highly complex and material sites of decision, judgment, and evaluation of the kind we were pointing to above. These decisions constitute the structure, frame, or program of the material support (the "software" that runs the media's "hardware") and they are already in place more or less independently of whatever "content" is fed into the apparatus. But only "more or less" for precisely because this structure is decisional, it has the character as well of a discursive operation, of an argument from reasons and assumptions even if these have been covered over by the repetition of use and seem to have taken on a virtually "natural" appearance. It is this always possible equivocation of the distinction between the "content" of a reproduced discourse and the structure or "form" of its reproduction that has to interest any theorization of the deconstruction or transformation of institutional limits. This interest is not just theoretical, as we say, but practical in the most concrete sense of the dissemination of a discourse, a writing, or another practice of inscription. This is also, therefore, the place at which evaluations of "difficulty," of what is or is not "receivable" or "accessible" to this or that public risk merely submitting to, without questioning or even remarking, the critical judgments already determining the conditions in which institutions, and first of all the institutions of the media, decide who says what where about the limits of those very institutions.

These conditions of journalistic coverage—the demand for immediate comprehensibility (but according to a standard of comprehensibility that cannot be made explicit, that itself remains "incomprehensible"), the projection of an "average" reader with "average" opinions (whatever these might be), the constraints of time and space—are always in force and affect, of course, far more and more crucial kinds of reporting than some stories about the current state of literary study in the university. All the same, these stories have perhaps displayed something else at work other than haste, mediocrity, and impatience. If we looked more closely at an actual article of this sort (which we'll admit to selecting precisely because we find it hasty, mediocre, and full of signs of its author's impatience with the subject), we might also be able to isolate in more specific terms some of the conditions that activate the evaluation of "difficulty," "obscurity," or "nonsense."

For this exercise, we select a brief article for the June 1991 issue of the French monthly magazine *Actuel*.[18] Although neither the magazine in which it was published nor the author of the piece will be familiar to most American readers, it offers a particularly dense number of openings for the sort of practical analysis we've described. The article, in fact, puts on stage and highlights the very situation in which it has been produced, the situation of an American journalist who addresses "average" French readers on the subject of the reception among "average" American academics of contemporary French thought (Lacan, Foucault, Derrida, and Baudrillard are the named representatives). In this situation, the journalist seizes the opportunity to make assertions like the following: "That Lacan or Derrida are, let's admit, rather difficult to digest, that is not their [i.e., American academics] problem, quite on the contrary. It is precisely their [i.e., Lacan or Derrida] indigestible side that makes them into idols. Americans, like other primitive peoples, don't like to appear stupid in front of foreigners and they are suspicious of what they understand too well." Having made such a boldly indefensible assertion, our American reporter does not hesitate to apply its lesson and, so as not to resemble his benighted countrymen who are afraid to appear stupid in front of foreigners, he invokes the contrary logic: he will be suspicious of what he *cannot* understand too well and of what is, by his own admission, difficult. He apparently believes that, in this way, he will demonstrate in front of his foreign readers his own civilized and sophisticated behavior. When he then goes on to compare the way Americans read Derrida to the way they judge French wine (they look only at the price tag), he strikes a note that is no doubt calculated to reinforce his sophisticated, nonprimitive profile, at least in the eyes of a certain kind of French reader. But what in fact could be more *primitive* than suspicion, fear, and finally loathing in the face of what one does not immediately understand? Applying this primitive logic, our reporter may easily put one in mind of a member of some tribe that considers the incomprehensible language spoken by another tribe or people to be proof of their barbarity and unreliability.

In fact, however, his own barbarity goes much further than that: He *assumes* that even those who speak or write this other language do not understand what they mean to say. Here is how he follows up his analogy to wine-tasting: "The same is true with Derrida. Americans cite him and recite him *without knowing* whether it has the taste of the cork" (emphasis added). And then he quotes a few sentences, leaving their source vague so as to better imply that they are typical of a certain genre: "In a book titled *Philosophy and Deconstruction: The Writings of Jacques Derrida,* one reads sentences of the following sort: 'Deconstruction accounts for these *constitutive* "contradictions" through the construction of arche-syntheses, or infra-structures, as we will call them hereafter. These infrastructures represent laws of distribution and disposition, economically minimal clusters of concepts, predicates, or possibilities of these "conflicting" concepts, levels of argumentation, or heterogeneous instances of discourse. Because of the incommensurability of the material possibilities that enter these syntheses and the specific structural arrangement of their features (a problem we cannot broach here), these arche-syntheses are non-unitary.' " The implication is that these decontextualized sentences are pure jargon, without content, without meaning, pure effect chosen, as our reporter will put it in a later moment of his tirade, to impress the "vulgum pecus": "what can the *vulgum pecus* do but be impressed when it hears talk about 'polysemia,' 'reinscription,' 'alterity,' 'espistemè' [*sic*], 'desitinerant' [*sic*]," and so forth. Once again, this journalist seems above all concerned to distinguish himself from the strategy of the vulgar who, in order better to dissimulate their vulgar ignorance, simply repeat—"cite and recite"— what they do not comprehend. (One could point out, by the way, that the "empty jargon" charge is hardly an original invention; rather it "cites and recites" one of the most common tactics in the genre we are examining.[19]) Meanwhile, of course, his own citation of the Latin expression does not altogether fit this counterstrategy since it may betray a similar urge to impress the common herd with a "jargon" that, as he writes of Derrida's readers and commentators, "makes them as mysterious as that of the legal and medical professions [*sic*]."

If we append a "sic" to these numerous grammatical or spelling errors, it is not just to point out an even more obvious vulgarity or "barbarity" of such writing practices. Rather we want to underscore the editorial conditions in which such unstable mixtures get distributed. It is possible, for example, that the mistakes we have signaled were introduced by a careless translator, whose negligence we have in turn translated back into English. But the point is that magazines of this sort do not generally indicate that a text is a translation. Indeed, one of the identifying features of this journalistic discourse is precisely the dismissal of the fact of language difference, and therefore the concrete specificity of any given language. We have seen how the presumption of a common and a common-sense language operates not only as a technical condition, but as the principal thematic of this discourse. The effects of such dismissal can only be measured by confronting one language with another, the original with the translation, an operation that the conditions of newspaper and magazine publishing do not permit. And even if they did, how many readers could be counted on to look at things more closely? For example, how many readers of Karpel's article in *Actuel* would be able to remark that the quotation from Rodolphe Gasché's essay, given above in the original, undergoes numerous distortions in its passage into French, any one of which would make a self-respecting translator blush for shame?[20]

The conditions we are highlighting, then, are ones that, at every point and concerning every detail, ought to put one on guard as to the reliability of the reasons given here for suspecting the other's supposedly incomprehensible language. So when we read an assertion to the effect that deconstruction "permits one to write absolutely anything" one must see there a peculiar and perverse irony at work. It is as if the author of this brief diatribe were declaring that, thanks to deconstruction, he can write anything he likes about deconstruction, of course, but also, why not, about anything else. But at the same time he is writing to censor the very permission he has been given, or he has taken, to write whatever he likes. This incoherence is given a cover or an alibi because the charge that others have somehow issued permission to write "absolutely anything" is serving as assurance that here, at least, that's not the way we do things: We have our standards! The implied protest against the lack of standards is thus standing in at the precise point where the standard of judgment is most suspect.

This kind of incoherence should make for a highly uncomfortable, indeed intolerable position, but in fact it seems to flow from the source of common sense.[21] Doubtless that is why the charge that deconstruction lets one say absolutely anything, or, in its alternate version, claims that no text has any meaning, has become the most commonly repeated charge in the sort of "reporting" we are considering. Let's take another example of the same tactic but chosen this time closer to home, therefore without the additional twist in the address to a non–American public. Moreover, our second example is an article that, unlike Karpel's, purports merely to relay a piece of information, according to the highest standards of objective journalism.

On September 25, 1991, the *New York Times* reported on its front page the formation of the organization Teachers for a Democratic Culture (TDC), which it describes as having been formed to "lead the counteroffensive" against right-wing attacks on so-called "political correctness," referred to in the article as "a new leftist orthodoxy." Among the founding members of the group, the article cites Stanley

Fish, Henry Louis Gates, Jr., and Gerald Graff, and mentions that they are among the thirty "notable scholars" who have signed an organizing manifesto. The journalist, Anthony DePalma, quotes once briefly from this manifesto, but the greater part of his article is taken up by paraphrase and summary of the history of the dispute, mixed with quotations from Graff, Dinesh D'Souza, and Stephen Balch, the president of the National Association of Scholars, an ultra-conservative group of university professors. The article, then, appears to conform to the standards of liberal journalism by presenting a balanced overview of a controversy. It is marked by the attempt to represent the positions of the several parties to the dispute as themselves reasonable and balanced. Accordingly, the "critics of the conservative onslaught," that is, TDC's founders or sympathizers, are said to concede that there have been incidents here and there on university campuses in which so-called "politically correct" advocates have in effect abrogated the academic freedom of their colleagues or fellow students. And the journalist mentions another concession: "The critics also concede that some radical literary theories, including deconstructionism—which says that no text can have a fixed meaning—can legitimately be criticized." This statement is not in quotes nor is it attributed to any of the interviewees, which would tend to lead most readers of the article to assume that it is a paraphrase of the group's "manifesto."

Indeed, that was my initial assumption when I read this article; it was corrected only some weeks later when I obtained a copy of said manifesto and found that there was no such "concession." "Deconstruction" is in fact mentioned there only once in a list with other "new literary theories and movements" whose "actual effects in classroom practice" have been the subject of "malicious distortions" in the representation of "our ideas and practices to the wider public." Did the journalist read this sentence and decide it would not be a "malicious distortion" simply to ignore it? Did one of the members of TDC contacted for the article go off the record with the remark about "deconstructionism"? And who is finally responsible for the seemingly authoritative gloss: "which says that no text can have any fixed meaning"? Try writing to the *New York Times* for answers: it will send you a form letter in reply that politely concedes your right to your opinion, thank you.

Once again, the ironies here are already obvious, but they bear repeating because of the important implications they carry for the effort to represent more accurately academic work to "the public," which is one of the major professed aims of Teachers for a Demo-

cratic Culture. "We think," declares the manifesto, "the very formation of such a group will be an important step in gaining influence
over the public representations of us and our work." The largest and
most discouraging irony, therefore, is the way in which the "very
formation" of TDC became, on the contrary, another occasion for
the kind of "malicious distortion" it was founded to combat. But,
as far as I know, none of the founding members of TDC made any
attempt to correct publicly the *New York Times* article.[22] Without
drawing any hasty conclusions about this de facto concession, one
may nevertheless be justified in wondering why the apparent political
intentions behind this initiative could be so quickly and so easily
hijacked.

A speculative answer to that question would take up the matter
of *difficulty,* which is presumed by both the *New York Times* and the
TDC manifesto to be a nonissue. Indeed, it is this presumption that
allows both organizations of public discourse to project something
like an ideal ground of communication on which to meet in a reasoned exchange of information. Neither a prominent daily newspaper
nor an obscure interest group formed primarily as a public relations
channel is prepared to recognize that among the questions at issue
may be some that cannot be dispatched in the form of information.
The TDC manifesto says as much: "We understand the problems of
any organization claiming to speak for a very diverse, heterogeneous
group of teachers who may sharply disagree on many issues, including that of the politics of culture. What we envision is a coalition of
very different individuals and groups, bound together by the belief
that recent attacks on new forms of scholarship and teaching must
be answered in the spirit of principled discussion." In other words,
it is not our place to represent the sharp disagreements "on many
issues" but only the "spirit of principled discussion," which acts as
a kind of umbrella, to recall the figure from Gerald Graff we analyzed
above (see pp. 17–20). But this is also to suppose that the task of
"clarifying our ideas and practices to the wider public—something,
it must be admitted, we have not done as well as we should,"[23] can
be accomplished under this umbrella *without difficulty*. By that is not
meant that the organizers naively anticipated theirs to be a simple
task, but rather that they envisioned a place in which "principled
discussion" could occur in public without overriding certain determinations of what is or is not "difficult." They quite patently do not
understand their task to include challenging, revising, or even questioning those prior determinations. Nor, therefore, by implication

do they understand that this might be precisely one of the "practices" in question which they propose to represent better to a wider public.

One result of all these assumptions, or rather concessions, is that the phrase "deconstructionism—which says that no text can have a fixed meaning" is able to pass into the public domain (it little matters on whose responsibility) as if it were on the program of this enlightened group. For the fact is that, in order to explain why such a phrase or its evil twin ("deconstruction allows one to write absolutely anything") is neither simply true nor false, another kind of practice *other than simply predicative discourse* (S is P) has to be undertaken. And it is this "other" that is judged to be too difficult, inaccessible, or out of place by *both* the *New York Times* journalist *and* the organization of scholars that has given him his story. In the absence or perhaps merely the bracketing deferral of this other practice on the site and the conditions of public discourse, the political effect of TDC's founding can be recuperated to what appears to be a contrary purpose.[24] And if this is as worrisome as it seems, then it ought to be prompting more attention from the advocates of the intellectual's public, political responsibility.

At least one objection to the foregoing might point out that there are many places—books, journals, academic conferences, the graduate seminar, or even the undergraduate and secondary school classroom—where what we have called this "other" practice can and does go on. These are places where the time and space required for "difficult" argument and effective, practical intervention is not restricted. So it is not as if this practice were being systematically prevented from developing its protocols and disseminating itself. Even if that were simply true, however, should this kind of concession to the prior determining judgments of what constitutes the public understanding of sense and nonsense, difficulty and accessibility, and so forth be made the grounds of a political responsibility of the "intellectual"? A second objection, but it is one we could readily accept and endorse, would emphasize that the said responsibility ought not to be thought of as reducible to a single axiom, since the "intellectual," whether or not we deplore her putative fall from the public space into the institution, is nevertheless always addressing herself to more than one addressee, reader, audience, or public.

It is, however, precisely this notion—or rather necessity—of plural address that has the power to dismantle and transform what we think we mean by "difficulty," "accessibility," or even "reception." For it must cause us to pose the questions that are being elided when the determinations of these concepts remain concealed in the very judgments they produce: What is determining here the limits of comprehensibility and for whom? What is "common" about a common sense that presumes the other to be speaking nonsense? But these questions need to be not just posed but allowed to open onto and into the whole diversity of public practices (that is, of any meaningful or symbolic act). It is then that a "move in the direction of the public," as a watchword of theoretico-political responsibility, would take up that responsibility as more than a concession to a totalizing judgment of who and what the public is at any given moment. If there is a difficulty here, it is not in recognizing, as Robbins and others willingly do, how any unitary concept of "the public" works to deny an irreducibly plural, differentiated "entity"; it is not, in other words, a difficulty at the level of concepts, but at the level at which one accepts or resists the conditions of one's *own* address, one's *own* meaning, one's *own* intention, and consequently one's *own* "self." At this level, where we are plugged into all the forces of unconscious desire, the division or pluralization in question challenges not comprehension but these powerful forces of denial. And yet the undeniable and the inevitable remain in force since division describes the very possibility of any address at all, whether or not it attempts to conform itself to whatever criteria are supposed to regulate "public address" or "public access."

The descriptive analysis of divided address, the fact that every act of meaning is possible only because it is impossible to guarantee its certain delivery at an intended destination, is not an interpretation that can be countered within a field of conflicting interpretations of meaning acts. It is rather what gives that field its very divided aspect, the possibility and therefore the necessity of interpretation. It also can only give us pause at whatever point we attempt to determine the "difficulty" of a discourse relative to some "public" or other. For finally any such a determination must rely on a unified figure of address that would have one and only one correct destination; if, however, an address is of necessity divided, by what standard can one decide when it has been received? What is the reception of an address? Are there not forms of reception that transform the "message"? And likewise forms of address that transform the conditions of reception? Is this not even what we mean or would like to mean by teaching? And above all perhaps by teaching "literature"? If we judge such questions and the analyses they call for to be "too difficult" or, worse, politically disabling because they complicate too much the model of effective public discourse, can we be so sure that

that judgment and the decisions it entails have not themselves installed the very limits on public access that everyone in a democracy must decry?

This division of address, then, would have to form the basis of any "reply" to the charge that deconstruction "permits one to write absolutely anything." Finally it is not the truth or the falsity of such a statement that can be determined (which is why it is at once both true and false), but only the effect of the division that gives such a predication to be read. For it says more and other than what it means to say. It is no sooner inscribed than it immediately loses any foothold it may have sought to gain in a region safely outside the dangerous interchangeability of absolutely anything for anything else. Instead, the assertion divides itself into a denunciation and an example of the very sort of perversion it would denounce; and with that, the position outside unlimited interchangeability—the position of Truth for which there is no substitute—collapses into, that is, *becomes interchangeable with* what it opposes. The single, irreplaceable Truth (about deconstruction, but also about "absolutely anything"), supposed to stand at an infinite remove from the movement of substitution—which is to say, of writing—cannot but be overtaken by the movement of its own inscription. And with that movement, places shift, reverse, collapse, but also something else gets inscribed: a displacement of the Truth in writing and by writing. And this displacement is anything but a destruction or a disappearance; on the contrary, it represents an altogether unprecedented demand for the written "truth," the literal "truth," the "truth" of "literature." And for its teaching.

PROLOGUE | THE IMPASSE OF LITERARY
HISTORY

The very bottom, the bottomless abyss belongs to art. And art is that deep which is sometimes the absence of profundity, of the foundation, the pure void bereft of importance, and sometimes that upon which a foundation can be given, but it is also always at the same time one and the other, the intertwining of the Yes and the No, the ebb and flow of the essential ambiguity. And that is why all works of art and all literary works seem to leave comprehension behind and yet seem never to reach it, so that it must be said of them that they are always understood too much and always too little.

Maurice Blanchot, *The Space of Literature*

ALTHOUGH we may continue to ask ourselves what sense to give it, literary studies in the modern Western university have a history. What is more, that history has itself been marked, or even dominated, by models of history, by historicisms old and new, to which literary studies have had recourse at times, and to which they continue to owe their legitimacy as a discipline of knowledge. As Timothy Bahti puts it, "The preponderance of historically defined teaching and research in the modern university's study of literature leaves history today a horizon beyond which we can scarcely think. Literary studies in the university are still the heir to the historicism after Hegel."[1] If this is true, then the periodically reasserted dominance of historical inquiry, whether or not it is seen as a counterbalance to some supposedly ahistorical or even antihistorical concern with literary theory, would be an anticipated effect of this history, one which it would be rather pointless to regret.

Nevertheless, histories or historicisms that take literary texts as their object, to the extent that they are engaged in the disciplinary project of knowledge or comprehension, will also continue to produce that odd conjunction remarked by Blanchot whereby one knows always too much and too little about a work that continues to present itself as "*sometimes* the absence of profundity, of the foundation, the pure void bereft of importance, and *sometimes* that upon which a foundation can be given." If we take foundation or ground here in the sense of the ground of history, the irreversible inscription of events to which Péguy, for example, appealed, then the fictions of literature are groundless, that is, without historical truth but also without effect on that truth, "the pure void bereft of importance." What does it then mean to assert that such groundless fictions are *at the same time* the basis on which history's ground can be given, that they are, in effect, the groundless grounding of that ground? And what are the implications of such an assertion for the historical study of literature in particular and art in general?

If history is not its own ground but rests on something else that has to do with fiction, then the historical study of literature can only ever give a partial picture of a work's historicality. More specifically, it will not account for the sense in which the work opens the possibility of a history, an opening that has its scene or its stage not in a finished and duly recorded past but always in a future. A literary work has a historical context, as we call it, but no more nor less than any document or artifact produced in the past; but the work, if it is still read and studied when this "context" will have subsided into archival compost, has a relation as well to a future, by which it remains always to some extent incomprehensible by any given present. This is the dimension of the work's *historicality*, which is therefore not to be simply confused or conflated with historical "context." It is likewise this historicality of what we call literature that the institutionalization of literary studies has largely and necessarily misrecognized, for it withholds from the putative object of that discipline the stability required of an object of knowledge. What we still call literature (but perhaps for not much longer) would be one means of this withheld stability of meaning, or to put it differently, it would be the *reserve* of every present, instituted meaning and thus the possibility of its transformation, that is, the possibility of a future. Furthermore, such reserve possibilities extend to the instituted meaning of literature and literary studies themselves. Despite the fact, therefore, that academic literary study has largely misrecognized this dimension of a, by definition, unknowable future "literature," the latter will nevertheless have been working to transform its own institution.

This dimension of literature's historicality, the groundless ground of history, is what we propose to approach, if not comprehend, by turning to one of the most enigmatic texts in the American literary

canon: Melville's *The Confidence-Man: His Masquerade*. More generally but also more implicitly, we will be attempting to look from
another angle at the formation of this canon, a process that can be
viewed through the lens of the emergence of Melville's work somewhere near the summit of that construction. In addition and more
generally still, we will take Melville's signature on this and other
works as an emblem of the *credit* for which every ambitious work of
fiction applies, in a dynamic of promise and interest that carries beyond any present or presentable moment of reading.

Beyond the present: what we are sketching with such a "return"
to Melville is the figure of an impossible step across or beyond the
impasse into which literary studies have been led by their own history
in the university. This history seems to have arrived at its end when
"literature" is determined predominantly as an ideological tool that
must be contained in the past, as a history that must be left behind.
The end of literary study is history. And as such, it has no future,
at least not in that name. That is the impasse.

A next step, if there is one, is the invention of a future—that is,
of a stranger, and even of a stranger "in the extremest sense of the
word." This description will be found on the first page of *The Confidence-Man,* to which, therefore, we turn as to an absolute other whose
provenance remains still to come.

MELVILLE'S CREDIT CARD

LITERATURE IN THE AGE OF CREDIT CARDS

The last major work Melville published during his lifetime, *The Confidence-Man: His Masquerade* (1857), has had, to say the least, a curious history. In 1984, the editors of the authoritative Northwestern-Newberry edition of Melville's writings summarized the adventure of this text as follows:

> Published on April 1, 1857, *The Confidence-Man* was a flat failure: it earned Melville not one penny, got little understanding or approval from reviewers, and until well into the twentieth century found few readers and certainly very few admirers. Now critics place it high in the Melville canon and list it among esteemed works of modern fiction. Yet no interpretation of the book is generally accepted, though many have been offered. There is disagreement about its author's intentions, its title character's identity and motives, its structure, the relation of the parts to the whole—*and even whether it amounts to a whole.* The book wins acclaim but resists critical consensus.[1]

Note the somewhat reluctant acknowledgment of the questions critics have raised concerning the wholeness of the book, whether its many parts "amount to a whole." It is as if those responsible for this integral and definitive edition of the work in question begrudged those of their colleagues who go so far as to say that *The Confidence-Man* does not hold together, is not a unified thing, *is* not therefore *a* thing at all. This is not just a question about *what* the thing is, a hermeneutical question, but *whether* it is, an ontological question. As such, it provokes some resistance even when, as here, the point is to remark how the book has resisted critical consensus.

This resistance will be noticeable again in the next paragraph when the editors venture a "brief description" of this book that may not be a whole, that may not form a consensus, therefore, even with itself.

A brief description may be ventured. The apparently plotless action of *The Confidence-Man* takes place aboard a Mississippi steamboat, the *Fidèle*, headed downstream from St. Louis towards New Orleans on April Fools' Day in 18–. A single passenger, the shape-shifting and name-changing title character, remains almost constantly on the scene. . . . This character—designated as "quite an original"—has more than ordinary, perhaps supernatural, capabilities. In the book's daylight first half (Chapters 1– 23), he masquerades in a total of seven (some would say six) successive guises, never reassuming the same one. Throughout its nighttime second half (Chapters 24–45), he assumes one further persona, that of "the cosmopolitan." . . . In all his appearances, both day and night, he pleads for confidence or its equivalent and argues winningly, however dubious his motives, against distrusting anything in human nature, physical nature, or the cosmos. Most of his listeners, it seems, prove too trusting, but a few too skeptical. Just which characters—those with warm soft hearts and heads or those with cold ones, "philanthropists" or "misanthropists"—have the author's approval is uncertain; perhaps none unqualifiedly. It seems to be left ambiguous whether, underneath everything, he calls for a difficult, even impossible, balance of heart and head or despairs of any trustworthy basis for moral judgments. . . . As the Confidence Man moves among the *Fidèle*'s passengers, seeking to work alike upon their trustfulness or their skepticism, Melville simultaneously challenges the reader's alertness. As bare a summary as the foregoing cannot avoid critical disagreement, for example about the number of guises the Confidence Man assumes *and even whether he is a single character*. (255–57; emphasis added)

Employing the same concessive syntax remarked in the first passage, the editors in effect acknowledge that their "bare summary" or "brief description" may be anything but the reliable, objective account it would purport to be. In particular, their assertion that "a single passenger, the shape-shifting and name-changing title character, remains almost constantly on the scene" bears the mark of an act of interpretation, indeed an act of faith since they then speculate that, if this single character can appear in so many guises, it is because he "has more than ordinary, perhaps supernatural, capabilities." Although their description goes out of its way at many points to accommodate the equivocation of its object, the assertion of the continuity of a title character through successive disguises is allowed to stand until the final clause of the final sentence, where this central trait of the description, the one that holds it all together, is itself challenged: "and even whether he is a single character." That challenge, however, is clearly marginalized by the rhetorical structure of this descriptive paragraph: It is marked as a little absurd ("even . . .") and is evidently not to be understood as one of the assumptions of the foregoing description; rather, it comes from elsewhere, somewhere outside the "critical consensus" formed by the four principal signatories of this "Historical Note."[2] Nevertheless, from this margin the possibility opens up that the editors have described not the object "itself," which they concede remains itself in question as precisely an "itself"; rather they have described but a *belief* concerning that object and shared by a certain mainstream of Melville scholars, the belief that *The Confidence-Man* is held together by the notion of a self who is selfsame.

With the figure of belief, one is brought back into the dynamic field on which the text in question deploys its forces: belief, confidence, faith, fidelity, credit, credibility, credulity. Or rather, that textual field would have already laid out the stakes of the very reading act one performs, no matter how minimally "descriptive" or "consensual" the act would aim to be. As if, everything being a matter of belief, confidence, or credit *in* the text, any statement about it (including this one) would be *part* of that which it describes, interprets, evaluates, judges—delimits. The delimiting trait, as Derrida has observed on many occasions, is divided: It does not pass simply between the object and some discourse on the object, but redivides the objectifying limit and traces figures of inclusion of the one in the other. This effect of *The Confidence-Man* has often been remarked and could be said to form part of a certain critical consensus about the book.[3] Accordingly, in its minimal description, the Northwestern-Newberry team of editors notes the doubling of the confidence/ no confidence alternative on the side of the reader: "As the Confidence Man moves among the *Fidèle*'s passengers, seeking to work alike upon their trustfulness or their skepticism, Melville simultaneously challenges the reader's alertness." This is one way of acknowledging that the reader is likewise thrown back on the alternative repeatedly staged by the plotted encounters between the fictional figures, an alternative that is never simply decided on one side or the other of the divided divide between the reader in the text and the reader of the text. Any minimal "description" of this text, if it is not to yield too quickly and too massively to mere consensual belief, must not only acknowledge this effect but try to account for it. Only then, perhaps, can the limits on the calculation of any such accounting or accountability be made to appear.

Let us attempt, then, another minimal "description" of the text that recenters (so to speak) its dynamic around the doubled trait of reading: *The Confidence-Man* represents a number of encounters between passengers on a steamboat going down the Mississippi on a first day of April. These meetings do not follow each other within the logic of any continuous intrigue; they are apparently almost wholly disconnected from each other, effects of the chance that has gathered a diverse group of characters in the same place for a precisely determined lapse of narrative time: from dawn to midnight. All the same, the encounters resemble each other in at least one aspect: Each time, one character, always a man, seeks to gain the confidence of his interlocutor and to receive a token of this confidence, usually some money. These money tokens take several forms: coins begged from passersby, a loan or a gift to a friend in need, a donation to charity, a purchase of stocks, a purchase of herbal medicines, a down payment for a promised service, an investment in some speculative venture, and so forth. The narrative description, meanwhile, multiplies the number of broad hints that let one believe, or at least do not exclude the possibility, that all these transactions are undertaken by a single and selfsame person who has managed to adopt several disguises in the course of the day. And since, in his various disguises, this master of masquerade speaks endlessly of the confidence men ought to have in each other, then no doubt he is the confidence-man named in the title, which is to say a swindler, someone whose appeals to confidence are themselves unreliable. But—and it is a very large but—whereas much seems calculated to lead one to this conclusion, the narrator and the narrative *never* directly confirm or contradict any of these reading suppositions. The latter are consequently suspended in the state of open hypotheses. What is important, indeed imperative, to acknowledge is that this effect of suspension is no less calculated than the other effect of doubt sustained concerning the probity of certain characters who may be the masquerades adopted by just one character. These two contrary effects are both to be credited to the text's narrative, which thereby maintains a kind of double-entry bookkeeping in its other transactions with the reader, if indeed they are in any simple sense *other*. As a result, this reader can never know whether she or he has been the dupe of an elaborate ruse, nor even what it could mean in this case "to be a dupe." The reader's relation to the text, therefore, duplicates that of the characters in relation to the supposed "confidence-man" encountered in the narrative.

That one must count on such a doubling of narrative relations is inscribed from the first in the text's title, which designates (perhaps) not only a set of characters in the fiction, who may or may not be a single character behind a series of masks, but also the very thing that gathers these characters together in a series or an apparent series, the text that calls *itself The Confidence-Man*. If there is a series, then, the text itself would be a part of it even as that text also designates the series it in some sense contains. The text "itself" is divided in its limiting trait and this makes for some strange configurations: The whole is also a part of "itself," the title of the series is also one of the members of the set it names in naming itself. What is more, if the text as a whole can be part of the possible series of swindles, then perhaps it has swindled one into believing that certain characters are swindlers who form a series. In other words, perhaps this title, *The Confidence-Man,* is itself a con.

But what might it mean to call a work of fiction a swindle or a confidence trick? Is such a judgment even possible? What prejudgments or presuppositions would have to be in place before one could read to that conclusion? And if that conclusion is determined by presuppositions, has one even read anything at all in reading such a fiction? It is as if this text did nothing more than expose its divided trait in order to suspend it at the very limit of the reading act. The divided, suspended trait of reading *in* the text and *of* the text—for it is precisely this difference that is suspended—doubles every mark, at every step. That is what one has to read and at the same time that is what one cannot read. From the moment the reading is part of what is read, from the moment the divide holding them apart must be crossed (and it must be crossed at every step, as we shall see), then all calculations are opened onto the incalculable, that is, onto a certain future. *The Confidence-Man,* in this sense, comes to us, if it comes at all, from this future. Its temporality is that of an always-yet-to-come, and it issues what may be called literature's unlimited credit card.

It is this structure of *writing on credit* that assumes prominence in Melville's last published major work, the one with which he signed off and checked out of the American literary establishment. Checking out, he left his credit card, which no one then wanted to accept any longer. (As the editors put it: "*The Confidence-Man* was a flat failure: it earned Melville not one penny, got little understanding or approval from reviewers, and until well into the twentieth century found few readers and certainly very few admirers.") And yet well after its expiration date, the card began not only to circulate and accrue interest, but to display on its surface, which is the surface of a certain carte blanche, the necessarily fictional or literary premises that ground accreditation and legitimation in general and, in particular, the accreditation and legitimation of literature as institution. Within that fictional structure, therefore, one may find inscribed the history of an institution that draws on the line of credit opened in Melville's name and, beyond perhaps, in the name of a certain American literature as a literature of the self.

Writing on credit: the phrase draws on two accounts of its possible meaning. Credit (its semantic register extending to belief, faith, confidence, as well as to the fiduciary uses of the term) would be in one sense a thematic support, that on which the narrative depends for a certain referential coherence. *The Confidence-Man,* being on or about credit in this thematic sense, has drawn many, indeed most, of its readers into critical debates about the book's "philanthropic" or "misanthropic" aim (see, once again, the editors' description above), that is, about whether or not, according to the intentions of this book's author, one ought to trust one's fellow humans. Given, however, the suspended movement of judgment as regards all the credit transactions portrayed in the narrative, such debates cannot get very far before they *must* invoke the very notion of belief or credit in question in order to advance toward one or the other response.[4] This is the principle we saw at work in the brief description of Melville's text quoted above in which a certain partiality of belief must be called upon in order to advance even minimal assertions about the text's identity. Credit or belief thereby carries over from this thematic register of the text to the register of reading that, unable to *make present* the certain value of its assertions, has likewise to proceed on credit. It is as if the deferred payment plan of *fiction*—by which we mean here not untruth but suspended reference—in carrying itself over from one register to the next, contaminated any attempt to arrest the movement or to call in the debt.

Writing on credit is from the very first a double writing that will deploy its thematic or narrative content as a kind of mask, alibi, or allegory of its own operation. This double writing does not present alternative ways of reading the text so much as it implicates necessarily the one in the other. The *Confidence-Man* can be said to be *about* credit only to the extent that it is credited as being about credit, and so forth. Although ultimately any text must apply for such credit, Melville's would seem to leave little space for doubt that that is what it is doing, at every step. In fact, it is all a matter of steps and spacing, of intervals left suspended between written marks. This interval, space, or suspension is (suspends) the essential mark of writing and of fiction, of writing as fiction, that is, of writing as that which demands belief but at the same time suspends it from the credit extended to a future that is always still to come.

We are making, then, some rather extravagant claims about *The Confidence-Man*. We are giving it a lot of credit, even unlimited credit, for we will insist that, *from its very first step,* this text engages not only writing and fiction in general, literature in particular, but the general structure of credit and its institutions: the institution of literature, to be sure, but also other political institutions as these come to be inscribed by the conventions of credit. These claims, which we will have to shore up in a moment, also draw from a certain credit account opened in a recent text by Derrida, *Given Time.* There it is a prose poem by Baudelaire, titled "Counterfeit Money," that implicates a reflection on gift and time, on the gift of time, with "the most serious stake of political economy":

> If there is something that can in no case be given, it is time, since it is nothing and since in any case it does not properly belong to anyone; if certain persons or certain social classes have more time than others—and this is finally the most serious stake of political economy—it is certainly not *time itself* that they possess.[5]

To say that "the most serious stake of political economy" is the unequal distribution of time—free time, time to live, lifetime—is to recall that the capital of capitalism is also stocked in the form of this temporal money; it is in effect to place the capitalist adage "Time is money" before the mirror of its own reversibility: money is time, money buys time which is thus anything but free, freely given. Time counted as wealth or possession, which permits one to say "I have time" even though time is nothing and belongs to no one, this time is always a time to come, a time not yet "spent," a future time or simply the future. It is not, in other words, a present time, right here and right now. This wealth, then, has no form that can present itself in the present and in that, apparently, it differs from money which, as substantial sign of value, must assume some presentable and present form: for example, the coin that the narrator's "friend" places in the hand of the poor man in Baudelaire's "Counterfeit Money," the coin that may be counterfeit. In this scene of a minor redistribution of wealth, the poor man is asking, he is asking to live, to be given his life—the time to live. And he is given in fact a mark, a sign, a token, that is, a coin without intrinsic value. The coin is without intrinsic value not because it is necessarily counterfeit, for whether

or not it is, as Derrida underscores several times, can never be affirmed, just as one can never establish the trickery or "counterfeiting"
of Melville's confidence-man. Rather it is because, true or false, the
coin's value is still determined by the network of conventions that
alone allows it to be exchanged for some goods, that alone, in other
words, allows it to buy some time. Whether the coin is legally minted
silver money or a simulacrum made from some other material, this
difference is itself finally immaterial because, true or false, the coin
only has value by way of convention, a web of conventions.

A web of conventions, which is to say, a system of credit. What
the poor man receives from the friend of the narrator is a token of
credit. He is given credit. Credit is one of the key words in *Given
Time:* on one side, its network is attached to the important chapter
from Mauss's essay *The Gift* that is titled "Honor and Credit," but
from this point it spreads out to take in finally all the considerations
that come out of the reading of Baudelaire's narrative. When he
comes to reflect on this globalization of the credit network, Derrida
writes:

> Everything is act of faith, phenomenon of credit or credence, of belief
> and conventional authority in this text which perhaps says something
> essential about what here links literature to belief, to credit and thus to
> capital, to economy and thus to politics. Authority is constituted by
> accreditation, both in the sense of legitimation as effect of belief or credu-
> lity, and of bank credit, of capitalized interest. (97)

If Baudelaire's text, named "Counterfeit Money," can be taken
for the counterfeit money it names, if it is in this way that it "perhaps
says something essential about what here links literature to belief, to
credit and thus to capital, to economy and thus to politics," then
may one not pursue this suggestion and continue to read across the
lines of the credit network in which the so-called literary text comes
to occupy a determined place? At the same time, it is in this place
and in the name of literature that an unlimited and undetermined
credit account has been opened, one that is guaranteed by nothing
more substantial than a signature. Or, to put it in the form of the
question that is thereby opened up: What of literature in the age of
credit cards?

If we pursue this question onto another shore of modernity, that
of nineteenth-century North America, one reason might be the more
rapid adoption than in Europe of that supplement to gold or silver
currency which is the bank note. It is also, of course, in the United
States that the first credit cards were to be put on the market (begin-

ning with Diners Club and then American Express in the 1950s), and it is American commercial banks that succeeded in selling the rest of the world on this new convention in the form of Visa and MasterCard. But, more important perhaps, our passage from the Old to the New World, by bringing us closer to the point of emergence of the economy of credit cards, will also help focus attention on credit as the common currency of that transaction called reading. So we turn to Baudelaire's contemporary, Melville, who will right away force us to reconsider in what sense one can speak of his contemporaneity.

We have already glossed several times the phrase "to write on credit." It is, we said, something like a check that draws on at least two possible accounts of reserved meaning. "Melville writes on credit" means at once that his subject or his theme is often credit, belief, faith, reliability, confidence, and so forth. But the same phrase mobilizes the sense of a transaction that defers payment of a debt to a future date, that accumulates interest as long as the account remains open, and that demands that one have faith in a promise for which the only guarantee remains a signature. The phrase "to write on credit" conjugates two scenes of the signature. In the vast credit network we are approaching, where, to recall Derrida's terms, "authority is constituted by accreditation, both in the sense of legitimation as effect of belief or credulity, and of bank credit, of capitalized interest," the concept of "signature" is one of the most obvious exchange points between "literature" as it comes to be determined in the course of the nineteenth century and the increasingly "dematerialized" forms of money (or credit) that, during more or less the same period, will come to displace currency based on gold or silver.

For this reason, one might be tempted to trace a sort of parallel development or conjunction between, on the one hand, the institution of the literary signature and, on the other, the emergence of a credit economy, namely an economy that replaces the conventions of minted metals with conventions of the signature. This is the temptation of what a "New Historicist" might perhaps today call "contextualization."[6] Here, to "contextualize" would mean to "contemporize," to configure diverse phenomena in the synchrony of a same time or a same period. Thus, a literary work would be contextualized when it has been conjugated with, for example, contemporary texts of the law. (In fact, this is more than an example among others since the domain of formal law provides the preferred context in this kind of study.)

This interesting and even necessary gesture, however, leaves untouched the question of what could be meant by the "same time" of a signature that, writing on credit, entrusts itself to a nonpresence of time and thus credits itself with a time that is altogether other than a present. How is one to measure the "same" of a "same time" for that which, by force of signing *on* credit, *right on* credit, is not even contemporary with itself? What context of "the same time" will keep sufficient account of the fact that a text goes on accrediting itself well beyond the limits assigned to any contemporary historical "context" in which it may be placed?

But the risk of overlooking the fact of the literary signature's credit structure is not one that can be simply avoided by a more meticulous historical accountability. Rather, it is precisely on the condition of a certain *unaccountability* that we read a text called literary; it is the condition to which we are referred by the still open credit of a signature whose accounts are not closed upon the death of the signatory, which are therefore not simply contemporary with a lived history. On the contrary, this credit opens onto an indefinite future where all the *interest* it attracts will be inscribed; it opens therefore onto the incalculability of an always deferred maturity date of the debt to the past. All the interest, that is to say, a whole history. For this scene of credit and debt, still opened and always suspended, *to interest us* beyond its apparent historical context, the text called literary must give us to read the ana-chronic historicality of an event that goes on reproducing itself, that is, that continues to renew its credit.

We will venture at this point to make two related assertions: first, this non-closed structure of the literary event is or comprises that of the credit card; second, it is not at all certain that this first assertion entails a metaphor or an anachronism. This because, *properly speaking,* the concepts of credit and debt designate the very transfer of value (or meaning) that we also call metaphor. Credit in the so-called proper or literal sense cannot exclude, indeed it immediately engages a metaphorization that carries it beyond the apparent distinction between literal and figurative. We may illustrate this with the example of the condition or the status of the very discourse we are using. According to well-recognized conventions of theoretico-academic discourse, the latter may give credit or recognize a debt or do one and the other indistinguishably. These conventional discursive moves, however, cannot be taken simply as metaphors "borrowed" from what would be their proper domain, for instance, finance or banking.[7] Before we can take the terms "credit" and "debt" to be metaphors in this context, we would have to know their nonmetaphorical value, their true worth as signs, the capital or collateral on the basis of which the figure borrows or takes out a loan. We would have to be able to keep straight this wholesale borrowing between different signifying accounts and for that we would need a measure of value whose worth is not itself borrowed or given on credit, but is intrinsic or inherent. And precisely because in place of that intrinsic or inherent value we have only convention, whether linguistic, monetary, or other, it is not at all certain that when we speak of a literary text as a credit card, we are merely using a metaphor or employing an analogy. It is to this irreducibility of the figure of credit that the literary text sends us *as* or *like* an unlimited and infinitely renewable credit card. Whence the always possible, always open, which is to say, always *historical* interest of the thing, namely that (and here let us venture a third assertion), in the age of credit cards "properly speaking," what is at stake is a certain credibility for which the fictive operation or transaction remains the best model. Perhaps, therefore, it is only by setting out from this model, the operations or transactions of the literary text, that those other, so-called literal credit card transactions can become, precisely, creditable. Everything comes down to knowing what one is doing when one gives credit.

To say that ours is the age of credit cards is, of course, a metonymic figure that designates a vast credit network by means of one of its most visible, concrete elements. These cards themselves, of course, are but a way of storing information in binary code so as to be able to enter it in the network of electronic telecommunications. The multiple supports for the writing of this code (magnetic tape and disks, laser disks, fiber optic wires, silicon chips, and so forth) are only readable by the appropriate machines and techniques. More precisely, the information that they carry becomes readable or even visible for human operators only after multiple translations and support transfers effectuated by these techniques. So many reading prostheses or postal relays. But, precisely, if the age of credit cards reinscribes in multiple ways the age of the post card, the one that goes from Socrates to Freud and beyond, what defers the presence of the human to itself in this beyond, what sends it off in a movement of irrecoverable debt is increasingly remarked or characterized by these new techniques, which are both more widespread and less manifest.

The indisputable and inevitable generalization of this technical network, which surrounds or subtends more and more ostensibly so-called human relations, does not fail to apply differential and discriminatory programs that are no less formidable for being quite familiar. We may evoke briefly just two indications of this programmatic application, without undertaking an analysis that is beyond the scope of this study.

The first indication comes to us from Los Angeles, this name of a city that now designates less a geographic entity than the grossly unequal conditions of life and death in our modern urban agglomerations. In the wave of analysis and statistics that broke after the fact over the civil disturbances of April–May 1992, one could find the following figures concerning the credit network: "In South Central L.A. [i.e., the large section of the city that has the highest concentration of low-income population and was the scene of the most widespread destruction], the number of banks in 1991: 14. The number of Savings and Loans in 1991: 5. The number of these institutions affected by the post-verdict violence: 3 damaged, 1 destroyed." Thus, only eighteen banking institutions remain in these most densely populated sections of the city. These statistics are accompanied by a commentary: "the lack of bank branches in these neighborhoods, where the average income of the inhabitants is much lower than elsewhere, forces those who receive checks from government assistance to go to check cashing stores to get their money. For this service, the check casher demands a commission (that is, a profit) that can be as high as 10% of the value of the check." Other statistics in the same report reinforce this picture of a system that effectively blocks access to bank credit and therefore to the most current system of value: "The number of check cashing stores in South Central L.A., 1991: 132. The percentage of L.A. banks that refuse to cash government checks for non-clients of the bank, 1991: 94%" (LA Weekly, May 8–14).

These percentages and statistics make one thing plain: at a time when the common global language is beginning to resemble more and more a generalized banking system, an electronic medium of credit and debt, this same system continues to invent ever more efficient means to discriminate among the modes of access to this economy or this general language, thereby restricting access to it in an always stricter fashion. There where it is strictest, there where the percentages effect the most ruthless punishment, the blockage can give rise to reversals, that is, to the negation of the very precarious laws that regulate access to property, value, wealth: in the language of those who police these laws, this negation is called "looting."

We could take as a second indicator of this differentiated generalization (or generalized differentiation) the process that has overburdened with debt those countries said to be "developing" in the so-called Third World. Begun in the 1950s, at a time when overproducing industries in the West, and particularly in the United States, needed to extend their markets beyond national borders, this process almost immediately entered into crisis, which did not prevent international banking and financing agencies from encouraging ever more important loans over the next thirty years.[8] To enter into any detail here of how this devastation has been accomplished would seem to take us away from our subject. Yet, how can one approach the question of credit in literature, already a vast subject, without acknowledging at least what "to extend credit" has meant on a worldwide scale for the last forty years, without interrogating the relations between the promises of future wealth (but for whom? and at whose cost?) and this unlimited credit account that was opened not so long ago in the name of literature? On more than one side, the threshold of that "World Bank" that regulates loans in direction of countries to be "developed" (a "World Bank" whose very name dissimulates its management of different worlds that must not be allowed to begin to resemble each other, to compete with each other) shares its delimiting feature with fiction in general. It would be the fiction of a shared distribution of wealth through a series of loans in the course of which the initial creditors are reimbursed (with interest, of course) by those who come later and so forth and so on, until the debt becomes overwhelming. One of the most acute analysts in the field does not hesitate to qualify this scheme as "a confidence game," a huge swindle.[9] This remark will bring us back to Melville's text.

The term "confidence-man" was, in 1857, the name recently given to a species of petty thief who banked on the confidence accorded by the victim in order to rob the latter right under his nose and with his cooperation. The expression had designated first of all a swindler, known primarily by the pseudonym William Thompson, whose exploits had been widely reported in the New York press beginning in 1849. Among his numerous reported schemes, Thompson, it seems, approached his victims in public and made some appeal to their confidence. If this appeal was answered, he then asked for the loan of some object of value, often a watch, which he promised to return the next day. But, of course, he and the watch were never seen again. This dishonest little game invented by the one called "the original confidence man" was apparently the beginning of the expression's adoption into the language. Very quickly, journalists of Melville's day seized on the expression "confidence man" to apply it widely, seeing in Thompson and his ilk the very type of the American capitalist speculator or politician.[10]

But it is to Melville that goes the credit for calculating certain links between the confidence game and the fictions of literature. We said that everything comes down to knowing what one is doing when one gives credit. What are we doing, then, by crediting Melville with this calculation? A brief reminder of his credit history will help to circumscribe that question.

We recall, then, that Melville's literary debut in 1847 with the exotic travel narratives *Typee* and *Omoo* had won him an enthusiastic public and favorable critical notice in the literary circle that called itself "Young America." Based in New York, the writers and publishers of this circle heralded the arrival of a new literature that would be American and democratic, "realist" instead of "romantic," based on "facts" rather than "speculations," and that would, therefore, not let itself be taken in by the transcendental reflections of the circle's *bête noire,* Emerson. It was in these terms that the members of the circle thought they recognized one of their own in Melville and on these conditions that a first credit account was opened in his name. Over the course of the ten years of his publishing career, until 1857 when *The Confidence-Man* appeared, Melville's name would be almost always accompanied by the phrase: "the author of *Typee* and *Omoo,*" these titles serving in sum as letters of reference or credit.

Very soon, however, Melville attempted to get rid of this reference by replacing it with another. But this effort quickly aroused the suspicion of the critics. After a first attempt of this sort and a first failure, the novel *Mardi,* Melville took up again the kind of writing accredited by his contemporaries in two new adventure novels, *Redburn* and *White-Jacket.* Here is how he describes them in a letter of the period:

> They are two *jobs,* which I have done for money—being forced to it, as other men are to sawing wood. . . . Being books, then, written in this way, my only desire for their "success" (as it is called) springs from my pocket, & not from my heart. So far as I am individually concerned, & independent of my pocket, it is my earnest desire to write those sort of books which are said to "fail." (259)

That was in 1849; subsequently, Melville would seek a kind of writing whose credit was undecidable, in other words, a writing that could cause a failure of the determination, according to the values in place, of what "to succeed" or "to fail" *could mean* in literature. Like the letter quoted above, in which the words "success" and "fail" are the only ones in quotation marks and both qualified by an "as one says," this writing would suspend reading between, on the one hand, the calculable and quotable market values of the day and, on the other, that which shows up on no market, and thus perhaps concerns only "me," as Melville writes, "individually and independently of my purse." It would be a writing with a false bottom, a kind of smuggler's suitcase that would hide its riches beneath banal appearances in order to get them by customs.

For the novel *Pierre, or the ambiguities* (1852), Melville thinks he has found the formula. That, at least, is what he tells his worried publishers: this book, he writes to them, would be "very much more calculated for popularity [than all he had written since *Typee* and *Omoo*]" (269). Nevertheless, in the novel he refers to in these terms, the young hero Pierre, having become a writer, will be treated as a swindler by the publisher who had advanced him money against the promise of a "popular novel." Putting his young character in the place of the discredited author, Melville delivers to him the following letter from his publisher:

> SIR: You are a swindler. Upon the pretense of writing a popular novel for us, you have been receiving cash advances from us, while passing through our press the sheets of a blasphemous rhapsody, filched from the vile Atheists, Lucian and Voltaire. (270)

If there is here a *mise en abyme,* if the novel *Pierre* gives one to read the letter that denounces its own swindle, one would still perhaps have to hesitate before crediting the notion of that other calculation, namely, the calculation of a popular "success" that would succeed in dissimulating the hidden bottom of its failure. Here, on the contrary, the failure of the popular genre seems to have been anticipated and displayed. When Melville writes of his "earnest desire to write those sort of books which are said to 'fail,'" he makes of failure the very measure of success. But how to calculate a success of the failure that would not resemble a failure of the success? This question, of course, would not have posed itself only to Melville, nor to him in the first place or the last. It is even, one could say, *the* question by which so-called modern writing would have tried to demarcate itself from everything that had made for the success of a previous literature.

A calculation of failure that must let itself be overrun by the incalculable: these are more or less the terms, for example, in which the "failure" of Genet has been described by Derrida. Recalling the title of an essay on Genet by Bataille, he writes:

> "Genet's Failure." What a title. A magical, animistic, scared denunciation. . . . But hasn't Genet calculated the "failure"? He repeats it all the

time; he wanted to make a success of failure. And now, through the simple provocation of his text, he constructs a scene that obliges the other to unmask, to stammer, to become unhinged. . . . It is this, the text (Genet) that traps, pursues, reads the reader, judgment, criticism.[11]

As we will see as we approach Melville's most calculating text, it is on the border of the scene, there where the other is convoked to engage a reading, that the calculation of failure will be overrun—by the failure, precisely, of any possible calculation. Which is why when we say that it is all a matter of knowing what we're doing when we give credit, we acknowledge by those very terms that we *cannot know*, and that is why we have to give credit.

A few more remarks about the fictive letter from *Pierre* that we've just cited: When Melville stages the failure of his character Pierre, when he puts *en abyme* the failure of the novel of the same name (it was, according to an historian of the affair, "a disaster for Melville's literary career . . . a total failure . . . condemned on every count" [*CM*, 269, 271]), this stage and this abyss open onto multiple questions of credit that are embedded one inside the other. First of all, quite obviously, it is a matter of the money advanced by a publisher who is thinking only of his future sales, who had extended credit to one whom he believed to be the author (at least potentially) of popular fictions. This belief is itself relayed by the supposition that one can extend credit to the other when he names and affirms what he is doing, for example, when he names what he is doing a "popular novel"; not only does one believe that he himself believes it and affirms it in good faith, but moreover that he understands the words he uses in their *common* sense, in other words, in their popular sense. At this level of the embedded credit pyramid, it is no longer simply a matter of a private contract agreed to by individual parties or signatories, but indeed of the general symbolic or linguistic contract. To contract to write for the popular sense is to agree to confirm, to repeat this general contract by keeping in circulation the common or conventional meaning of the terms that guarantee the contract.

It is thus a matter of performing an act of public faith, and it is because he failed to perform this implicitly promised act that Pierre's publisher accuses him of being a swindler. More precisely, Pierre failed in his duty to reiterate the faith it is appropriate or conventional to have in the signs of religious faith. (Recall here the second title of *Pierre:* "or the ambiguities.") It is finally God who guarantees or ought to guarantee all symbolic contracts; so by dispensing with this ultimate guarantor, by trying to put into circulation his "blasphemous rhapsody," Pierre failed to fulfill his contract. He had accepted money in exchange for his explicit or implicit promise to emit only those signs that carry the accredited emblem of the credit that one can, with confidence, extend to them, the emblem of the religious, symbolic convention. Instead, he sent to the printer a currency struck with the image of those "vile Atheists, Lucian and Voltaire," which he is trying to pass off as common currency, and first of all that with which he plans to pay his debt to the printer! In this embedded chain of credit, in this piling up in a pyramid of belief, symbolic and explicit contract, faith, and confidence, God would be one part or one piece, an exchangeable piece among others, with others, and *at the same time* He is supposed to support and guarantee with His infinite credit the whole pyramid. The blasphemy of which Pierre is accused would be unavoidable from the moment God is a part of the contract to be credited; for what is to blaspheme if not to make of God a part, just a part, and thus to broach the infinite credit of the whole, to put a price on it or exchange it for money? The pyramid, like a great swindle, is threatened by collapse from within by the very thing that should never lend itself to such schemes.

In *The Confidence-Man,* as we shall see, it will often be a question of this broaching of a divine infinity that is dragged into a series of credit speculations, beginning with the first sentence of the first chapter.

A Black-Letter Text

Before coming to that sentence and taking the first step onto the decks of floating credit evoked by the riverboat's very name, *Fidèle,* there is another text by Melville that similarly turns on credit and belief as a central dynamic of reading. Unlike *The Confidence-Man,* however, it appears to put an end to the suspension of judgment that it installs and to close the narrative by making good on all the debts it has floated. It may serve, therefore, as a contrast against which to measure the radical credit operation of the *The Confidence-Man.*

Serialized in three installments by *Putnam's Monthly Magazine* in 1855, the novella *Benito Cereno* is one of Melville's best-known tales. As the story of a quelled rebellion on board a Spanish slave ship, Melville's rewriting is faithful to the main outline of the account given by Captain Amasa Delano, in his *Narrative of Voyages and Travels in the Northern and Southern Hemispheres* (1817), of the revolt aboard the *Tryal* in 1805, which he and his shipmates helped to put down. Although *Benito Cereno* takes its title from the name of the slave ship's defeated captain, it is narrated for the most part through Delano's uncomprehending point of view. This device of a deluded observer, who entirely misses the significance of what he witnesses, situates the principal interest of the tale: not only does it preserve narrative suspense, until the truth is revealed so suddenly and violently that not even the unseeing Delano can deny it any longer, but it focuses the narration on the operations of belief and credit, even credulity. In this fashion, it implicates the act of reading the text in the acts of blind faith performed by Delano; indeed, it makes of the unsuspecting reader an accomplice in those acts whose significance is shown to depend on a blindly credited system of belief.

As already mentioned, *Benito Cereno,* unlike *The Confidence-Man,* stages a scene of judgment. The inclusion of depositions from the court trial in Lima of the rebel slaves appears to close the incident of the revolt, although the text does not end at that point, but flashes back to an intervening scene between the revolt and its definitive judgment. This twist given to the narrative temporality is curious; it is as if there were some reluctance to leave the final word to the state-appointed court of judgment, even as it has to concede that the law will rule in any case.[12] Moreover, the tale's narrator goes into eclipse when the trial is presented in the form of the deposition by Benito Cereno taken down by the court recorder. When he returns for the last few pages, he feels he has some explaining to do and he confides to the reader as follows:

> Hitherto the nature of this narrative, besides rendering the intricacies in the beginning unavoidable, has more or less required that many things, instead of being set down in the order of occurrence, should be retrospectively, or irregularly given; this last is the case with the following passages, which will conclude the account: . . . (114)

The irregularity of the narrative, however, concerns not only the temporal order of events but the positioning of this narrator with regard to those events, and more specifically, with regard to the interpretation or reading of those events. This irregularity has produced considerable havoc within the history of critical readings of the novella, as critics have found it necessary either to absolve Melville, via his narrator, of the racist assumptions that drive the story, or on the contrary to ascribe them to the author/narrator, who in this regard would be only slightly less blinded than Delano.[13] In question, finally, is the credit that has been extended to one of the greats of the American canon. But if this question has been raised and even summarily decided here and there, still to be settled are the questions of credit and judgment as raised in the text, or rather *as* they constitute the very text we read.

That it is a matter of reading is made clear by a striking image Delano hits upon at the height of his confusion. Unable to sort out the signs he is getting of Don Benito's ambiguous mastery over the servant Babo who attends him so closely, Delano is tempted by the idea that the Spanish captain is an impostor, "some low-born adventurer, masquerading as an oceanic grandee" (64). As he will do repeatedly, however, the American retreats from his own "ungenerous surmises," which he fears he may have to regret if he credits them too quickly. Instead, he decides to give the other captain the benefit of doubt, which decision is expressed with a typographical image: "In short, to the Spaniard's black-letter text, it was best, for awhile, to leave open margin" (65). The Spaniard's "text" is his appearance and his behavior before his guest, which the latter has difficulty reconciling with what he expects from a fellow captain in trouble to whom he has just offered rescue. To "leave open margin" would seem to mean leave him room to write more, to write to the end before judging the text. But it is a "black-letter text," the color working a pun here between the typographical character and the suspected "blackness" of Don Benito's imposture. This is not all, of course, that is signaled by the mention of color, one of the many instances in the novella where whiteness or blackness is evoked as indicator of some moral quality. When Delano—or is it rather the narrator?—has recourse to the metaphor of the "black-letter text" to designate the reading problem, he names without knowing it the cause of that problem: the fact that the text he has been given to read is written black on white, black over white, which corresponds to a typographical standard but also, for him, to a moral aberration. It is this aberration that is blocking his ability to read this black on white text, the text written by a blackness that is less the "color" of Don Benito's imposture than it is the conventional designator of the race to which the text's real author, Babo, belongs. Whereas he is willing to extend to the fellow white man the blank margin of innocence, he is unable to credit what he reads in clear black letters: the black authorship of the very plot he is acting out, his role written for him in advance by the slave whom he takes to be a savage illiterate. He reads black on white, but he still chooses to see white on black, white over black, and credits the latter since it alone fits the larger cultural text. Delano's credulity is tested by these contradictions, but it always rebounds by virtue of the faith he has in the "natural" order of white over black. This credulity is itself scripted by the black plotters. They count on the American's inability to decipher the black on white signs, on the fact that, in a larger and more important sense, it is he who is illiterate.

Because Delano is a bad reader, too willing to believe what he believes rather than what he sees, the reader is likewise at risk of being led into the errors of bad reading as soon as she or he credits the "natural" justification for the enslavement of one race by another, as soon as she or he reads white on black there where the text is printed black on white. But how does this negative image (in the sense of a photographic negative) get printed on the page? The narrator's "irregularity" has a lot to answer for in this regard.

The narration generally adopts the mode of free indirect discourse, espousing at times explicitly Delano's thoughts without marking any distance of the observer.[14] Accordingly, the third-person "objective" view tends to disappear at these moments; or is it rather that Delano's view becomes indistinguishable from the narrator's? An example:

> There is something in the negro which, in a peculiar way, fits him for avocations about one's person. Most negroes are natural valets and hair-dressers; taking to the comb and brush congenially as to the castinets, and flourishing them apparently with almost equal satisfaction. . . . And above all is the great gift of good-humor. . . . When to this is added the docility arising from the unaspiring contentment of a limited mind, and that susceptibility of bland attachment sometimes inhering in indisputable inferiors, one readily perceives why those hypochondriacs, Johnson and Byron—it may be, something like the hypochondriac Benito Cereno—took to their hearts, almost to the exclusion of the entire white race, their serving men, the negroes, Barber and Fletcher. But if there be that in the negro which exempts him from the inflicted sourness of the morbid or cynical mind, how, in his most prepossessing aspects, must he appear to a benevolent one? When at ease with respect to exterior things, Captain Delano's nature was not only benign, but familiarly and humorously so. . . . In fact, like most men of a good, blithe heart, Captain Delano took to negroes, not philanthropically, but genially, just as other men to Newfoundland dogs. (83–84)

The passage begins sententiously, with no mark of mediation; the sententious pronouncements are not lent to Delano, nor are they read as reflections of his own observations. The first sentences in particular have all the marks of an extradiegetic narrator, and here one who merely reads off the lessons of common wisdom, who states what *is:* "There is something in the negro. . . . Most negroes are . . . There is, too . . . And above all is . . ." This is discourse for the

MELVILLE'S CREDIT CARD | 187

benefit(?) of the reader. It aims, in effect, to explain another factor in Delano's misapprehension of the scene he is witnessing: the factor of a common belief in a certain "nature" of the "negro," a belief presumably shared by Delano. The series of statements, however, cannot be attributed to Delano through free indirect discourse. Or can they? At this point, can one tell? We learn by the end of the passage that Delano was particularly susceptible to the apparent geniality of "the negro," but this was his nature: "Captain Delano's nature was not only benign, but familiarly and humorously so." In other words, his nature plus the nature of "the negro" equals geniality, trust, and harmony between the races. This equation, of course, depends on one of the sides being guaranteed by the narrator's opening ontological gambit, his statements as to "the negro"'s natural propensities and character. These are generalizations about "the negro." On the other side of the equation, one has not a generalized nature, but a differentiated one: Delano's nature is not only benign, benevolent, but humorously so. This benign nature is differentiated from Johnson's and Byron's, "those hypochondriacs," those "morbid and cynical minds" who nevertheless "took to their hearts, almost to the exclusion of the entire white race, their serving men, the negroes, Barber and Fletcher." So, if "the negro" can be spared even the "inflicted sourness of the morbid or cynical mind, how, in his most prepossessing aspects, must he appear to a benevolent one?"

This reference to Johnson and Byron seems clearly marked by the intervention of the narrator. That is, we have little reason to believe that it is Delano who goes through this series of deductions to arrive at his own susceptibility. And even less reason to believe that Delano is capable of these literary references. These are therefore supplied by the narrator, a literary type. Delano is simply behaving true to form, true to his nature, which is unsuspecting, benevolent, the opposite of cynical and morbid, therefore little given to the sort of reflections here laid out. Subtract the literary references, however, and Delano is clearly capable of thinking along the same lines. The narrator, it would seem, intervenes merely to shore up the verisimilitude of Delano's credulity by adding the context of cultural belief and literary history concerning the nature of "the negro." But the question is: Who assumes that belief? Who credits it? Delano for one, or so we are meant to believe, even if he is not entirely capable of articulating it in the form given by the narrator. This same narrator, however, here and there steps back from his observed subject as if he did not want to be confused with him. For example, when Delano observes a black mother nursing a child, he is said to compare them to a doe and a fawn and then to reflect on this comparison: "There's naked nature, now; pure tenderness and love, thought Captain Delano, well pleased. . . . These natural sights somehow insensibly deepened his confidence and ease" (73). When this kind of "primitive" thinking is directly attributed to Delano, as it is here, the narrator allows himself a laugh at his expense by remarking that Delano was well pleased with himself. The episode is broadly drawn and leaves no doubt that Delano's complacency is being mocked. Elsewhere as well, and in general, inferences of this sort—as to the "nature" of anything—are attributed to Delano, as for instance, when he tries to resolve the contradiction between what he sees—the blacks' brutality toward the whites—and what he is told by Cereno, that the blacks on the whole have behaved better than the whites. Delano sorts this information through the grid of his assumption that, if there is some plotter aboard, it has to be the white captain. "The whites, too, by nature, were the shrewder race. A man with some evil design, would he not be likely to speak well of that stupidity which was blind to his depravity, and malign that intelligence from which it might not be hidden? Not unlikely, perhaps" (75).

Delano proceeds from a faulty assumption, or rather from the inherent fault of the racist generalization: whites are shrewder than blacks by nature. His own shrewdness in resolving plausibly the observed contradictions of this assumption is thus put in question, because he sets out blindly, stupidly from the stupidity of the racist maxim. All of this is quite clear. What is less clear is the narrator's own shrewdness or stupidity. The narrator seeks to draw the (white) reader into the very illusion experienced by Delano, and one of his devices—as it is the principal device of the black mutineers—is the racist generalization and general white stupidity about race relations. Like Babo, the narrator counts on the (white) reader being unable to read black on white, he counts on the (white) reader drawing on the same set of maxims, and he will supply these if need be, in order to mistake the scene.

The narrator, it seems, is playing quite a dangerous and duplicitous game: on the one hand, as the sententious voice of white man's reason, he lends his own considerable credit to a chain of faulty logical links, and thereby shores up the cover story of the "natural" relations between masters and slaves; on the other hand, however, he leaves here and there a critical or ironic space between Delano's complacent belief in such a "nature" and its contradiction by the history of relations between whites and blacks, a history that has to lead any thinking person to reject complacency outright. After all, as we will learn from Don Benito's later deposition, it was because he believed his friend the slaveowner Aranda's assurance that the slaves put in his charge were all "tractable" and could be allowed to sleep on deck without chains that the uprising was possible. Aranda's error, Don Benito's error, Delano's error, and potentially, the reader's error are all consistent with the refusal to acknowledge a terrifying history in favor of a belief in tractable "nature." But although the same error cannot simply be imputed to the narrator, who is alone in knowing how the story must end before it begins, he is clearly willing to play the card of complacent "nature" and to echo the racist ideology in order to heighten the effect of the tale's surprise denouement. He is willing, in other words, to play dumb not only about the outcome of the tale, which is the minimal condition of the narration, but also about the history and thus the reality of enslaved-enslaver relations.

Was it this necessity to feign stupidity in order to write so-called popular novels that sent Melville in quite another direction?[15] Perhaps, but precisely because the game is duplicitous, things may not be quite so simple.

In any case, the narration also labors to supply all kinds of indications that the credit given "nature" is misplaced. These signs are not only the ones that Delano considers, in his more suspicious moments, but they also occur at a level that could be called unconscious, the level that Delano himself seems incapable of formulating, for "he was a man of such native simplicity as to be incapable of satire or irony" (63). He is truly baffled by duplicity, by the idea that things may not always be what they seem, that people do not have a nature that prescribes their action, and that consequently the motive for action may not be transparently visible. Blacks are naturally servants and happy in their role, and so forth. He is incapable of worrying very long the possibility of duplicity and quickly reverts to his native simplicity. Here is a typical sequence of his thoughts: Are not Spaniards "as a nation . . . all an odd set; the very word Spaniard has a curious, conspirator, Guy-Fawkish twang to it. And yet, I dare say, Spaniards in the main are as good folks as any in Duxbury, Massachusetts" (79). Or again: "And among the Malay pirates, it was no unusual thing to lure ships after them into their treacherous harbors, or entice boarders from a declared enemy at sea, by the spectacle of thinly manned or vacant decks, beneath which prowled a hundred spears with yellow arms ready to upthrust them through the mats.

Not that Captain Delano had entirely credited such things. He had heard of them—and now, as stories, they recurred" (68). A final example:

> But the Spaniard was a pale invalid. Never mind. For even to the degree of simulating mortal disease, the craft of some tricksters had been known to attain. To think that, under the aspect of infantile weakness, the most savage energies might be couched—those velvets of the Spaniard by the silky paw of his fangs. From no train of thought did these fancies come; not from within, but from without; suddenly, too, and in one throng, like hoar frost; yet as soon to vanish as the mild sun of Captain Delano's good-nature regained its meridian. (64–65)

In this last passage, the suspicions are said to be impressed on him "not from within, but from without," that is, from what he sees without seeing it; it is not Delano's nature, in other words, to have such thoughts; they do not come from within but are forced upon him suddenly and he just as quickly dissolves them in the warmth of his nature. But this is the narrator's intervention as well, telling us almost that Delano is not even thinking these things for himself, of himself.

Another clearer instance of this form of the narrator's intervention is given when Delano observes a Spanish sailor engaged in "tarring the strap of a large block." He is said to be struck by an incompatibility between something "superior" in the man's figure and his menial task. The narrator then comments:

> Whether this haggardness had aught to do with criminality, could not be determined; since, as intense heat and cold, though unlike, produce like sensations, so innocence and guilt, when, through casual association with mental pain, stamping any visible impress, use one seal—a hacked one.
>
> Not again that this reflection occurred to Captain Delano at the time, charitable man as he was. Rather another idea. Because observing so singular a haggardness combined with a dark eye, averted as in trouble and shame, and then again recalling Don Benito's confessed ill opinion of his crew, insensibly he was operated upon by certain general notions which, while disconnecting pain and abashment from virtue, invariably link them with vice.
>
> If, indeed, there be any wickedness on board this ship, thought Captain Delano, be sure that man there has fouled his hand in it, even as now he fouls it in the pitch. (71–72)

The passage is a good demonstration of the narrative structure. What could not be determined is whether the haggardness of the sailor is a sign of guilt or innocence. But Delano does not consider this lack of determination "at the time," which suggests that later, after the key is put in the lock, he does consider it and realizes, too late, his mistake in supposing haggardness to be a simple sign rather than an ambiguous one of the sort analyzed by the narrator. This analysis is inserted here like a kind of road sign to the alert reader, a warning not to make Delano's mistake, not to proceed as credulously as the hero does in crediting the version of things told him by the Captain. There is a dissociation, then, between the narrator's suspension of judgment and Delano's rush to judgment, but without going so far, of course, as to openly challenge the judgment that Delano made "at the time," a challenge that could be made only on the basis of what is later learned, for that would destroy the narrative suspense. Just enough is said for the reader to hesitate, if she or he knows how to read what is written in black and white, and to remain suspended there where Delano rushes to judge and decide.

This dissociation is the mark of the textual, and it is not a mere coincidence that Melville turns once again to a printing metaphor— that of the hacked seal—to remark this textuality. Whereas Delano is the reader in the text, he cannot simply be assimilated to the reader of the text without disregarding such marks of textuality, which are always double. That, at least, is the wager of this dangerous game. Delano is simplicity, the reader is his double. Delano constantly effaces the marks of duplicity as they arise or occur to him; whenever he considers that what he is seeing may be a fiction, an elaborately mounted design or device, a play staged for his benefit (or rather at his expense), he rushes to decide or to dispel the specter of the "as if." This explicit syntax of the hypothetical, or fictive, occurs on almost every page of the story.[16] Delano's double, the reader, is thereby constantly being reminded of the possible fiction (which is thus doubly fictive) that Delano wants to reduce to the simple appearance of truth. If the reader is attentive to the *as if*'s, she or he will double back over the hypotheses that Delano too quickly credits. Or, once again, that is the wager.

There is, however, a device in place that is also blocking this reading of duplicity: the credit extended not only by Delano but here and there by the narrator to the tropic pattern of black and white. As in the passage just cited, black is the color of vice and wickedness, all that which Delano can suspect behind the white man's haggard expression and "dark eye." But it is precisely because Benito Cereno is a white man that the association with evil blackness occurs to Delano. The reality of the relation between blacks and whites aboard

the *San Dominick* remains hidden to Delano by the habit of a fundamental tropic asymmetry, which maps exterior racial characteristics
onto interior moral qualities, but always in an uneven or unequal
fashion: the white man's superior intelligence makes him capable of
the blackest of crimes, whereas the black man is, as it were, exempted
by "nature" (which is to say, by this tropic pattern of "natural"
qualities) from the very intelligence imputed to the man who can
foul his hand in wickedness as surely as he fouls it in pitch. According
to this unequal distribution of paired binary distinctions—which in
fact sustains and reinforces every form of so-called natural inequal-
ity—the white man can conceal a wicked or "black" soul because
his whiteness confers a superior intelligence; blackening himself in
the pitch of iniquity is but another sign of whiteness. But this pattern
is not reversible: the black man's intelligence, if it permits him to
plot and dissimulate, is not a sign of whiteness, that is, of equality
with white superiority, but only again and always of his inferior
blackness. The pattern of tropological substitution between black and
white and between their internal and external values is incomplete
or blocked. As a result, Delano is literally incapable of reading what is
written in black *and* white; he sees only white against white, without
difference, and the appearance that results is therefore literally unreadable, its differentiations or textuality effaced in a sea of whiteness.

But here is the problem: If Delano had been a better reader, less
credulous, less willing to credit the authority of the trope of "nature,"
he would most likely not have survived the encounter with the *San
Dominick,* nor would any of the ship's remaining crew. It is to his
credulity, simplicity, "good nature," and bad reading that he owes
his survival. He acknowledges as much at the end, in the conversa-
tions with Don Benito as they sail toward Lima after the mutiny has
been put down: "Had it been otherwise, doubtless, as you hint, some
of my interferences might have ended unhappily enough. Besides
those feelings I spoke of enabled me to get the better of momentary
distrust, at times when acuteness might have cost me my life, without
saving another's. Only at the end did my suspicions get the better
of me, and you know how wide of the mark they then proved"
(115). The narrative is in fact strung together as a series of Delano's
failures to read the signs all around him, preferring instead to credit
the "good nature" of all those on board. Even when one of the
Spanish sailors thrusts a fantastically knotted rope in his hand and
murmurs to him "Undo it, cut it, quick," Delano retreats from the
sense of an intrigue to be unraveled and turns to a more reassuring
thought: "All this is very queer now, thought Captain Delano, with

a qualmish sort of emotion; but, as one feeling incipient seasickness, he strove, by ignoring the symptoms, to get rid of the malady. Once more, he looked off for his boat" (76–77).

This kind of scene is repeated many times, often closing as this one does with Delano seeking out a sign that his boat, *Rover,* is making good progress toward the *San Dominick.* Seeing it, he is reassured by the familiarity it recalls for him. This is made plain in the next paragraph, where the boat is compared to a pet dog: "that boat, *Rover* by name, which, though now in strange seas, had often pressed the beach of Captain Delano's home, and, brought to its threshold for repairs, had familiarly lain there, as a Newfoundland dog; the sight of that household boat evoked a thousand trustful associations, which, contrasted with previous suspicions, filled him not only with lightsome confidence, but somehow with half humorous self-reproaches at his former lack of it" (77). It is certainly not through any carelessness, on the contrary, that Melville will reemploy the simile of the Newfoundland dog a few pages later, but this time as a term of comparison for the friendly negro: "In fact, like most men of a good, blithe heart, Captain Delano took to negroes, not philanthropically, but genially, just as other men to Newfoundland dogs" (84). This tropic pattern, which is meant to shore up Delano's wavering confidence, takes the dog to be the touchstone of faithfulness, a Fido that one can confidently take into the family. Yet, whereas the transfer of "a thousand trustful associations" from the dog to the boat operates metonymically—boat and dog have both lain on the threshold of Delano's home (and both perhaps were named not Fido but Rover)—there is no such link cited for the association of dog and "negro." Instead, dog and "negro" are assimilated by an implied resemblance, a resemblance that is not stated but taken for granted, that is, on credit. This is, in other words, another instance of the credit extended to the ungrounded trope of "nature," specifically the nature of "the negro," which is here propped up on the nature of Newfoundland dogs. Neither, it is supposed, will ever bite the hand that feeds them.

But once again we must ask: Who is speaking? Who is offering up these unreliable tropes and eliciting trust in their sure value? Is the narrator here to be understood as merely recording the credit transactions by means of which Delano negotiates with his own misgivings? Is it, therefore, Delano who recurs to the image of the faithful dog as he watches *Rover* approach as well as when he observes the servant's ministrations to his master? Or is it from the narrator's own account that these tropes are drawn and then transferred to

Delano's? We still cannot answer this question; we still cannot decide between extra- and intradiegetic third-person narration. What we can remark, however, is that this undecidability is of the same order as that experienced by Delano throughout his experience on the *San Dominick*. His wavering between confidence and suspicion, faith and mistrust corresponds to an indecision as to whether or not to credit the principal narrator of the ship's tale, Benito Cereno, whose account is inconsistent on so many points. But while the Spanish captain's narration inspires little confidence in the hero, the latter nevertheless repeatedly resolves to extend credit to it, not because of Cereno's own authority (very soon after meeting him Delano begins to question whether this authority is not a charade: "Is it, thought Captain Delano, that this hapless man is one of those paper captains I've known, who by policy wink at what by power they cannot put down?" [59]), but because of that larger authority that is the order of nature and that comprises the order of men. Delano, in effect, never questions this great, anonymous narrator of the story; he places all his trust in and gives full credit to this invisible source of all he sees and hears; from that source, he draws the reassuring associations of familiarity with which to banish from his thoughts all the strangeness that assaults him. This willingness to accept on credit the currency issued by this authority is what is called his "good nature," and it is, as we have already remarked, that which preserves him from the violence unleashed all around him. Indeed, it preserves not only him, but finally the very system of belief in which he has placed his confidence. Having survived his encounter with the *San Dominick,* Delano returns to his own command, from where he can order the suppression of the mutiny aboard the Spanish slaver and bring the mutineers, those "unnatural" slaves, to their judgment and condemnation in Lima before the vice-regal tribunal. The question we are asking, then, is how far the narrator of the tale one reads coincides with or imitates this great narrator in whom Delano, an exemplary nonreader, places all his confidence.

It is significant that, once Delano has his eyes opened for him, the narrative shows little interest in the character whose deliberations have been the sole focus of the tale until that point. It is as if the American captain simply disappears into the background of the reestablished order of command, his confidence in nature's narration vindicated and therefore fully restored. It is only in the final pages, after the long citations from the depositions presented at the trial, that Delano is figured once again in dialogue with Don Benito. This exchange confirms what we have just advanced: that Delano has merged with the anonymously ordered nature that he sees as having repaid the trust placed in it. For Delano, in other words, it is as if *nothing happened,* no story, no history, only nature taking its course.

We pick up the conversation at the point at which Don Benito has just recalled the irony of his being mistaken by Delano for a monster when he is in fact "the most pitiable of all men." He then draws the moral:

> "To such degree may malign machinations and deceptions impose. So far may even the best man err, in judging the conduct of one with the recesses of whose condition he is not acquainted. But you were forced to it; and you were in time undeceived. Would that, in both respects, it was so ever, and with all men." (115)

Delano, however, is not one to "moralize" his experience. That is, he does not want to draw any lesson about the possibility of judging when even "the best man [may] err." Instead, true to his good nature, he urges forgetfulness:

> "You generalize, Don Benito; and mournfully enough. But the past is passed; why moralize upon it? Forget it. See, yon bright sun has forgotten it all, and the blue sea, and the blue sky; these have turned over new leaves."
>
> "Because they have no memory," he dejectedly replied; "because they are not human."
>
> "But these mild trades that now fan your cheek, do they not come with a human-like healing to you? Warm friends, steadfast friends are the trades."
>
> "With their steadfastness they but waft me to my tomb, señor," was the foreboding response. (116)

In this exchange, Delano's indomitable Yankee confidence, his enterprising welcome of the "trades" that carry them away from a dreadful past toward an always bright future runs into the Spanish fatalism of Don Benito for whom the past will not pass. For Delano, each new day turns over a new leaf, a white page, and begins a new story that, like the others before it, will be forgotten. Sun, sea, sky, and wind: these are his trusted, "steadfast" narrators; they write without memory of debt, guilt, error, whether inflicted or suffered; they write, therefore, with unlimited credit. Turning over a new leaf here, in Delano's sense, means anything but applying the reading lesson he has just been given.

But it is Don Benito who is represented as having the last word in this exchange, a last word so unfathomable it leaves only silence around it. Delano, taken aback by the previous "foreboding response" of his interlocutor, rejoins:

> "You are saved," cried Captain Delano, more and more astonished and pained; "you are saved: what has cast such a shadow upon you?"
> "The negro."
> There was silence, while the moody man sat, slowly and unconsciously gathering his mantle about him, as if it were a pall.
> There was no more conversation that day.

Don Benito's reply would seem, on a first level, to refer to Babo, the leader of the mutiny and the author of the plot to deceive Delano. That Don Benito does not name Babo here is consistent with the pathological aversion he has shown, since boarding Delano's ship, to look upon the man who had pretended to be his devoted personal servant. Babo is forever lodged in Don Benito's memory and there stands before his mind's eye in the indistinguishable guises of menacer, accuser, judge, and humble, humiliated slave. "The negro," Babo, is a kind of black hole that pulls into its bottomless depths all human relations ordered around mastery and slavery, white and black, captain and underling, colonizer and colonized, Old World and New—in short, the whole framework of that "natural" order that Delano, with his fortunate amnesia, cannot imagine being upset even after the experience on the *San Dominick,* where his faith was shown to be utter credulity. When Don Benito refuses the consolation of nature's new leaf, it is because "the negro" so blackens the pages of his memory that he will never again be able to turn the page. His fatal awareness, in other words, is that "the negro"—not just Babo, but the whole enslaved black race—*is* memory, human memory, that which distinguishes the human from what is only "human-like" nature. Human history is written black on white, white against black, and its traces are preserved, remembered no less by the black man than the white. No less, indeed immeasurably more.

And this is what the white man Delano would forget. But what about Delano's double, the reader of the tale? Doesn't she or he turn the page as if nothing has happened, nothing but a fiction, a novel? If Melville's narration of these bloody events can be described as a wager, then surely the stakes of that wager must be something rather than nothing. Or perhaps there is a sense in which this nothing nevertheless happens?

For there is still a puzzle left unsolved at the end of the tale: the fact that a bad reading is held out as a good or at least a fortunate reading, the fact that Delano is wrong, and in that he is right. He is right to be wrong, and would have been wrong to be right. This circumstance of the fortunate error—but fortunate for whom?—considerably complicates the conditions of judgment and the significance of the credit extended or refused in this text. A passage from the narrative's first pages, which opens this credit account, seems to have some bearing on all this.

It is the first reference to Delano's "undistrustful" character, prompted by his initial sighting of the *San Dominick,* which is behaving strangely even when seen from a distance. Specifically, it "showed no colors" as one would have expected a peaceful fellow ship to do upon entering a remote harbor.

> Considering the lawlessness and loneliness of the spot, and the sort of stories, at that day, associated with those seas, Captain Delano's surprise might have deepened into some uneasiness had he not been a person of a singularly undistrustful good nature, not liable, except on extraordinary and repeated incentives, and hardly then, to indulge in personal alarms, any way involving the imputation of malign evil in man. Whether, in view of what humanity is capable, such a trait implies, along with a benevolent heart, more than ordinary quickness and accuracy of intellectual perception, may be left to the wise to determine. (47)

How is one to take the implicit question regarding the "quickness and accuracy of [Delano's] intellectual perception," which is "left to the wise to determine"? We can read there the implication that the question of Delano's intelligence is not the narrator's concern, who defers it "the wise." This narrator, then, would be declaring that he will not presume to make such a determination, that he will not assess or judge the captain's "intellectual perception." The narrator is thereby defining what must be his role in the story: to defer judgment on the wisdom of Delano's reasoning from the basis of his "good nature." This deferral of judgment is, as we have been saying, indispensable to the structure of the suspenseful tale. But perhaps as well, the narrator's deferral to the wise should be read as more than just tinged with irony: the statement "leave judgment to the wise" would mean leave it to those who presume "quickness and accuracy of intellectual perception" to be paramount signs of wisdom. However, is such wisdom always very wise?

The latter question is raised by Delano's "benevolent heart," which guides him through the mined labyrinth aboard the *San Dominick* better than his often slow-witted and inconsistently accurate intellectual assessment. His wisdom, if he has any, is certainly not prudence; as Don Benito remarks at the end of the novel, his behavior consisted of "smilings and chattings, rash pointings and gesturings. For less than these, they slew my mate, Raneds . . ." (115). It is the heart, then, a "singularly undistrustful good nature," that generously extends the credit which the head, the seat of calculated "accuracy of intellectual perception," would withhold. But, in fact, as we've seen, Delano's actions and judgments throughout are based on a "good nature" that comprises as one of its tenets the "natural" submission of the black race. It is this belief that blinds Delano up to the last moment, until he sees Babo rush at Don Benito's heart with a dagger. "That moment, across the long-benighted mind of Captain Delano, a flash of revelation swept, illuminating, in unanticipated clearness, his host's whole mysterious demeanor, with every enigmatic event of the day, as well as the entire past voyage of the *San Dominick*. He smote Babo's hand down, but his own heart smote him harder" (99). Delano is judged by his heart at this moment, but does it smite him for a crime of the heart or the head? Is it finally his usually benevolent heart that fails him and then condemns him, or does the "flash of revelation" illuminate the failure of his "intellectual perception"? What Delano finally sees and reads is the strife that pits black against white, which shows up not as a contrast or difference in *nature,* but as a *history* of brutal conflict, "the entire past voyage of the *San Dominick,*" a slave ship. The belief in the "nature of the negro" belongs to the category of neither heart nor head, neither the wisdom of benevolence nor the wisdom of intellectual accuracy. In both heart and head, Delano has been wrong.

Melville's narrative of deferred revelation and judgment works almost like a mechanical device, wound tighter and tighter until it unleashes the flash that smites Delano, and perhaps the reader as well. The force driving the machine is the energy generated by the compression of historical conflict into natural distinction, the whole discourse by which "good nature" is credited with the authorship of things human and which, even when revealed as the source of devastating error, prevails by turning another page, by wiping out what events have written. In the language of Melville's narrator, it leaves an always open margin to the black-letter text. This narrative structure, then, embeds within itself its own repetition, the apparently infinite resource and the unlimited credit of the blank page on which to begin again without debt owed to what has come before. This is a certain model of the literary text as a self-canceling structure of repetition, of always renewable credit, that Melville up to a point exploits here with particular skill. (It is also, as we will see, the model that he will set aside when he comes to write *The Confidence-Man*, for example.)

But there is, in addition, what we have called the wager of this text, the chance taken that this "black-letter text" will leave an ineffaceable, disfiguring mark on the figural chains it credits for the space of the deferred judgment. In short, the wager is that something will happen *other* than repetition, something like an irreversible impress of the "black-letter" that is not the province of the judging, calculating, crediting subject, nor even of the wise, but of the force of history's material inscription.[17] The wager is to let such an inscription be enacted without or before the judging subject. Delano's, the narrator's, or the reader's deferral of final judgment (right or wrong? wise or unwise?) can never make up for the *delay* to which they owe their very position as judging, crediting subjects. The so-called subject of history, of the black-letter text, is the instance of a belatedness with regard to this material inscription. The risk taken in *Benito Cereno* is with a narrative mechanism that calculates a certain delay of judgment as if the judging subject had all the time in the world to master events and were not the afterthought of history inscribing itself.[18]

Benito Cereno has a possible postscript, or perhaps "interscript" would be the better term. To another tale, "The Bell-Tower," probably written just after *Benito Cereno* but published two months earlier also in *Putnam's Monthly*, Melville gave an epigraph "from a Private MS" that seems to shuttle between the two texts and to point to a kind of allegorical translation of the one in the other: "Like negroes, these powers own man sullenly; mindful of their higher master; while serving, plot revenge." There would be several ways to read the "powers" in question with reference to "The Bell-Tower": the creative, inventive ambitions of the tale's principal character, the architect Bannadonna, but also the inventions themselves, in particular what was to have been his crowning achievement, the automat he calls Talus, "the new serf," "iron slave to Bannadonna and, through him, to man." It is the prototype of Talus that is mounted on the bell-tower to strike the hour. At what was to have been the unveiling of his creation and the first demonstration of its mechanical performance, Bannadonna becomes absorbed in perfecting a sculpted figure on the bell. He is consequently struck and killed from behind by the automat he had created to strike at precisely that moment and precisely that place. "And so pride went before the fall," in the final words of the text.

It is possible to read this tale as at least partially composed out of some misgivings leftover from *Benito Cereno,* from the mechanism wound up and put in place there. In a manner that cannot simply be mastered by Melville, or any other subject, the plotted revenge of the black-letter text blindsides at the point of greatest calculation, the moment of deferred revelation. In any case, this overlay of the two texts suggests that Melville probably had few illusions about being able *himself* to win whatever wager *Benito Cereno* might have represented.

INCALCULABLE ADVENTS

We said that *Benito Cereno* could provide contrast for the radical credit operation undertaken in *The Confidence-Man.* The former has essentially the structure of a credit account opened and closed, however misleading or even finally impossible this closure proves to be. This rather straightforward device of suspense may exact its own costs, as, for example, the ambiguous assumption by the narrator of the discourse of "nature." And yet Delano, for one, can seem confident that his account has been settled and the slate wiped clean.[19] When *The Confidence-Man* discards such a device, dispensing with the pay-off of an intrigue unknotted or a secret revealed, the question of credit or confidence is displaced from out of this narrative closure, which appears to resolve it or contain it. Instead, it is carried over the edge of a fictional representation, with its calculations and reckonings. With this step over the edge, a certain *incalculability* comes to the fore.

Before leaving *Benito Cereno,* however, we might remark another resemblance with the later text. Because both take place aboard a ship, that privileged venue for Melville's invention, each is defined by a moment of entry into this highly circumscribed world. *Benito Cereno* accompanies this moment, when Delano first steps aboard the *San Dominick,* with a general reflection:

> Always upon first boarding a large and populous ship at sea, especially a foreign one, with a nondescript crew such as Lascars or Manilla men, the impression varies in a peculiar way from that produced by first entering a strange house with strange inmates in a strange land. Both house and ship, the one by its walls and blinds, the other by its high bulwarks like ramparts, hoard from view their interiors till the last moment; but in the case of the ship there is this addition; that the living spectacle it contains, upon its sudden and complete disclosure, has, in contrast with the blank ocean which zones it, something of the effect of enchantment.

The ship seems unreal; these strange costumes, gestures, and faces, but a shadowy tableau just emerged from the deep, which directly must receive back what it gave. (49–50)

Between boarding a ship at sea and stepping into the "unreal" of a fiction, the difference is unremarkable, especially when fiction takes as its invented locale the very enchantment of this bordered space that emerges from the surrounding blankness. This passage, however, from the blank depths over the bulwarks that delimit the small space of human drama is not only to be *compared* to the passage into writing, from the blank margins to the black-letter text, but the very forms thus delimited and configured emerge *as* writing and from writing, as the movement of a certain spacing or stepping action.[20] And by the same token, these forms, "these strange costumes, gestures, and faces," are always on the verge of sinking again into the formless, figureless blankness, the sea of white ink.

In *The Confidence-Man,* this stepping action is engaged with the first line of the text in a way that immediately calls attention to the strange power of writing to bring figures out of blankness. The first sentence of the initial chapter, titled "A mute goes aboard a boat on the Mississippi," marks and makes a sudden appearance: "At sunrise on a first of April, there appeared, suddenly as Manco Capac at the lake Titicaca, a man in cream-colors, at the water-side in the city of St. Louis." Every element of the sentence remarks a border: the artificial border of the first day of a month, the natural transition of day to night, or still again the geographic frontiers of a town's riverfront or the shores of a lake. But it is also or first of all writing that comes on stage as suddenly as a sun god and begins to narrate— and to narrate *itself,* to double itself according to an allegorical figure that is already, with this first step, inexhaustible. The writing figures itself as "a man in cream-colors" and opens an account in his name to which interest begins to accrue. It is he, we are told, who appears suddenly and begins to move.

With a particularly, even absolutely, strange step, this figure goes aboard the steamer *Fidèle.* "In the same moment with his advent, he stepped aboard the favorite steamer *Fidèle,* on the point of starting for New Orleans." Critics have often remarked the odd diction of this text, its persistent attenuation of affirmative statement, or its tendency toward what R. W. B. Lewis in 1964 called a "self-erasing prose" (346). In this sentence, however, affirmative description or assertion itself is rendered odd by the strange temporality introduced by the phrase "in the same moment," which is the same moment of an advent, without precedent, that advances a step as it comes into view. The sentence enacts a kind of collapsing of narrative time, the time of successive events, advents, or appearances.[21] Instead of succession, it is as if, in the same moment, the same figure appeared on both sides of a border to be crossed, at once outside and inside the vehicle that begins to carry him or it from the moment an appearance is doubled or shadowed by a certain step. Or more precisely the advent announced here would be that of a spacing interval that strangely divides the first appearance of a man at daybreak.

And indeed, the man in cream-colors ("His cheek was fair, his chin downy, his hair flaxen, his hat a white fur one, with a long fleecy nap"), accompanied by neither baggage nor friends, will be received on board by the crowd already waiting there to depart as, "in the extremest sense of the word, a stranger." He is a stranger in the midst of strangers, but stranger still than the others, and even extremely, absolutely strange. And thus, absolutely without credit—or, what amounts to the same thing, with unlimited credit—come from nowhere and advancing on a way that is without example. Let us follow his steps: They lead him

> until he chanced to come to a placard nigh the captain's office, offering a reward for the capture of a mysterious impostor, supposed to have recently arrived from the East; quite an original genius in his vocation, as would appear, though wherein his originality consisted was not clearly given; but what purported to be a careful description of his person followed.

The writing whose traces we are following figures an arrest of its own movement and points to a written object as if to a kind of self-portrait. That object is called a placard. Everything that follows is going to come out of this placard, which, as its name indicates (from *plaquer* or *placken*), forms a kind of recess where one surface has been applied over another. Accordingly in French, *placard,* besides meaning a poster or printed sign (but it is also the printer's term for a galley proof), is a closet or cupboard, a covered recess in a wall.[22] Doubling itself at this point again, applying or folding one written surface over another, the text puts aside a certain reserve within its own borders out of which to draw ingredients as needed. An inexhaustible storehouse, the placard will cover all the bets one might place on the identity of the "mysterious impostor" in the closet. Like a universally accepted credit card or an unlimited line of credit, the carte blanche of the placard permits every sort of exchange in all kinds of currencies. Thus, as we said, everything to follow will come out of this placard or closet, but on a certain condition: the condition of not being able to guarantee against the imposture that is posted or signaled there. This condition is announced or denounced at the very place, at the very moment that the writing figures itself as writing. In other words, at the point at which writing figures the written object in this placard, the condition of irreducible doubling is both described and displayed. Such display does not suspend the condition; on the contrary, the announcement of possible imposture has all the more power to *impose* itself on the crowd: "As if it had been a theatre-bill, crowds were gathered about the announcement . . ."

The passing allusion to the theater and the stage acts as another kind of warning to look out for the illusion of representation. Drawn to the placard "as if it had been a theatre-bill," readers impose a referential, punctual frame on the text before them when they take it as announcing a representation to come on some other stage, when, in other words, they read it as referring reliably to the unreliability of a fiction. But of course nothing can reassure them that, for example, the "careful description" published of the impostor has itself not been taken in by the very imposture it would denounce. In that case, it would be in error and would lead into error beyond anyone's will or knowledge. Or again, since it is not clear "wherein his originality consisted" and therefore what exactly this imposing genius is capable of, there is no guarantee that the placard itself is not a fraud or a counterfeit, and that the "careful description" has not been calculated to mislead the very pursuit and capture called for.[23] But all these possibilities of error (and one could enumerate still others) are raised to the next power by their *reprise* or doubling on the other scene that at once includes and is included in the one we are reading, the scene, in other words, of precisely our own reading where we, like the passengers of the *Fidèle,* also read a placard, that is, these printed pages gathered under the title *The Confidence-Man.*

With this raising to the next power of writing's power to impose, any calculation of a possible imposture very quickly approaches the impossible. And this because there is a *mise en abyme* of a warning as concerns the credit one can or must give to writing. But precisely because it posts its capacity for imposture, the writing here also deploys the other capacity of its "original genius," the capacity to *tell (itself as) the truth.* It is deployed, then, between the two faces, the two surfaces of this truth-telling. Everything is entered on both registers that are stuck together back to back, like a poster on a wall. Thus, on one side, there is the poster on which one reads: "Look out, readers! There is an impostor who is perhaps circulating among you, even now as you read. Believe what I tell you." On the other side, and while "you" give yourself over to this warning, you forget to pay attention to what is going on behind your back where, as we read, "certain chevaliers," that is pickpockets, are free to ply their trade unsuspected. Showing the two faces of the coin back to back, displaying mistrust outsmarted by a fundamental trust in the written word, the writing here showcases all its tricks, pours out equivocal allusions and doubly encased ironies that tumble in free fall onto the page.

> As if it had been a theatre-bill, crowds were gathered about the announcement, and among them certain chevaliers, whose eyes, it was plain, were on the capitals, or, at least, earnestly seeking sight of them from behind intervening coats; but as for their fingers, they were enveloped in some myth; though, during a chance interval, one of these chevaliers somewhat showed his hand in purchasing from another chevalier, ex-officio a peddler of money-belts, one of his popular safe-guards . . .

Laugh as we might at the congress of mistrust that can never be too mistrustful, that nevertheless places trust in safeguards of all sorts, the last laugh is held indefinitely in reserve and returns to no one—least of all, perhaps, to Melville, who shows his hand here more than anyone else.[24]

In the meantime, we can isolate a few more indications of how, in its first pages, this text sets out to catch the confidence or the credit one cannot fail to place in the other from the first approach, from the moment one boards the writing vehicle—that is, from the first moment there appears anything at all with the first rays of the sun, as soon as the stranger arrives. The latter is the figure of a sort of white writing, the writing of the early morning, unencumbered by memory, but also a saying without said or without speech.[25] For, as revealed in the title of the chapter, the stranger is mute, a condition that will be confirmed when he positions himself beside the placard in order to show the crowd another writing.

> Pausing at this spot, the stranger so far succeeded in threading his way, as at last to plant himself *just beside the placard,* when, producing a small slate and tracing some words upon it, he held it up before him *on a level with the placard, so that they who read the one might read the other.* The words were these:—
> "Charity thinketh no evil." (4; emphasis added)

One reads, in other words, the first of Saint Paul's famous aphorisms on charity from his first letter to the Corinthians. Notice, however, the insistent notations concerning the position of the mute and his slate relative to the placard. He stood "just beside the placard" and held the slate "on a level with the placard, so that they who read the one might read the other." The whole suspensive technique of this text is to be found in these precise indications, which nevertheless leave room for and give rise to infinite speculations. The relation between the two written surfaces is put in place in such a way as to leave a blank or an interval between the signs, between all the posters, placards, notices, announcements, and cards scattered throughout the text. Between these two figures of the written object, the writing at the same time poses and suspends any possible relation of meaning connecting one to the other, the placard to the slate; or, to put it in other terms, it *lends* a meaning to this relation on the basis of nothing other than a pure spacing. This is the trap set for a reader who cannot read the placard without also reading the slate, who cannot not leap over the blank that holds them in relation by holding them apart.

In the face of this posed relation, how is one to avoid the hypothesis of a meaning to be credited and according to which one written sign is repeated, represented, canceled, or renewed in the other? How is one not to make a *series* of the signs one reads one after the other, one beside the other? Like the man in white who crosses a threshold at the same moment he appears, the blank separating the signs is crossed as soon as it is put in place. And from the simple spacing, one passes over into a whole rhetoric of possible metonymies with which to lend meaning to this blank and mute writing.

From one sign to the other, the blanks multiply the hypotheses of meaning. We can enumerate a few of them quickly: The relation that is posed would be one of opposition, the charitable words inscribed by the man in white, which remind readers of the duty to think no evil of their neighbors, would be opposed to the notice on the placard, which warns readers to beware of a possible impostor in their midst. In this way, the mute's sign would seek to send the notice on the placard off course in some way. Or rather, the inscribed words do not seek to do anything at all; it is their scriptor, their author who must have a reason for writing what he writes, unless he is altogether without reason, that is, simple-minded. This latter hypothesis is in fact the one preferred by a good number of the *Fidèle*'s passengers who take him for "some strange kind of simpleton" and draw the conclusion of "the singularity, if not lunacy, of the stranger." But we must not forget the other register where this scriptor, so quickly written off as mad and thereby refused the very charity he publicizes, would be but the relay of another who perhaps still deserves to be credited with having a reason for his writing acts, for these blanks. Crediting him with reason, giving him carte blanche,[26] one moves to the next set of hypotheses: The mute, which is to say the writer, would be acting out of charity toward his fellows who, if they follow the inspiration of the fascinating placard, might well suffer and make others suffer from lack of charity; or else, the writer, which is to say the mute, would himself be an impostor who is attempting to inspire a spirit of charity in the crowd so as to profit from it as circumstances permit and so as to be in greater security among them.

None of these reading hypotheses is to be rejected, all warrant some credit, but that credit can never be taken off the books by a repayment of the borrowed meaning. In what follows, one will never learn exactly what to make of the man in white, neither where he comes from, nor what he wants, nor finally at what point or how he leaves the stage, if indeed he does leave it. For the hypothesis remains opens that his apparition at the beginning of the trip signals the first step of an impostor who is going to metamorphose many times during the course of the voyage. As for the narrator, he will advance the hypothesis (but for what reason?) that the mute disembarked after having fallen asleep on deck and been forgotten by the crowd. In the next chapter, this supposition is slipped in at the turning of a phrase: "two or three random stoppages having been made, and the last transient memory of the slumberer vanished, and he himself, *not unlikely,* waked up and landed ere now . . ." (8–9; emphasis added). Like that of the mute, this writing advances on credit and always leaves something on the slate, here for example the notation "not unlikely" that grants its charity to the mute who "not unlikely [has] landed ere now."

In itself, the word "slate" introduces the whole scene of credit and debt in which we are engaged: "Put it on the slate," that is, charge it to my account. And by the way it is inscribed there, the writing on the slate underscores a debt that will not be effaced. After the man in white has traced (no doubt in white on the black or gray background) one after the other the aphorisms that all begin with the word charity ("Charity suffereth long, and is kind," "Charity endureth all things," "Charity believeth all things," "Charity never faileth"), not without exposing himself at each turn to the humiliation of the scornful crowd, the narrator notes that "The word charity, as originally traced, remained throughout uneffaced, not unlike the left-hand numeral of a printed date, otherwise left for convenience in blank" (5). It is as if this blank and mute writing were miming its own state of indebtedness to an original trace, left uneffaced on the slate that supports it. And it would be that same support that receives indifferently all our reading hypotheses, not unlike charity that "suffereth long," "endureth all things," and "believeth all things."

The list of hypotheses concerning the one who writes on the slate could be extended much further without leading out of the alternative already in place, namely: Either one has confidence in the infinite credit of God and thus in his messenger, angel, lamb, or spiritual son that is the man in fleecy white; or else, on the contrary, one mistrusts the credit sought by an impostor who, while preaching charity, is counterfeiting the lamb's innocence. Several generations of Melville's readers have not failed to divide themselves more or less neatly along the lines of this alternative.[27] One question debated at length is whether or not the man in white is part of the series of supposed impostures or disguises that are presumed to unfold in subsequent chapters under the noses of the passengers/readers. Meanwhile, the belief that there is indeed a series, that certain characters are so many masks of a single and selfsame confidence man, rests exclusively on variations of the metonymic association we have just considered between the man in white and the impostor described by the placard. In other words, there are only blanks articulating the elements of the supposed series, blanks through which one must draw a continuous line in order to make of the dispersed elements the outline of a same face behind a series of masks. To the question "Whose is the face behind the mask?" every answer can be made credible by a reading of selected elements.[28]

Or *almost* every answer for, let us note it in passing, in the considerable critical literature by so many experts of imposture, nowhere does anyone venture the hypothesis of a supplementary disguise behind which the confidence man would be in fact not a man but . . . a woman. It is as if andromorphism were not an element of possible disguise among others, but were outside all speculation: sexual difference as transcendental ground of interpretation. Which is to say that sexual difference, unlike other differential signs, would not be suspended by the text's confidence games; on the contrary, it would form the frame and the limit on those games, the trait setting the fiction of reference, in all its uncertainty, apart from a reference that does not call on belief, credit, confidence, or faith but, going beyond all appearance and possible imposture, is what it says and says what it is in a coincidence of self with itself.[29]

Perhaps, however, it is this extratextual position of identity, and first of all sexual identity, that is being put on the line when the man in cream colors steps off the solid ground at the same moment he appears. The question of whether he is or is not part of the series of impostors would translate an anxiety that arises at the very first steps of this strange blank writing. At that moment, that strange "same moment" of the advent of a spacing step, the disquieting suspicion begins to stir that none of this holds up or together, that it is from the first step divided and therefore full of blanks and bottomless holes, to the point that one gets lost, I lose myself—the "I" loses itself. In order not to lose myself, in order not to get swindled out of that greatest treasure, I take out the loan of a reading hypothesis, I give myself the credit of certain suppositions, not only as concerns the supposed structure of this text, or, a still more hypothetical thesis, as concerns its final meaning, not only as concerns "what-the-author-Herman-Melville-intended," which comes down to the same thing, but also with regard to that which *interests* me first of all, which allows me, *a* me and a me that would be one, to have an interest in what I read, what I therefore, by the same token, have a part in, am a part of and a party to. Giving myself the credit of my reading hypothesis, I connect the unconnected dots and, as in the child's game, I draw a line, the contour of a closed and rounded-off form that can finally be identified as the trace of some object or subject or other. If I give myself the credit of myself, and if I am not to lose myself by taking part in this serious game, then it all has to come back to me in the final accounting.

But, precisely, it doesn't come back, there is no return on this investment unless I continue making loans one after the other, one on top of the other. Nor will all this lending activity be checked at the other border of the text. In the final lines of the ultimate chapter, the one who is called the cosmopolitan and the last supposed avatar of the supposed series of confidence-men, Jack Goodman, makes his exit and leaves the last word to the narrator:

> "I have indifferent eyes, and will show you; but, first, for the good of all lungs, let me extinguish this lamp."
>
> The next moment, the waning light expired, and with it the waning flames of the horned altar, and the waning halo round the robed man's brow; while in the darkness which ensued, the cosmopolitan kindly led the old man away.

And then one reads—it is the last sentence of the text—: "Something further may follow of this Masquerade." This sentence, added after the expiration of the light, closes the book without closing its accounts; on the contrary, it lets the speculation run on beyond the final period toward an endless sequel. It is a somewhat too obvious way of saying that all is perhaps not yet said, a final word whose finality is carried off or carried away, postponed to an unspecified future date, an unlimited extension of credit.

It is important to note that the mode of this final sentence marks a contrast with the rest of the preceding paragraph and the description of the dying light. The final line describes nothing, names nothing: It is rather a notice posted at the end of the text and addressed to the reader, not unlike the placard displayed on the first page. Moreover, that placard, which gives notice of a possible imposture, in effect says the same thing: "Something further may follow of this Masquerade." It is as if one had not moved from the spot of one's initial fascination before the placard, as if one had remained glued there dreaming of the impostor who is perhaps going to continue his masquerade, who is sought by the authorities, and whose capture promises a reward. The desire of the dream, sharpened by the promise of a reward, would have spellbound the reader eager to witness the capture and thus all the more disappointed to find himself or herself, at such a late hour, still in the same place, having taken so many steps and followed so many paths only in a dream. Did nothing at all happen? At what point did I start to dream? And now, is the dream over and am I really awake? Let's take it from the beginning again.

Everything seems to begin with the advent of the stranger at the break of day. Is it then he, this heliographic apparition, who, despite his apparent, exhibited innocence, initiated the series of possibly crooked loans and credits that can be closed out only by an infinite refloating of all this accounting? What happens? The stranger arrives in front of the placard and reads there, as does everyone else, the description of "a mysterious impostor, supposed to have recently arrived from the East," that is, who has arrived as well with the sunrise, but already *before* the advent of the man in white. The latter, whose first steps trace the first movements of the writing we read, would thus be inscribed as coming *after* this mysterious earlier arrival. As a result, there is a kind of twist at the beginning of the narrative, where the first to come arrives after the other. This other arrival, this other beginning, has been displaced, via the placarded announcement, to a position within the narrative, and from there it sets itself apart, signaling or re-marking an exteriority and an anteriority that the narrative can only figure without including. This is what the placard does when it describes the one who is sought as "quite an original genius in his vocation, as would appear," although, as the narrator must add, "wherein his originality consisted was not clearly given." In this figuration of an origin that it does not name, or rather does not *give,* the writing of the fiction has its point of departure, which is a kind of false start, a departure in a secondarity that comes after in order to figure the true start, the true, the start of the truth. Now, if the originality of the original trait is buried in the closet of the placard, and if the finality of the final trait is carried off by an irrevocable postponement ("Something further may follow of this Masquerade"), then one can only *give credit*—to oneself, to others, reflexively *and* reciprocally, that difference being suspended, precisely, by the structure of an original credit that is given in the place of the original *itself,* an original that would be present to itself, fully accounted for and not on credit. Here then is the credit account opened at the origin, at sunrise. It makes no sense to seek to verify its good standing; on the contrary, sense is made only on credit; it gives (itself) credit. A certain confidence and trust is engaged at the beginning and from the beginning; that is the condition of any beginning at all.

One is thus in advance obliged to extend credit and perhaps especially there where it is a matter of announcing or declaring that no credit is the rule. This is made plain in the first chapter of *The Confidence-Man* when it juxtaposes a third moment (which is to say, already a fourth if one counts the always anterior original moment of the "quite an original") to the two (three) preceding ones, all of which are moments in which writing is put on display. We have already examined the first juxtaposition of the placard to the slate of the man in white, in which a spacing relates or refers the second to the first and thereby opens all the possibilities of a relation of meaning. We can now add to what we have already said that the opening is in this manner referred back to the recess hollowed out within the text where an inaccessible exteriority, originality, or "firstness" is put in reserve. Now, there is a second (third) juxtaposition: the man in white's slate, which displays the uneffaced debt on its charitable support, is in effect replaced by "a gaudy sort of illuminated pasteboard sign" that the boat's barber hangs in front of his shop "next door but two to the captain's office." Recall that the placard hangs "nigh the captain's office," and the slate is held up "just beside the placard." The spacing notations are as precise as ever, and they point to an increasing distance from the captain's office, which would be something like an anchoring reference point. (Here, another line of speculation could open up—but we'll confine it to parentheses—in the spacing that juxtaposes the placard and the sign on a door that says "Captain." The question is: At what point does the spacing of signs cease to produce meaningless blanks? Where is one to situate the limit on speculative confidence? Is the captain of this ship, who never appears "in person," also perhaps a part of the scheme? Who can answer that question? Who's running this ship? Who's in charge?) On the barber's sign there are two words: "No Trust." The narrator describes the effect this sign produced on the crowd:

> An inscription which, though in a sense not less intrusive than the contrasted ones of the stranger, did not, as it seemed, provoke any corresponding derision or surprise, much less indignation; and still less, to all appearances, did it gain for the inscriber the repute of being a simpleton.

Of satiric import, these lines point to the complacency of those who place their confidence and faith above all in cash, in face value, and are therefore prepared to extend credit quite naturally to whomever displays the same belief, which is to say, the same lack of belief. As if it were altogether natural to credit the reason of anyone who refuses to give credit. The barber's sign, in other words, is a sort of decoy or lure for reason insofar as it seems to *oppose* itself to the inscriptions of the man in white, as one might stop payment on a check or suspend a credit card in order to prevent them from circulating any further and contracting unwanted debts.[30] The barber's sign lures reason into the oppositional frame from the moment it announces and solicits belief that one can, *by means of a general and inaugural rule,* refuse in general to give credit. And yet, far from putting a stop to it, the sign renews credit, a certain unavowed credit of the credulous crowd, but also the credit that this writing extends to itself as it proceeds out of the placard and its warning against imposture. To put it in the most domestic terms: By setting the barber's sign beside the man in white's slate, by making of their juxtaposition an opposition, one takes out of the closet a comfortable pair of old shoes with which to cushion the steps of the writing's credit/no credit procedure, its advance/no advance that opposes one sign to another and in this way gets no further than the threshold of the recess out of which it comes. And so it would go until the final threshold of the text that, as we have seen, leaves us wondering, as in a dream, whether anything happened at all—anything other than the strange steps of a narrative that give one to speculate about what may be hidden in its closet.

SOMETHING FURTHER . . .

Yet, there, at the same time, where nothing happens, this *nothing* also happens. To recall Blanchot's terms: at the same time "the pure void bereft of importance" and "that upon which a foundation can be given." The "at the same time" configures, rather than an alternative, a conjunction in time that measures a certain step. It is the step of a "man in cream colors," or a "white" man, into a black-letter text. Instantly, two things happen at once: (1) a dividing line is drawn and therefore a border must be crossed, and (2) this line divides the "white man" in two, who at that moment appears. "In the same moment with his advent, he stepped aboard the favorite steamer Fidèle . . ." Which one then steps aboard, the angel or its double, perhaps an impostor? Doubled in that singularly dividing step, the singular "who" is irretrievable at the origin of this writing: irretrievable because it is the *same* step that gives the writing its movement. *There is* first of all the divided writing, and it divides itself from the origin at its first appearance, or rather *his* appearance—for the step also steps into the figure of a man, and the allegory of writing is engaged in that split second. The appearance of the figure, as suddenly as a god's, an appearance, therefore, that is already doubled by a likeness, is called an "advent": "In the same moment with his advent, he stepped aboard . . ." An advent is a coming, the *event* of a coming of the absolutely other into the experience of the same. And at that moment the singular event is doubled by the language of likeness or sameness. The incalculable occurs, it comes about by this crossing of innumerable *singular* events into the representation of sameness, that is, of the more than one. The calculation of these events can then begin as story or history, a narrative series of spaced transactions that nevertheless remains open at both ends, in the anteriority of its *singular* beginning, and in the posteriority of a final revelation of the "Masquerade," its *singular* end or destination.

Between these two unique poles of experience, a proliferating *crowd* of figures, all of which appear out of nowhere or nothing, just *like* the inaugural angel, the initial messenger from the "pure void." The angelic event proliferates, but precisely because it multiplies, it appears to disappear into the more than one. This movement of multiplication can be traced clearly in Melville's successive chapter headings, beginning with the initial chapter, which, as we've already seen, has tucked away in its closet an anterior originality, "quite an original genius . . ." Chapter 2 is headed: "Showing that many men have many minds" and chapter 3: "A variety of characters appear." What has appeared, in other words, is the more than one, which is also the *other than one:* the other, some other. But who or what is it? And what has happened other than the spacing of a step, a sign, a slate of letters?

MELVILLE'S CREDIT CARD | 213

Nothing happens except the spacing step of an advent and therefore everything is possible. The other appears as the possibility of the future, and therefore from the future, as the future's event. What to call this event, which is a stranger "in the extremest sense of the word," what to call it in a language that knows only how to say the stranger as the same, as the already familiar? Between this always anterior advent of the one, in chapter 1, and its disappearance into the more than one, in chapter 2, there is another step over the blank space, and into a proliferation of names.

"Odd fish!"
"Poor fellow!"
"Who can he be?"
"Casper Hauser."
"Bless my soul!"
"Uncommon countenance."
"Green prophet from Utah."
"Humbug!"
"Singular innocence."
"Means something."
"Spirit-rapper."
"Moon-calf."
"Piteous."
"Trying to enlist interest."
"Beware of him."
"Fast asleep there, and, doubtless, pick-pockets on board."
"Kind of daylight Endymion."
"Escaped convict, worn out with dodging."
"Jacob dreaming at Luz." (7)

Called "epitaphic comments," these lines are lent at the outset of chapter 2 to a "miscellaneous company": "Such the epitaphic comments, conflictingly spoken or thought, of a miscellaneous company . . ." The event of nothing but the other's doubled appearance is the possibility of the crowd of possibilities represented here in a list that is necessarily cut short of the infinity to which it would have to extend before the representation came to an end. The comments, because they do end in a finite list, are "epitaphic," legends inscribed over the one who has disappeared. Only to come again, perhaps, in another figure. How can the same *one* appear at the same time as the more than one? This is the question of how to "impart the particular,"[31] and we are taking it to be Melville's as well, by whom we mean the singular instance of the writer who takes in or takes on the stranger, who *welcomes* it or him or her as absolutely other. " 'Odd fish! . . . Jacob dreaming at Luz' ": each of the nineteen entries on the incomplete list, applied to the sleeping figure of the man in cream colors, applies *by the same token* to the allegorized step into writing that is Melville's. A singular experience signs this text, but it is to the event of the other's appearance and thus to a certain doubling that the singular is consigned or co-signed. "Melville" signs the text as another, and thus it is signed more than once, indeed many times, at least nineteen times and still counting. "Odd fish!" . . . "Uncommon countenance" . . . "Humbug!" "Singular innocence." "Means something" . . . "Trying to enlist interest" . . . "Beware of him." If we cannot decide which of these epitaphs should be erected over the finite experience that lies buried beneath them, if incalculable multiplicity is the rule from the first highly calculated step, that impossibility has nevertheless to be reckoned as the affirmation of nothing other than the other. This "nothing other than the other" happens as credit extended to an appearance, a credit that already has to have been extended so that the appearance can appear. Prior, then, to any judgment, as the very possibility of decision, is this affirmation that is not the affirmation of this or that, of some content or some theme, but of the articulating space in which figures can appear—and disappear—to each other, as each other. It is this space that is measured out allegorically in *The Confidence-Man,* which speaks in public (*agoreuein*) otherwise (*allos*), from the place of the other, elsewhere than in the present.

Arresting this multiplicity at a calculable number, or better yet reducing it to just one, is the work of literature's institution. That institution, we now may perhaps better understand, will have taken the form of the human figure, the human face, or in a still more determined reach for calculable stability, the human body. It is these forms that, through a series of reversals and substitutions, have supplied the content of literary study over its brief history and continue to do so. Literature has come into its institution or its catachresis in human form, but at the same time the "original genius" withdraws into the placard and is kept in reserve. The reserve is an irretrievable past, which can never be made present, which can only be credited therefore. And by the same token of credit, the reserve holds a future, it gives the future as other. In this sense, the text's application for credit, which we will have already approved even before we begin reading and even if we begin reading under the apparent sign of "No Trust" ("Humbug!" "Beware of him"), is the support of literature's institution, "that upon which a foundation can be given."

Here, foundation is given to the American experience of writing as the advent of a stranger, "in the extremest sense of the word."

To what extremes can we take this notation? Can we go to the extremes of an other that is not even human, at least does not have the familiar guise of human figure and body? At what point does the extremely strange begin to melt altogether into an undifferentiated sea of meaninglessness? Is it at the point at which the figure of man merges into some blankness, for example "some sugar-snow"?

> Gradually overtaken by slumber, his flaxen head drooped, his whole lamb-like figure relaxed, and, half reclining against the ladder's foot, lay motionless, as some sugar-snow in March, which, softly stealing down over night, with its white placidity startles the brown farmer peering out from his threshold at daybreak. (6)

The American literary institution has repeatedly answered that man is the measure and the ground. In that figure and form it has sought a stabilization of its object, but also of its project, or perhaps one should say of its projection. A text like *The Confidence-Man* serves as a kind of blank screen, a ground blanketed in snow that can take for a time the imprint of a worker in the field, but only eventually to absorb it like the deep "which," as Melville puts it in *Benito Cereno,* "directly must receive back what it gave." Its figurative possibilities are endless unless held in check, framed by the one figure that surveys and orders the scene: "the brown farmer peering out from his threshold at daybreak."

The complex allegory in this passage is marked at the point of the transfiguration of the lamblike figure into some sugar-snow, the pivoting point of the word "as": "as some sugar-snow in March." Called into the picture at that point is a nonhuman realm of elements, frozen water of "white placidity." What is being named by this newly appeared figure? And who will name it, from which point of view? The brown farmer, whose brownness is perhaps the signal that he is the most ill-used of men? Will he tell us what he sees beneath the cover of "snow," the figure's mere appearance behind which is hidden its real face? But the farmer is startled by the appearance, as if struck by the muteness of the sleeping lamblike figure. This silent transfer of silence occurs metonymically, by what we have been calling the spacing step of the text. In the transfiguring step from the man in cream colors to the brown farmer, who are merely juxtaposed to one another, the transfer is accomplished on a field of white, which comes unexpectedly in March (and the spacing step marches on). What comes is unnameable and is given (by whom?) the soft, sweet name of sugar-snow. Naming the unnameable event with a general rule will always be impossible except in this metonymic, catachrestic way. What is said or written in the black-letter text first appears as that which is not said or written at all, by anyone, any human subject, any identifiable intention. It appears *as* snow, *like* snow: it appears, in other words, *as* the possibility of the *as:* appearance and name. This is the event, the coming into language of nothing but its own possibility as the dividing step of differentiation. What comes with that step is the other of the name and of the human language that puts a face to its names: the absolutely other, which is always the future of the name "human" or "man" or "woman" or "black" or "white" or "brown." The absolutely future other comes as the grounding possibility of all these guises, which is also the impossibility of their singular presence without guise, without doubles, without multiplicity.

"Many men have many minds": the multiplicity that appears with the first step of representation is counted out among men, the differences between individuals in any "miscellaneous company" or collective society. But the same phrase—in a chapter heading, bordered on both sides by blanks, its context thus suspended—can also be read as asserting or affirming that there are many men who each have many minds, who are each of different minds within themselves. They are themselves not themselves, but other and other than a self or an identity. Other than self is the possibility of the other's event, and this is what the text affirms by performing its stepping movement: for example, from the sleeping lamblike figure, to the sugar-snow, to the startled brown farmer, to the "grotesque negro cripple" of chapter 3, "In which a variety of characters appear."

As in *Benito Cereno,* the troping of white and black, but also of human and inhuman gives its impetus to this movement and it is the powerful impetus we analyzed above of "nature" made as familiar as a Newfoundland dog: "owing to something wrong about his legs," the grotesque figure of chapter 3 has been "cut down to the stature of a Newfoundland dog."[32] This "attractive object"

> was making music, such as it was, and raising a smile even from the gravest. It was curious to see him, out of his very deformity, indigence, and houselessness, so cheerily endured, raising mirth in some of that crowd, whose own purses, hearths, hearts, all their possessions, sound limbs included, could not make gay.
> "What is your name, old boy?" . . .
> "Der Black Guinea dey calls me, sar."
> "And who is your master, Guinea?"
> "Oh sar, I am der dog widout massa." (10)

Without master, without name, without house, without purse, without bodily wholeness: "Black Guinea" appears as a without-ness, a face given to a dispossessed blackness cut down low to the ground, made humble, less than human, "der dog widout massa." It is as if the engendering step of repetition, which multiplies figures as they appear and so that they *can* appear, had just had its legs cut out from under it: the grotesque result is a set of frozen oppositions (perhaps having been chilled by their passage through the snow) that set slavish, inhuman figures below human ones. This advent, nonetheless, repeats the advent of the lamblike figure, only this time the figure speaks, rather than writes on a slate. He speaks, however, *almost* in another language, which is *almost* unrepresentable in standard English orthography. And he makes "music, such as it was." Nevertheless, the crowd answers his music with smiles, made gay and mirthful by the appearance of without-ness, which is thereby affirmed, like the eternal return. There is affirmation, then, before, or rather as the possibility of opposition, of negative and positive. The other, the stranger, the inhuman appears *as* and *to* the same, and that is the possibility of any meaning emerging from the deep blankness of limitless space.

But this emerging step is immediately doubled or split, as was the lamblike figure's. This repetition blackens the page, but also cripples the movement of a certain address. What has happened to the address—which also means the grace of movement—between the first step on(to) the page and this second, repeating step? In other words, how, when, and where did Black Guinea lose the use of his legs and thus his address?

To those questions, there is a whole history as answer and all of history to answer for. It is in history and as history that the address of the other to the same is written in an almost unrecognizable language, that the grotesque distortion of the other's idiom is answered with projection and ejection beyond the limits of human sameness. This is the projecting mechanism of identification, the movement by which sameness constitutes itself *by means or mediation of* the other. This mediation by the other, thanks to the other's appearance, is the affirmative *possibility* of self, but it is not self or a self. The "self" rather is that which is first *called to,* much like the music "such as it was" raises a smile even "from the gravest," those who are preoccupied by possessing what they possess. There is first the address or call of the other.

In the Black Guinea episode, as with the lamblike figure's quotations from Paul, the address appeals to charity. But consider what has happened to this appeal or call from one figure to the next. In chapter 1, Paul's injunctions are repeated as the law of charity, that is, as addressed to everyone and to no one in particular, not even perhaps to any human identified as such. For the law as written does not say "The charitable man thinketh no evil," or "The charitable man believeth all things," but rather Charity thinketh and believeth, suffereth and endureth, and finally never faileth. Charity itself does these things, but charity itself is no one; it is a giving without giver, and what it gives is what it does not have, a self.[33] The law is given or addressed to everyone by no one, by the without-ness that can be figured either in black or white, written as it is in black and white. But in the movement from white to black, that is, in the very movement by which the law is written into history, something happens to the address of the other, which has *given the law to be written*.

Black Guinea speaks from the humbled place of the beggar. He addresses from below. Once again, Melville is careful to mark the spatial relation, which, from the horizontal juxtapositions of placard, slate, and barber's sign, has here been turned onto its vertical axis:

> cut down to the stature of a Newfoundland dog; his knotted black fleece and good-natured, honest black face rubbing against the upper part of people's thighs as he made shift to shuffle about . . .

In this lowered position, Black Guinea becomes the object of charity, or rather its *target* in a game that requires a certain address:

> suddenly the negro more than revived their first interest by an expedient which, whether by chance or design, was a singular temptation at once to *diversion* and charity, though, even more than his crippled limbs, it put him on a canine footing. In short, as in appearance he seemed a dog, so now, in a merry way, like a dog he began to be treated. Still shuffling among the crowd, now and then he would pause, throwing back his head and opening his mouth like an elephant for tossed apples at a menagerie; when, making a space before him, people would have a bout at a strange sort of pitch-penny game, the cripple's mouth being at once target and purse, and he hailing each expertly-caught copper with a cracked bravura from his tambourine. (11)

The emphasis on the word "diversion" is Melville's, and this technique for drawing the reader's attention is very rare throughout the text. Pairing the stressed word with the key term "charity" ("a singular temptation at once to *diversion* and charity") signals precisely a diversion or turning aside of charity's address. The result is a twisted or crippled grotesque. What has happened is that the law's address, by no one to everyone, in chapter 1 has been specified in chapter 3, given direction and destination. To be more exact, it has taken aim at a target and, "whether by chance or design," this ballistic specification diverts charity's balm or gift into its opposite: a painful assault.

> To be the subject of alms-giving is trying, and to feel duty bound to appear cheerfully grateful under the trial, must be still more so; but whatever his secret emotions, he swallowed them, while still retaining each copper this side the oesophagus. And nearly always he grinned, and only once or twice did he wince . . .

This crippling event seems to befall the Other, that is, Charity, as soon as it repeats its step, as soon as its eventness or singular firstness is doubled or simulated in a second appearance. Hence the question debated among the *Fidèle*'s passengers regarding Black Guinea and the true nature of the game (a man with a wooden leg "began to croak out something about [Black Guinea's] deformity being a sham, got up for financial purposes, which immediately threw a damp upon the frolic benignities of the pitch-penny players" [12]), but also, as we've seen, the question that has bedeviled *The Confidence-Man*'s critics: is the lamblike figure part of the series of repetitions or not? That question, we may now suspect, attempts to save the "white man" as the singularly innocent origin that stands outside the series and does not get caught up in its blackened patterns of doubling. But we can perhaps also see now the other force of this question, which arrives in the wake of an advent or an event that is at once doubled and diverted. This other force is, precisely, that of the other-than-the-same, which is diverted into the structure of representation by a kind of folding back or *application*.

The law of charity *is* nothing until it is applied. If it is nothing and no one, however, how can the law apply to it? By whose authority, by what *prior* law does it demand that charity or credit be extended to it?

> "Charity thinketh no evil."
> As, in gaining his place, some little perseverance, not to say persistence, of a mildly inoffensive sort, had been unavoidable, it was not with the best relish that the crowd regarded his apparent intrusion; and upon a more attentive survey, perceiving *no badge of authority* about him, but rather something quite the contrary—he being of an aspect so singularly innocent; an aspect, too, which they took to be somehow inappropriate to the time and place, and inclining to the notion that his writing was of much the same sort: in short, taking him for some strange kind of simple-

ton, harmless enough, would he keep to himself, but not wholly unobnoxious as an intruder—they made no scruple to jostle him aside . . . (4;
emphasis added)

This intruder "of a mildly inoffensive sort" wears no badge of authority, shows no sign that he comes and writes as a delegate of the
law. Indeed, when he is surveyed more attentively, read more
closely, something rather "quite the contrary" is perceived about
him. Quite the contrary of authority and of the law's demand is a
demand, an address of another sort, an other demand that is the
petition of the other. That petition is "singularly innocent," innocent
in being, precisely, singular, without likeness, without double, without mask or master, exactly what it appears to be. But it appears
"somehow inappropriate to the time and place." Or rather, "*they
took [it] to be* somehow inappropriate to the time and place." In this
"taking-to-be" occurs the fold of the application of a supposedly
prior law to this instance, to this singularly innocent appearance. The
prior law is (taken to be) the law of self-presence in time and place,
the law of identity of time and place with one self, with oneself.
What they take to be (the law) is being present, what they take to
be appropriate is appropriation. This gesture of *taking* the present, of
appropriating it away from the other, executes a swerving motion
back to the same, to the principle of likeness: "and *inclining* to the
notion that his writing [i.e., "Charity thinketh no evil"] was of much
the *same* sort." In this "inclining notion" they "jostle him aside." He
is thus projected and ejected out of appropriate, present time and
place. And so is his writing that is taken to be of much the same
sort: inappropriate, that is, untimely, out of sync, from some other
time and place. The petition from the writer is thus read but rejected,
shunted off, *diverted* into an address that one can safely ignore as long
as it kept to itself "but not wholly unobnoxious as an intruder."
(Charity, thy name is also Bartleby.)

Shall we then say that *The Confidence-Man* is this not wholly unobnoxious intruder in American literature insofar as the latter takes
itself, identifies itself as literature and as American? Yes, we *shall* say
it, affirm it inappropriately as inappropriate to the time and place.
This novel masquerade figures always the inappropriation of the
present in which it is taken to be this or that, or in which it is
subjected even to "more attentive survey" and studied closely. The
text projects another time and place than the present. It petitions
from this nonpresence to be given a future, to be given time. The
petition is put forward by its singular aspect and its appearance "quite

contrary" to the law. But there is the rub of this petitioning affirmation, which is neither positive nor negative but the possibility of both: quite contrary to the "badge of authority" may also mean a petition made *against* the law, a fraud, a confidence trick. For on whose or what authority does he write what he writes? In whose name does he come but his own? But his own name has no authority as the law, to speak the law of its own name: it is but an instance to which this law of the proper name is applied. Melville's *Confidence-Man* attempts to sign itself in this swerving movement of the law, in the other time and place of present law.

That signature gives American literature and literary studies a future and a past, an opening to the other's singular appearance as another time and place. The opening, however, also opens this construct "American literature and literary studies" to its transformation by the other that appears. *The Confidence-Man* enacts and reenacts, in an apparent series of repetitions, this event of appearance "suddenly as Manco Capac at the lake Titicaca." The repetition, if there is any, repeats a petition. But which comes first, repetition or petition? How do we read the sudden appearance of an advent of the other in the same, in the same moment another time and place? Of the petition in the repetition?

We might say that *The Confidence-Man* -petitions. It marks a space within re-petition for the step of appearance that immediately, "at the same moment," repeats the other in the same. As another reader has remarked, Melville shows a marked affinity for the punctuating hyphen.[34] *The Confidence-Man,* beginning with its title, is not an exception; beyond the title the hyphen will be remarked in, for example, the transformative figure of the "sugar-snow" (or, for that matter, the "black-letter text" or "The Bell-Tower"). The hyphen is a signature of the most inappropriate kind, a mere mark, a singularly innocent trait. The minimal or liminal event of writing, it partitions names and events, divides them, and partakes of the names it imparts to all the figures it traces. It scans the rhythm of a step from another time and place, the possibility, therefore, of a coming transformation. And it confides itself to this transforming possibility, to the future and to the other. It is this confiding movement, this confid-ance or confi-dance that carries it step after step, for forty-five chapters to the sign-off message: Something further may follow of this Masquerade.

It is possible, of course, to read in this final affirmation the only real question Melville is posing in an allegory of his inappropriate, powerless, laughed-at, and perhaps soon-to-be-forgotten signature, the question of whether something further will or will not follow.

Will he be given any further credit on presentation of this -petition, of this mere marking step of writing? Perhaps the allegorical vehicle carrying the signature confidence-man is the last boat and thus the last chance to arrive at its destination? Yes, certainly, that is possible. But first the question supposes that we know already the destination of the signature Melville or the signature American literature. It supposes that we know its address and what is addressed to whom. Above all and first of all, however, it supposes that *there is* address and that we know that there is address. But this grounding supposition is put in place by a swerving motion whereby the address is affirmed when it is *taken* to be address. The address is affirmed and diverted, in other words, when it is taken to be pure address and nothing more, the pure nothingness of address—when it is taken and thereby given to be what it is. There is something given—presupposed—and something taken, but are they the same? Forcibly not if the same means identical in time and place, contemporaneous, coincident, two identical singularities, because that is the logical impossibility. But, yes, the same all the same, although at some remove within that sameness, not coincident in time and place, preserving a reserve of incalculable difference as in a placard or a closet. The "yes," here, is an affirmation quite the contrary of an authoritative knowledge; it is given-taken in a re-petition that repeats a difference in or as a sameness. There is a step, an interval, a space, or a hyphen: re-petition.

What is the address of this writing? Because that question is left open to countless possibilities, American literature and literary studies in America are given a future.[35] They are given a future by the other's time and place, and are thereby given or rather promised the other-than-itself, other than American and other than literature. This deconstructive opening occurs as affirmation of the transforming power of the other, a power that is also strangely powerless, an imposition and an intrusion that cannot impose itself behind the badge of any authority. Something further may follow of this Masquerade: Before it floats a question of his value or creditworthiness to past or present contemporaries, before it asks for an evaluation, a credit rating, an interpretation, the last line of Melville's last novel enacts the swerving affirmation of re-petition. So that something more *may* follow. So that the stranger may still come aboard, cross all the borders both natural and artificial, human and inhuman. So that institutions of the present—American or literary—do not appropriate all time and place to themselves.

EPILOGUE | *A FUTURE FOR IT—*

OUR PLAY has concluded: the catachresis of literature has come on stage as the principal subject and hero of that new City called the modern University. This subject has proceeded, once on stage, to do the properly Oedipal thing: it educates itself in its own genealogy and violent history. Having put out its I's, it now wanders blindly across the devastated stage of History, not dead but dying just like the rest of us. The theater is closing, it's time to get out and go home.

Then one of the actors comes out in front of the curtain and addresses a short poem to the spectators, who turn back toward the stage under the force of this apostrophe. Although "Literature"'s play is concluded, we return to this repetition of its history under the force of an address without certain destination.

The actor repeats a version of the poem she already recited at the end of act I:[1]

> Knows how to forget!
> But—could she teach—it?
> 'Tis the Art, most of all,
> I should like to know—
>
> Long, at it's Greek—
> I—who pored—patient—
> Rise—still the Dunce—
> Gods used to know—
>
> Mould my slow mind to this Comprehension—
> Oddest of sciences—Book ever bore—
>
> How to forget!
> Ah, to attain it—
> I would give *you*—
> All other Lore—

There cannot be, there ought not to be any commentary before such an event. The audience rather is turned by a pure address, a pure void without importance, an art that is not yet a *kind* of address, but purely itself: an essential ambiguity. "And art is that deep which is *sometimes* the absence of profundity, of the foundation, the pure void bereft of importance, and *sometimes* that upon which a foundation can be given, but it is also *always at the same time* one and the other, the intertwining of the Yes and the No, the ebb and flow of the essential ambiguity." Before this commentary can begin, before the audience starts to murmur its approval or dismissal, the actor repeats: "I would give *you*—All other Lore—" and the voice stresses *you*. What is this proffered and promised gift?

It is offered in the name of one who would be a teacher, if she could. She knows how to forget, but could she teach it? Or rather (and we begin to repeat, to imitate the tone of the punctuation) "But—could she teach—it?" which reproduces the spacings and the questioning of a certain "she." The essential ambiguities of this tone imitated by the punctuation begin to rain onto the page. They—in their irreducible plurality—start to gather at the turning of the line of this address, that other apostrophe which is purely spatial: "But— could she teach—it? / 'Tis the Art, most of all . . ." On either side of the turn, there is an "it," but are they the same? Do they refer to one and the same referent? There has been an elision at the turning of the repetition, at the point of a pure spacing of punctuation: " ? / '." a sequence of marks, to which has been added, among other things, the " " in order to signal or indicate, as with a tracing index finger, that I am quoting and not speaking in my own voice. I am copying down the address of another, who signed Emily Dickinson. In order not to forget that as you read, you must pay pretty close attention to all the punctuation marks. Rather tiresome, really, to have to remember to look at these little marks, especially when the play is over, and everyone's ready to go home. Moreover, what one has to remember is the elision of an "I," which differentiates "it" and " 't" on the page. They are and are not the same, that is, "also *always at the same time* one and the other, the intertwining of the Yes and the No . . ." " 'Tis the Art, most of all, / I should like to know": is "it" the art of *teaching* how to forget or the art of *forgetting?* Perhaps they are the same? Could an epilogue to the play of literature's cata- chresis teach this essential division—non-division—of "it"? Could it teach it? But which "it" is that, which "it" is it?

There is the discouraging experience of learning to hear the long dead voice of the other, "it's Greek." The futility of commentary:

after poring patient over the intricacies of diacritical spacing and punctuation, "I" rise "still the Dunce." They were gods who used to know Greek, but still it's Greek to me.

"It" insists once more in the final stanza in this epilogue that is already commentary, repetition, re-petition of the address:

> How to forget!
> Ah, to attain it—
> I would give *you*—
> All other Lore—

Two possibilities are set before us in the final lines that speak of a conditional gift. The first, and perhaps grammatically most plausible, is an exchange: if I could attain "it," what I most want to know— how to forget or how to teach how to forget—I would give or leave to you, in exchange, every other knowledge, "All other Lore." That is, I would rather know how to (teach how to) forget what I know, so if I had to choose I would leave every other positive knowledge, which knows what it knows, to you. There would thus be the proposal of a kind of reverse Faustian bargain. But another, more elliptical sense is overlaid on this offered exchange: if I could (teach how to) forget, then I would *be able* to give you all other lore. Forgetting would not be the alternative to lore, but rather its condition. This other possibility, in other words, grounds lore in a certain forgetting, rather than opposing them as different terms that can somehow be exchanged against each other. But this would be to understand that positive lore—and we mustn't forget that "Lore," which carries the stress not only of the last word but of the only true rhyme, implies always an act of teaching or learning, a *lernen*—is given or instituted by forgetting as its grounding condition. With this understanding, the apparent structuring tensions of our epilogued address—knowing and teaching, knowing and forgetting—are rearranged in a still more complex design, one which cannot finally be comprehended by an analysis into its simple elements. For if Lore is instituted as knowledge or precept, *Lehre,* by a forgetting of its condition, then it teaches above all or first of all how to forget. Lore is an instituted forgetting of its institution. Teaching or lore would always entail, in a fundamental and conditioning sense, teaching how to forget. Why, then, should there be any question about whether "she could teach it"?

It is late, everyone's tired and wants to go home, but an actor still speaks; so we linger awhile even though Literature has been played out to its end and the hero set wandering offstage without destination. The epilogue speaks of what "I would give *you,*" in the conditional. We are still asking whether to stay and listen, whether the play of Literature has anything more to say to us or to give us, or whether we should just forget it and go home. Impatient to get out of the theater of Literature's representation, we have perhaps let our attention wander too quickly to the end of the epilogue and to its final ambiguous offer, where stress is laid on the "you" of address.

But in the third of its four moments, there is another performance of address:

> Mould my slow mind to this Comprehension—
> Oddest of sciences—Book ever bore—

If we read the tone or mood of address in this syntax, then it sounds like a prayer, a supplication: "Mould my slow mind . . ." The syntax of "mould" as imperative verb, the grammar of address, is also, however, immediately divided between two requests: mould my mind, that is, imprint on my mind a repetition of the modeled voice, speaking in Greek or in some other language, which I hear or rather read on the page if I look closely. But this mould is a homogram of the other, the mould of disintegration, that which moulders in the earth. "Mould my slow mind to this Comprehension," therefore, both "imprint my mind so this comprehension will not be forgotten" and "disintegrate my mind with this comprehension." The first sense implores comprehension, but of what? Of the fact that comprehension is forever placed beyond the reach of my mind by its own finitude, by its slow mouldering and promised disintegration.

That this incomprehensible division falls on the word "mould," which marks the phrase as address, is a detail that cannot be given too much importance. At the precise point where the poem pivots toward its end or decline, the first word of the third stanza, it turns and supplicates a replication, which is immediately duplicated but as disintegration, as the end of the integrity or identity that says "my slow mind." The implored comprehension would seek to comprehend what no "I," even if it used to be a god, can encompass or know but only *address* to another. This is indeed the "Oddest of sciences" for it knows only on the condition of repeating to another that it cannot comprehend. Which is to say that it does not know, but it *teaches,* it addresses speech, language, and "all other Lore" that "Book ever bore" along the dividing line of moulding finitude.

This place of address—book, theater, poem, Literature, teaching, science, lore—is not a place in the ordinary sense; rather it gives place and space to the event of an unexpected appearance just when you thought the play was over. It gives "it": an essentially ambiguous gift, the entwined Yes and No. "It" has no name other than the catachrestic, wandering displacement of the "I" and the subject.

Three years later, in 1865, the displacement will inaugurate a repetition and a transformation:

> Knows how to forget!
> But could It teach it?
> Easiest of Arts, they say
> When one learn how

Between the earlier and the later inscription, the elided, catachrestic "It" has taken over, or perhaps recovered the place of a certain "she": "But could she teach it?" has become "But could It teach it?" A kind of folding in of an elision affects and forms these opening lines, the turning movement of their punctuation. "Knows how to forget!" is a statement without subject, as if the opening line already came after another, were repeating only the predicate in a partial echo of some other's speech, with a change of grammatical person: "I know how to forget" would have become "——— knows how to forget!" Repeated as by an echo or a quotation, this knowledge of forgetfulness that is itself forgotten in the repetition gets displaced onto or into an art of teaching. "Could It teach it?" Easiest of Arts, they say. Nothing to it, just repeat: "It" then "it." At the turning point of this elliptical figure there is repetition, teaching, and a question raised about the possibility of repeating the other in the same. However, *in* the poem, "It" holds the place of what lies uncomprehended outside or before the poem, an unrepeatable, singular, finite other, an incomprehensible, inappropriable It at the limit of acquisition by any science.

> Dull hearts have died
> In the Acquisition
> Sacrifice for Science
> Is common, though, now—

Now—the actor continues after this word. But we stop here, at the point where she begins to repeat the lesson: "I went to School. . . ." We went to the theater of Literature's representation and *now* we're leaving. Our epilogue will have been an allegory of this coming, lingering, but inevitable departure under the sign of the poem's "now," the word that, perhaps more than any other in all our languages, speaks the division of "literature" and the possible future of its address.

N o|t e s

INTRODUCTION: CATACHRESIS AND INSTITUTION

1. Charles Baudelaire, "Notes nouvelles sur Edgar Poe," in Poe, *Nouvelles histoires extraordinaires* (Paris: Garnier-Flammarion, 1965), 42; my translation.

2. See "The Poetic Principle," where Poe inveighs against "a heresy too palpably false to be long tolerated, but one which, in the brief period it has already endured, may be said to have accomplished more in the corruption of our Poetical Literature than all its other enemies combined. I allude to the heresy of *The Didactic*. It has been assumed, tacitly and avowedly, directly and indirectly, that the ultimate object of all Poetry is Truth. Every poem, it is said, should inculcate a moral; and by this moral is the poetical merit of the work to be adjudged. We Americans, especially, have patronised this happy idea; and we Bostonians, very especially, have developed it in full" (Edgar Allan Poe, *Essays and Reviews,* ed. G. R. Thompson [n.p.: The Library of America, 1984], 75). See also "Never Bet the Devil Your Head: A Tale with a Moral" in which Poe mocks the demand that "every fiction *should have* a moral," as well as the tendency of critics to interpret a moral in whatever they read (*The Short Fiction of Edgar Allan Poe,* ed. Stuart and Susan Levine [Indianapolis: Bobbs-Merrill, 1976], 369).

3. Paul de Man, "The Resistance to Theory," in *The Resistance to Theory* (Minneapolis: University of Minnesota Press, 1986), 5.

4. On this episode in de Man's early career and the reactions to its rediscovery, see my "A Violent Dawn at *Le Soir,*" in *Responses: On Paul de Man's Wartime Journalism,*" ed. Werner Hamacher, Neil Hertz, and Thomas Keenan (Nebraska: University of Nebraska Press, 1989), 255–65.

5. Jacques Derrida, "Différance," trans. Alan Bass, in *Margins—of Philosophy* (Chicago: University of Chicago Press, 1982), 11.

6. On the interlocking mechanisms of these decisional institutions as they affect the consolidation of what will count as "serious" American fiction of the last thirty years, see Richard Ohmann's incisive essay: "The Shaping of a Canon: U.S. Fiction, 1960–1975," in *Canons,* ed. Robert von Hallberg (Chicago: University of Chicago Press, 1984). Ohmann demonstrates persuasively how the middle-class concerns and middle-brow

judgments of university professors of English effectively regulate the major organs of book reviewing and publishing.

7. For a succinct review of the narrowing sense of "literature," see Raymond Williams, *Key Words: A Vocabulary of Culture and Society*, rev. ed. (New York: Oxford University Press, 1983), 183–88.

8. Jean-Luc Nancy, *The Inoperative Community*, ed. Peter Connor, trans. Peter Connor et al. (Minneapolis: University of Minnesota Press, 1991), 4. Nancy's analysis draws extensively on Bataille, in particular his notion of sovereignty. I have elsewhere shown a similar "logic of the absolute" to be at work when Rousseau's *Social Contract* breaks off at the point at which it would be necessary to consider the external, foreign relations of the sovereign State; see my *Signature Pieces: On the Institution of Authorship* (Ithaca: Cornell University Press, 1988), 73ff.

9. See, however, the obsolete English verb *agence*, which seems to have had a similar genesis and range.

10. On this relation between force and form in formalist literary criticism, see Jacques Derrida, "Force and Signification," in *Writing and Difference* (Chicago: University of Chicago Press, 1978).

11. "A politico-institutional problem of the University: it, like all teaching in its traditional form, and perhaps all teaching whatever, has as its ideal, along with an exhaustive translatability, the effacement of language. . . . What this institution cannot bear is for anyone to tamper with language, meaning both the national language and, paradoxically, an ideal of translatability that neutralizes this national language. Nationalism and universalism. What this institution cannot bear is a transformation that leaves intact neither of these two complementary poles. It can bear more readily the most apparently revolutionary, ideological sorts of 'content,' if only that content does not touch the borders of language and of all the juridico-political contracts that it guarantees." (J. Derrida, "Living On: Border Lines," trans. James Hulbert, in *Deconstruction and Criticism* [New York: Continuum, 1979], 93–95; trans. modified).

12. To take a well-known case, consider the terms of the debate at a preeminent California university over a core curriculum that had from its inception integrated only works from the Western canon. Despite widely publicized opposition (including that of the secretary of education, William Bennett) to any change in this tradition, the arguments for revision prevailed and a new syllabus was adopted that allowed students to choose to study non-Western works alongside the canonical texts. We can only imagine how that debate and even its outcome might have been different if all the parties to the dispute had not agreed, as they apparently did, that a fundamental transformation—for good or for ill—would be effected within the university's ideological structure by adding or substituting more works *in translation*, that is, in English. There was, in other words, a common accord across the deep division: both the defenders of the canon and the revisionists accepted the principle that a *single* language could also be universal, the lan-

guage of the university. As Derrida pointed out in 1979 (see preceding note) and as this example confirms, the *uni*-versity presumes an ideal of *translatability* and accepts as a principle of knowledge transmission the effacement of language difference, which is to say, of language itself and therefore of the very possibility of differentiation. To argue, on the contrary, that translation is not an ideal but a practical constraint (i.e., for general undergraduate education, one cannot reasonably require students to be able to read in more than one language) merely gives rise to another question: why is such a constraint deemed acceptable, and especially so in the United States? And that question immediately begets another: what kind of "diversity" can we teach to and learn from each other if American English is considered the language into which all others can be translated without a significant loss to the diversity of meaning? The fact that such "impractical" questions can be raised ought not to discourage in the least the necessary efforts to diversify curricula, but neither should they be ignored so that we can better enjoy the comfort of good conscience.

13. Samuel Weber, "Ambivalence: The Humanities and the Study of Literature," in his *Institution and Interpretation* (Minneapolis: University of Minnesota Press, 1987), 148.

14. Two other studies that we will not discuss but that have had an important influence on recent discussions of the Third Critique are Pierre Bourdieu's *Distinction: A Social Critique of the Judgment of Taste*, trans. Richard Nice (Cambridge: Harvard University Press, 1984), and Barbara Herrnstein Smith *Contingencies of Value: Alternative Perspectives for Critical Theory* (Cambridge: Harvard University Press, 1988).

15. It is to this dividing division of the Third Critique, between the work of art and all that is not the work, or between "distinterested," pure aesthetic judgment and impure judgment, that Derrida first pointed in his essay "Parergon" (trans. Geoff Bennington and Ian McLeod, in *The Truth in Painting* [Chicago: University of Chicago Press, 1987]). Geoffrey Bennington has also pursued the figure of the "frontier" in Kant: see "The Frontier: Between Kant and Hegel," in Geoffrey Bennington, *Legislations: The Politics of Deconstruction* (London: Verso, 1994), and "La Frontière infranchissable," in *Passages des frontières: Autour du travail de Jacques Derrida*, ed. Marie-Louise Mallet (Paris: Galilée, 1994).

16. Gerald Graff, *Professing Literature: An Institutional History* (Chicago: University of Chicago Press, 1987), 3.

17. For example, in Gerald Graff, *Beyond the Culture Wars: How Teaching the Conflicts Can Revitalize American Education* (New York: Norton, 1992), "Teach the Conflicts," in *The Politics of Liberal Education*, ed. Darryl J. Gless and Barbara Herrnstein Smith (Durham: Duke University Press, 1992), and the brief note, "Vital Signs," *Village Voice Literary Supplement*, October 1988.

18. The fact that Graff endorses the "argument for . . . a more explicitly historicized and cultural kind of literary study" (258) may indeed

indicate this place quite clearly. Since a certain kind of historical study has been, historically, a party to the disputes that Graff proposes should be studied historically, then "history" or "historicism" can hardly constitute the terrain of a neutral observer.

19. For another kind of journalistic account that pinpoints some of the methods of disinformation in the writings of Roger Kimball, Dinesh D'Souza, Allan Bloom, as well as their avatars in the press, see Michael Bérubé, "Political Correctness and the Media's Big Lie," *Village Voice Literary Supplement,* June 1991.

20. A brief list would include: Tony Bennett, *Outside Literature* (New York: Routledge, 1990); Franklin E. Court, *Institutionalizing English Literature: The Culture and Politics of Literary Study, 1750–1900* (Stanford: Stanford University Press, 1992); Jonathan Culler, *Framing the Sign: Criticism and Its Institutions* (Norman: University of Oklahoma Press, 1988); Antony Easthope, *Literary into Cultural Studies* (New York and London: Routledge, 1991); Gless and Smith, eds., *Politics of Liberal Education;* Bruce Robbins, *Secular Vocations: Intellectuals, Professionalism, Culture* (London and New York: Verso, 1993); William V. Spanos, *The End of Education: Toward Posthumanism* (Minneapolis: University of Minnesota Press, 1993); Evan Watkins, *Work Time: English Departments and the Circulation of Cultural Value* (Stanford: Stanford University Press, 1989). The "genre" was perhaps inaugurated in 1976 by Richard Ohmann's now classic study *English in America: A Radical View of the Profession* (New York: Oxford University Press, 1976). One could cite numerous other works that preceded Graff's and on which he relies to some extent.

21. Curiously, however, Guillory's extensive reliance on Bourdieu omits reference to two of the latter's works that would seem most pertinent in this context: *Homo Academicus* (Paris: Editions de Minuit, 1984) and *Les règles de l'art, Genèse et structure du champ littéraire* (Paris: Editions du Seuil, 1992).

22. For a counterexample of just how empty such sociologism can be, see Michèle Lamont, "How to Become a Dominant French Philosopher: The Case of Jacques Derrida," *American Journal of Sociology* 93, no. 3 (November 1987), 584–622. While Guillory is in general far more attentive to his object than Lamont, who not only makes numerous factual errors but relies extensively on the dogmatic reproduction of a wide set of unexamined concepts, his own procedures and assumptions largely conform to the central tenet of this kind of analysis, which Lamont states as follows: "The legitimation of theories results more from a complex environmental interplay than from the intrinsic qualities of theories themselves. Theories cannot thus be considered in isolation, even if they are experienced through their own logic and in their own cultural realm by their producers and consumers" (614–15). This assertion about legitimation itself presumes the legitimacy of a field of academic inquiry, the sociology of theoretical discourse,

which proceeds by emptying "theories" of their "intrinsic qualities" or their "own logic." The a priori assumption of such inquiry is that this emptying maneuver is possible without significant loss to understanding because it concerns what Lamont calls so blithely "interpretive theories," that is, merely interpretation and not hard science (or even mushier social science).

23. John Guillory, *Cultural Capital: The Problem of Literary Canon Formation* (Chicago: University of Chicago Press, 1993), 45.

24. In a review of *Cultural Capital,* Bruce Robbins specifically disputes Guillory's claims that canon revisionism is a displacement of "real politics." On the contrary, "the ability to get one's own experience reclassified as part of cultural capital—which is one description of what multiculturalism is all about—should also be classified as a genuine if not necessarily momentous redistribution of power" (" 'Real Politics' and the Canon Debate," *Contemporary Literature* 35, no. 2 [1994]: 373).

25. This definition places an extremely reductive frame on Guillory's analysis. "Theory" is first defined to mean "deconstruction," which is in turn defined to mean the thought and writings of Paul de Man. I have commented at length on this reduction in the essay on which I am drawing here: "The Division of Literature," *Diacritics* 25, no. 3 [1995]: 53–72.

26. Although all of Derrida's earliest work in particular insists on the deconstructibility of the opposition to *teknē*, perhaps the most forceful demonstrations in this regard are to be found in "Plato's Pharmacy." There has also been much important work by others that follows in this path and surveys new ones, most recently Bernard Stiegler, *La faute d'Épiméthée* and *La désorientation,* vols. 1 and 2 of *La technique et le temps* (Paris: Galilée, 1994, 1996); David Wills, *Prosthesis* (Stanford: Stanford University Press, 1995); Jean-Luc Nancy, *Les Muses,* trans. Peggy Kamuf (Stanford: Stanford University Press, 1996); and Avital Ronell, *The Telephone Book: Teletechnology—Schizophrenia—Electronic Speech* (Lincoln: University of Nebraska Press, 1989). Stiegler's comprehensive analysis, which cites Blanchot's warning in 1969 that the danger "is not in the unusual development of the forces and domination of technology, but first in the refusal to see this epochal change and to consider the meaning of this turning point," opens as follows: "Philosophy, at the dawn of its history, isolates *teknē* and *epistemē,* which in Homeric times remained indistinct. This gesture is determined by a political context in which the philosopher accuses the Sophist of instrumentalizing *logos,* as rhetoric and logography, a means of power and a non-place of knowledge. It is against the backdrop of this *conflict* in which the philosophical *epistemē* struggles against the sophistic *teknē,* thereby devalorizing all technical knowledge, that the essence of technical beings in general is enunciated" (15; my translation). Likewise, Nancy's study sets out from the tension between two concepts of art: " 'art' never appears except in a tension between two concepts of art, the one technical and the other sublime—and this tension itself remains in general without concept."

27. Samuel Weber, "Introduction," in his *Demarcating the Disciplines: Philosophy, Literature, Art* (Minneapolis: University of Minnesota Press, 1986), x.

28. See Weber's introduction to his *Institution and Interpretation* (ix–xv), where he addresses the question of the institutions of scientific knowledge.

29. In the final analysis, the only concrete justification Guillory can cite for this argument is a single use of the term "subversion" by Paul de Man in an interview: "I think that only what is, in a sense, classically didactic, can be really and effectively subversive" (quoted in Guillory, *Cultural Capital*, 240–41). With this kind of technique, his framing of "deconstruction" (see above, n. 25) shows its most vulnerable and tendentious side. Even if one *could* read de Man's statement as a disavowal of institutionalized practices, which is certainly not indicated, it cannot counterbalance the substantial work on pedagogical institutions, particularly the university, that deconstructive thought has been compiling for decades and to which Guillory makes no allusion. The references here would be numerous, but ought to include at least a massive collection (659 pages) of Derrida's essays on the subject (*Du droit à la philosophie* [Paris: Galilée, 1990]). Likewise, the essays collected in *Logomachia: The Conflict of the Faculties* (Lincoln: University of Nebraska Press, 1992) could serve to debunk the notion that when American literary "deconstructionists" write of the university institution, they are able to think only in terms of some hoped-for but unlikely "subversion." Such a conclusion, however, is also based on tendentious or quite simply mistaken interpretations of texts that Guillory does cite; for example, on p. 242, he imputes to a passage from a text of mine a statement that it never asserts and that is manifestly not its intention. The passage in question is recruited as evidence that the generation of de Man's "disciples" was busy disavowing the "institutionalization" of the master's work, whereas one of the points of my essay, and the passage quoted, was quite nearly the contrary. There are, moreover, two serious errors in the transcription of the brief passage quoted.

30. Tony Bennett, *Outside Literature* (New York and London: Routledge, 1990), 151.

31. Drawing on Howard Caygill's study of the Third Critique in the context of eighteenth-century British moral philosophy (*Art of Judgement* [London: Basil Blackwell, 1989]), John Guillory has argued quite persuasively that Bennett and others regularly overlook the fact that Kant almost never speaks of value in that text. They thus perpetuate a confusion of the economic term with the aesthetic term of "taste," whereas the Kantian aesthetic discourse should be read as attempting to regulate a pervasive market value; for this critique of Bennett specifically, see Guillory, *Cultural Capital*, 274–77.

32. Smith, *Contingencies of Value*, 54–84.

33. With this stress on the fictional structure of the assumption, I am once again drawing on Samuel Weber's incomparably attentive reading

of the Third Critique (in particular, 150–51), but also the whole nexus of *annehmen* that he traces through a dense layering of texts in "The Debts of Deconstruction, and Other, Related Assumptions," in *Institution and Interpretation*.

34. Immanuel Kant, *Critique of Judgment*, trans. J. H. Bernard (New York: Hafner Press, 1951), 15.

35. See, for example, Jean-François Lyotard, "Judicieux dans le différend," in *La faculté de juger* (Paris: Minuit, 1985): "But the value of signs for the critical watchman, once one accepts that it leaves the play of judgment free in respect to them (find the case for the rule and the rule for the case), does indeed presuppose a kind of intention (of finality) on the part of that which signifies. One must admit, and this is what Kant does under the name of nature, a kind of subject, an *as if* subject that would signal at least to the philosopher . . . that a quasi-phrase has taken place, in the form of this or that sign, one whose meaning cannot be validated by the applicable procedures of knowledge. Can one judge on the basis of signs without presupposing, even as a problematic, such an intention? That is to say, without prejudging?" (p. 216; my trans.). The problem of reflective judgment is also close to the center of Lyotard's thinking in *Le différend* (Paris: Minuit, 1983) and *L'enthousiasme: La critique kantienne de l'histoire* (Paris: Galilée, 1986).

36. Bennett here is in part paraphrasing Frank Lentricchia, who in turn is paraphrasing Foucault. The final phrase in quotation is Lentricchia's.

CHAPTER ONE: THE UNIVERSITY FOUNDERS

1. Jacques Derrida, "Mochlos; or, The Conflict of the Faculties," trans. Richard Rand and Amy Wygant, in *Logomachia: The Conflict of the Faculties*, ed. Richard Rand (Lincoln: University of Nebraska Press, 1992), 29.

2. Ibid., 30; trans. modified.

3. William Bennett, "Completing the Reagan Revolution: A Resumption of Responsibilities," *Vital Speeches of the Day* 52, no. 20 (August 1986): 610–13.

4. On some of these points, see Bennett's speech of March 1985 to the National Press Club: "Educators in America," *Vital Speeches of the Day* 51, no. 9 (April 1985) 128–32.

5. As to why this didn't happen, the conservative *National Review* offers two opinions. Lawrence Uzzell blames the entrenched liberal ideology of education "science," which, once it had hold of a major federal bureaucracy, was not about to let go ("Education's Mad Science," Apr. 11, 1986); Chester E. Finn, Jr., the assistant secretary of education for research and improvement, defends the department's right to exist and even argues for the "virtues of centralization." He also notes that, although the liberal establishment created the department, since William Bennett took it over,

some representatives of that same establishment have called for its abolition ("Two Cheers for Education's G-Men," Aug. 15, 1986).

6. Trans. Mary J. Gregor (New York: Abaris Books, 1979), 153.

7. On the significance of this *teilnehmen* in Kant's thinking of humanity and the humanities, see above, Introduction, pp. 32–34.

8. See Jean-François Lyotard, *L'enthousiasme: La critique kantienne de l'histoire* (Paris: Galilée, 1986), 45–77, and *Le Différend* (Paris: Minuit, 1983), 232–46; also Peter D. Fenves, *A Peculiar Fate: Metaphysics and World-History in Kant* (Ithaca: Cornell University Press, 1991), 255ff.

9. This term occurs in the first sentence of the paragraph immediately following the one I will quote and in a manner that suggests that, in the foregoing, Kant has been penetrating disguises. "Another disguise, which is easily penetrated indeed, but is one to which a nation, nevertheless, is legally committed, is that pertaining to the true nature of its constitution." The note to the passage on the British monarchy makes it clear that by disguise or concealment, Kant means the lack of publicity, maintained by censorship, concerning a certain state of affairs.

10. The freedom or autonomy of the philosophy faculty, in contrast to the doctrinal constraint that characterizes the "higher" faculties of theology, medicine, and law, is one of the central arguments of *The Conflict of the Faculties*: "Now the power to judge autonomously—that is, freely (according to principles of thought in general)—is called reason. So the philosophy faculty, because it must answer for the *truth* of the teachings it is to adopt or even allow, must be conceived as free and subject only to laws given by reason, not by the government" (43). On Kant's argument concerning the autonomy of philosophy in the university, see Derrida, "Mochlos," 25ff., as well as Timothy Bahti, *Allegories of History: Literary Historiography after Hegel* (Baltimore: Johns Hopkins University Press, 1992), 20–24.

11. It is at such a point, perhaps, that Nietzsche breaks out laughing at what he called "Kant's Joke": "Kant tried to prove, in a way that dismayed 'everybody,' that 'everybody' was in the right:—that was his secret joke. He wrote against the learned, in favor of popular prejudice; he wrote, however, for the learned and not for the people" (*Joyful Wisdom,* trans. Thomas Common [New York: Frederick Ungar, 1960], aphorism 193], p. 195).

12. Rousseau, *Oeuvres complètes* (Paris: Gallimard, Bibliothèque de la Pléïade, 1969), 4:246.

13. See the "Repères chronologiques" in Bronislaw Baczko's excellent anthology *Une éducation pour la démocratie: Textes et projets de l'époque révolutionnaire* (Paris: Garnier, 1982), 59–62. I have also relied on the richly documented study by Robert J. Vignery, *The French Revolution and the Schools: Educational Policies of the Mountain, 1792–1794* (Madison: State Historical Society of Wisconsin, 1966), which includes the best available bibliography of the subject. For translations of some earlier eighteenth-

century texts as well as of Condorcet's "Rapport," see F. de La Fontainerie's *French Liberalism and Education in the Eighteenth Century* (1932; New York: Burt Franklin Reprint, 1971). For interesting juxtapositions of revolutionary texts on education with those of the Third Republic and of contemporary French commentators, see *La République et l'école, une anthologie*, ed. Charles Coutel (Paris: Presses Pocket, 1991).

14. See Catherine Kintzler, *Condorcet: L'instruction publique et la naissance du citoyen* (Paris: Minerve, 1984) and Michèle Crampe-Casnabet, *Condorcet, lecteur des Lumières* (Paris: Presses Universitaires de France, 1985).

15. By pointing to this distinction, however, I am not endorsing Jean-Claude Milner's assertion that one can simply oppose Condorcet's "activist" knowledge to Kant's spectatorship or to the division of the First from the Second Critique; see Milner's introduction to Kintzler, *Condorcet*, 12.

16. Baczko, *Une education*, 181. All further quotations are from this edition and are my translation.

17. On this point, see Kintzler, *Condorcet*, 239ff.

18. On this distinction, see Baczko's introduction, *Une education*, 30ff.; see also Coutel, *La République, et l'école*, 26ff., who derives the distinction from a critique, by Condorcet and then later by Jules Ferry and Jean Jaurès, of the Spartan principles of education.

19. Vignery is probably correct when he attributes this shift in part to the deposing of the constitutional monarchy (Vignery, *French Revolution and the Schools*, 43).

20. Although Robespierre did not himself draft any of the proposals of the Committee on Public Instruction, he endorsed the proposal of Lepeletier and presented it to the Convention after the death of the latter. This proposal, which went further than any other in the direction of state control, would have assumed complete responsibility for children between the ages of five and twelve.

21. In fact, the "Rapport," in contrast to the "Mémoires," accepts the idea of separate education, at least in primary schools: "In the villages where there will be only one primary school, children of both sexes will be admitted to it, and will receive the same instruction from the same teacher. If a village or a town has two primary schools, one of them will be in the charge of a mistress, and the children of the two sexes will be separated. This is the only arrangement concerning the education of women that we have made in our preliminary work. Their education will be the subject of a special report" (212). This special report was never written.

22. Condorcet, *Oeuvres complètes* (Paris: 1804), 9:80.

23. In his "Rapport" as well, Condorcet warns against fostering a "spirit of emulation which would make professors desire to increase the number of their students" and which "does not proceed from sentiments so exalted that we may permit ourselves to deplore its loss" (202), while on the other hand he proposes measures to encourage a worthy emulation that would make scholars aspire to the highest achievement of science (205, 206, 209).

24. From poem 433 in *The Poems of Emily Dickinson*, ed. Thomas H. Johnson (Cambridge: Harvard University Press, 1955).

CHAPTER TWO: THE RHETORIC OF RUIN

1. Cf. Freud's famous analogy between the apparatus of perception-consciousness and the "mystic writing pad" (*Standard Edition of the Complete Psychological Works of Sigmund Freud*, ed. and trans. James Strachey [London: Hogarth Press, 1959], vol. 19), as well as Derrida's deconstruction of the analogy's distinction between memory and its external supplements in "Freud and the Scene of Writing," in *Writing and Difference*, trans. Alan Bass (Chicago: University of Chicago Press, 1978).

2. Michel de Certeau, Dominique Julia, and Jacques Revel, *Une politique de la langue: La Révolution française et les patois* (Paris: Gallimard, 1975). Along with incomparable analyses, the volume contains both Grégoire's report and a large selection of responses to his survey on the use of patois in the provinces.

3. *Oeuvres de l'abbé Grégoire* (Liechtenstein: KTO Press, 1977), 2, 229; my translation.

4. Grégoire makes this point explicitly on the next page. His plan, he writes, "will present the multiple advantage of facilitating postal service, commercial traffic, the orientation of travelers, the exercise of the police, and the collection of taxes" (160).

5. It is first of all, of course, the prescriptive force of the law that must be preserved without the loss occasioned by translation into dialects that are "absolutely devoid of terms relating to politics . . . . This inevitable poverty of the language that restricts the mind will mutilate your speeches and your decrees, provided that it does not make them untranslatable" (234).

6. The fact that 9 Thermidor (the end of the Terror) had fallen in the interval separating the report on the patois and the one on vandalism shores up this appearance of a reaction to the violence of the Jacobins. For an analysis of Grégoire's rhetoric mobilized against vandalism, see Anthony Vidler, "Grégoire, Lenoir et les monuments parlants," in *La Carmagnole des muses: L'homme de lettres et l'artiste dans la Révolution*, ed. Jean-Claude Bonnet (Paris: Armand Colin, 1988), 131-54.

7. It is, of course, Jacques Derrida who has shown the systematic persistence of this topos; see especially *Of Grammatology*, trans. Gayatri Chakravorty Spivak (Baltimore: Johns Hopkins University Press, 1974), part I, chap. 1, and "Plato's Pharmacy," in *Dissemination*, trans. Barbara Johnson (Chicago: University of Chicago Press, 1981), 171ff.

8. Jean-François La Harpe, "L'espirit de la Révolution," in his *Lycée, ou Cours de littérature ancienne et moderne* (Paris: Deterville, 1818), 14:444-45; all translations from La Harpe's essays are my own.

9. On the conditions of this appointment, see Michel Collot,

"L'Ecole normale de l'an III," in *Ecole Normale Supérieure* (Paris: Presses Universitaires de France, 1994), 14ff.

10. Jean-Marie Goulemot has retraced the particular influence La Harpe's *Cours* exerted on the formation of certain commonplaces about the *philosophes* in the history of ideas; see his "Le *Cours de littérature* de La Harpe, ou l'émergence du discours de l'histoire des idées," *Littérature* 24 (December 1976), 51–62.

11. For example, "this period that everlasting justice will entitle *the reign of the monsters*," "De la Guerre déclarée par les Tyrans révolutionnaires à la Raison, à la Morale, aux Lettres et aux Arts [On the war declared by the revolutionary tyrants on reason, morality, letters, and the arts]" in *Lycée* (Paris: Agasse, An VII), 8:12. La Harpe frequently uses italics, as here, to imply a distance from the words he is using, consistent with his maxim: "There are men whom one cannot mention without sullying one's speech" (8).

12. The next paragraph begins "Let us speak without figures," as if La Harpe had himself forgotten that he was already supposed to be speaking "without figures."

13. Jean Paulhan, *Les fleurs de Tarbes, ou la terreur dans les lettres* (Paris: Gallimard, 1941), 41; emphasis added; my translation.

CHAPTER THREE: THE WALLS OF SCIENCE

1. Quoted by James C. Axtell in his introduction to *The Educational Writings of John Locke* (Cambridge: Cambridge University Press, 1968), 73.

2. A certain utilitarianism would of course later serve as an argument for literary education in England and then America. See Franklin Court, *Institutionalizing English Literature: The Culture and Politics of Literary Study, 1750–1900* (Stanford: Stanford University Press, 1992), chap. 2.

3. Morelly, *Essai sur le coeur humain, ou principes naturels de l'Education* (Paris, 1745), 224.

4. On Hegel's digestive "metaphors," see Timothy Bahti, *Allegories of History: Literary Historiography after Hegel* (Baltimore: Johns Hopkins University Press, 1992), 80–133, where he observes that "digestion is for Hegel the assimilation and appropriation of an outer into an inner, and as such a figure for dialectic in general" (110).

5. Hegel, *Werke* (Frankfurt: Suhrkamp, 1970), 4:316; my translation.

6. Jacques Derrida, *Glas,* trans. John P. Leavey, Jr., and Richard Rand (Lincoln: Nebraska University Press, 1986), 9.

7. See as well the preceding paragraph in the same address that explains, in different terms, the incorporation of religious instruction into the school's curriculum. This was also done in compliance with "the most gracious orders" [*allergnädigste Befehle*] of state authorities (329). For a discussion of *Bildung* throughout Hegel's thought, see John H. Smith, *The Spirit*

and Its Letter: Traces of Rhetoric in Hegel's Philosophy of "Bildung" (Ithaca: Cornell University Press, 1988).

8. Although not focused on the university institution as such, David Simpson's *Romanticism, Nationalism, and the Revolt against Theory* (Chicago: University of Chicago Press, 1993) provides pertinent frames for the comparaison of British, French, and German national literary institutions at the beginning of the nineteenth century.

9. For a précis of Taine's influence, especially on his student Saussure, see Donald Preziosi, *Rethinking Art History: Meditations on a Coy Science* (New Haven: Yale University Press, 1989), 88–90; see also Hans Aarsleff, *From Locke to Saussure* (Minneapolis: University of Minnesota Press, 1982).

10. On the history of the discipline of history in the French university and, especially, its relation to literary history, see Antoine Compagnon, *La Troisième République des Lettres, de Flaubert à Proust* (Paris: Editions du Seuil, 1983), part I. Although Gerald Graff's *Professing Literature* (see above, introduction, pp. 16–20) covers the same period in less detail and without comparable attention to the relations among the nascent disciplines, it makes clear that literary study in the United States was subject to a similar requirement to "be scientific."

11. Hippolyte Taine, *Philosophie de l'art* (Paris: Fayard, 1985), 18; my translation.

12. For example, Taine writes: "In short, in the literary work as in the pictorial work, it is a matter of transcribing, not the sensible exterior of beings and events, but the set of their relations and their dependencies, that is to say, their logic. Thus, as a general rule, what interests us in a real being, and what we ask the artist to extract and to render, is its internal or external logic, in other terms, its structure, its composition and its organization" (29). For Diderot's notion of *rapports,* see especially his "Recherches philosophiques sur l'origine et la nature du beau" in *Oeuvres esthétiques* (Paris: Garnier, 1988).

13. In a long note to "The Double Session," Derrida outlines the "extremely complex system of Plato's concept of *mimesis,*" and concludes that it forms a "kind of logical machine [that] programs the prototypes of all the propositions inscribed in Plato's discourse as well as those of the whole tradition. According to a complex but implacable law, this machine deals out all the clichés of criticism to come" (in *Dissemination,* trans. Barbara Johnson [Chicago: University of Chicago Press, 1981], 186–87, n. 14). On some later avatars of this "machine," see Philippe Lacoue-Labarthe, *The Subject of Philosophy,* trans. Thomas Trezise et al. (Minneapolis: University of Minnesota Press, 1993), and *Typography: Mimesis, Philosophy, Politics* (Cambridge: Harvard University Press, 1989).

14. A way to avoid this unwelcome thought would be to replace the fourth term "science" by a Creator, either Nature or God. But it is precisely such transcendence that is no longer available to the scientific histo-

rian for whom human history must carry its own meaning, immanently. This problem is one that Charles Péguy (see chapter 5) repeatedly charged his contemporary historians and sociologists with neglecting.

15. The opening move of Heidegger's *The Origin of the Work of Art,* which replaces the question "What is art?" within the circle of the production of such questions that seek knowledge of some thing, can be understood as itself coming out of the bind of Taine's positivistic analogy.

16. Compagnon, *La Troisième République des Lettres,* 59; my translation.

17. Quoted in Compagnon, *La Troisième République des Lettres,* 57-58; emphasis added.

18. First published in the *Revue du Mois,* 10 Oct. 1910, "La Méthode de l'histoire littéraire" is the opening essay in the collection of Lanson's writings edited by Henri Peyre, *Essais de méthode, de critique et d'histoire littéraire* (Paris: Hachette, 1965). Our quotations are from the latter edition.

19. In fact, in 1912 Lanson began to write a weekly literary column for the newspaper *Le Matin.* Charles Péguy, one of Lanson's and the "method"'s most acerbic critics, analyzes at length this "event" of the "great professor of literature" at the Sorbonne who accepts to become a "petty journalist." In chapter 5, we will consider in detail Péguy's assessments of the relations between the university and a certain kind of journalism.

20. A study should be made of the coincidence between the delegitimation of nonscientific criticism under the name "impressionism" and the appropriation of that label by both painters and writers at about the same period. An indispensable reference for such a study would be Michael Fried's work on literary impressionism in Crane, Conrad, Norris, and, soon, others. See his *Realism, Writing, Disfiguration: On Thomas Eakins and Stephen Crane* (Chicago: University of Chicago Press, 1987) and "Almayer's Face: On 'Impressionism' in Conrad, Crane, and Norris," *Critical Inquiry* 17 (Autumn 1990), 193-236.

21. It would seem that Lanson's contemporaries did not fail to pick up on this problem. Compagnon refers to an article by Emile Faguet the following year and its assessment that "Lanson's earlier position, which distinguishes strictly *knowing* from *feeling,* was more coherent" (Compagnon, *La Troisième République des Lettres,* 347, n. 18). More coherent, perhaps, but with a coherence that merely preserves logical categories.

22. Aristotle *Poetics* (New York: Hill and Wang, 1961), 9:68.

23. Timothy Bahti has examined closely what is probably the most crucial chapter in the history of this displacement by history, that of German idealism before and after Hegel; see his *Allegories of History,* especially chaps. 1-4.

24. See Graff, *Professing Literature,* as well as his essay "The University and the Prevention of Culture," in *Criticism in the University,* ed.

Gerald Graff and Reginald Gibbons (Evanston, Ill.: Northwestern University Press, 1985); see also Jonathan Culler, "Literary Criticism and the American University," in *Framing the Sign: Criticism and Its Institutions* (Norman: University of Oklahoma Press, 1988).

CHAPTER FOUR: PÉGUY AND THE EVENT OF HISTORY

1. With this figure of appeal, we are recalling Walter Benjamin's description of the original text as one that calls for translation and thus depends on translation for its very survival as original, in that mode which Derrida has called "sur-vivre" or living on; see Benjamin, "The Task of the Translator," trans. Harry Zohn, in *Illuminations,* ed. Hannah Arendt (New York: Schocken Books, 1969), and Derrida, "Des Tours de Babel," trans. Joseph F. Graham, in *Difference in Translation,* ed. Joseph F. Graham (Ithaca: Cornell University Press, 1985).

2. In 1904 the faculty of the Ecole Normale was integrated into or "attached" to that of the Sorbonne.

3. The important exception to Péguy's institutional independence was his fidelity to the army. He enlisted in 1892, when he was 19, and for the rest of his life would spend several weeks a year in training exercises. When he was mobilized in August 1914, he had attained the rank of lieutenant.

4. For example, Péguy would describe himself as outside the "boîte," literally the "box" or the enterprise, which was the education system: "When we say to our friends on the other side of the school door that one has to have suffered in the street and have been buffeted by the distress of the street to know what it is to be miserable and what it is to be honest, because inside the box, within the company, one has never been tempted so to speak" (2:693). Likewise, he will insist that the *Cahiers* is "the only enterprise . . . that has ever been founded to struggle against the power of money in the publishing world" (2:685).

5. Charles Péguy, *Oeuvres en prose complètes,* ed. Robert Burac (Paris: Gallimard, Bibliothèque de la Pléiade, 1987–92), 1:831–32; my translation. All references to Péguy's work will be to this three-volume edition.

6. The text that announced Péguy's vigorous dissent and denounced the "perfectly unbearable pacifist hypocrisy" (2:43) was "Notre patrie," published Oct. 22, 1905, in the *Cahiers.* The title signaled a response to the position taken by the Socialist intellectual Gustave Hervé in his essay "Leur patrie," published in May of the same year. Hervé, in calling for a general strike if a mobilization was ordered, had written: "we recognize only one war, civil war, social war, class war." It should be noted, however, that Georges Sorel, whom Walter Benjamin credits with having first theorized the proletarian general strike in his *Réflexions sur la violence* (1909), was a frequent contributor to the *Cahiers* and one of Péguy's closest allies until 1913, when they had a falling out. See Benjamin, "Critique of Violence" in *Reflections,* trans. Edmund Jephcott (New York: Schocken Books, 1978), 291ff.

7. One may thus subscribe in principle to the dominant concern of David Carroll's reading of Péguy, in his *French Literary Fascism: Nationalism, Anti-Semitism, and the Ideology of Culture* (Princeton: Princeton University Press, 1995), 42–70. Carroll places Péguy resolutely in the position of what he calls a "father of French literary fascism," even though he acknowledges "the problem of the cultural and political implications of his work is quite complex" (46) and the fact that Péguy's "fascist" legacy is not an uncontested one. Nevertheless, inasmuch as Carroll relies almost exclusively on several thematic "implications" to decide that finally Péguy indeed deserves the title of progenitor of literary fascism, our reading here departs from his in significant ways. Without avoiding these themes or their frequently sinister resonance, the questions we take up here concern more the historical conditions of our own reading of these texts.

8. See, for example, Marcel Péguy's *Destin de Charles Péguy* (Paris: Librairie Académique Perrin, 1946), which is bathed in anti-Semitism and labors to explain away Péguy's Dreyfusism. Its initial publication date of 1941, under the strict censorship of the Nazi occupation, in itself makes clear the intent to harness Péguy's legacy to the cause of the occupiers. Robert Burac, the editor of the new Pléiade edition of Péguy's works in prose, writes in his recent biography about the "history of the posthumous destiny of Péguy": "By occulting whole sections of his work, by truncating it for partisan purposes, by mixing up its chronology through publications out of order, there were those who succeeded in making it say the opposite of what it meant to say. A false image, which has gotten engraved in public opinion, has been the result, and still today it discourages many potential readers. Consequently one of the greatest writers in our literary tradition is today widely unrecognized" (*Charles Péguy: La révolution et la grâce* [Paris: Robert Laffont, 1994], 314). Despite Burac's overconfident identification here of what these texts "meant to say" and thus of their false image, there is little doubt that Péguy's literary legacy has been manipulated by many forces, including the selective re-editing of his work. Burac's meticulous edition of the prose writings, however, does not entirely reform this habit: by separating out the prose texts from Péguy's considerable poetic works on Jeanne d'Arc, Chartres, and the Christian mysteries, this new edition works to dispel the image of Péguy as primarily a Catholic writer, one whose books were and still are routinely reprinted in editions appropriate as gifts for first communion.

9. Curiously, however, Péguy uses this same expression to explain and defend his recourse to the vegetal figure of the tree for humanity. Immediately after the paragraph just quoted, which ends with the words "perpetually arborescent humanity," Péguy goes on to protest vigorously and humorously that he is not "perpetrating literary comparisons" with this figure. Instead, he writes, "it is like an indication; but this indication is capital. I am simply retaining a sense, an indication of a sketch, an indication of a rhythm, a launching, an inclination, a getting under way of a certain

rhythm, a setting of the tone, like a hand gesture, perhaps a little less than a direction, at least as much as a direction for takeoff, a way of going about things, a flick of the wrist, a *coup de pouce,* a stroke of the modeler's or sculptor's thumb, etc." (2:943–44).

10. In the same passage, it is said to be "séant," that is, fitting or seemly, to cover over the "totally unwashed" event. Péguy's language and tone thus sounds a note of class difference in this description, one that is rarely absent from his evocations of the bourgeois "parti intellectuel." Silhouetted by this critique is Péguy's own refusal to be totally assimilated or "débarbouillé" by the class that educated him.

11. Maurice Reclus, in his volume of recollections of Péguy, recounts the following incident. As they were descending together a staircase where some painters had been working, Reclus on a whim picked up a paint can and began to carry it down the stairs. When Péguy saw what he was doing, he ordered him sharply to put it back where it belonged, saying "One must always treat with respect objects that are used for work" *Le Péguy que j'ai connu* (Paris: Hachette, 1951), 81–82.

12. Péguy refers to the manner in which *Le Matin* "announced to us rather pompously that it was about to associate M. Lanson to its staff" (3:869) in its issue of June 30, 1912. This announcement read: "From now on it is M. Gustave Lanson, professor of French literature at the University of Paris, who will bring to the pages of *Le Matin* his studies of major recently published books and, in this regard, will inform our readers of the diverse tendencies and currents of contemporary literature. Everyone knows the good taste and the knowledge [*science*] that M. Gustave Lanson brings to his examination of the works of the past in his eloquent courses at the Sorbonne as well as the authority that he has acquired by his teaching, in France but also abroad. He has earned no less authority from his justly well-regarded books. Whether in writing or in speaking, his criticism is always free, original, rich in novel and vast insights . . ." (3:1700–1701). Although Péguy comments no further on the pomposity of this announcement, he is clearly correct when he points to the newspaper's attempts to borrow the legitimacy conferred by Lanson's "scientific" credentials.

13. Péguy's retrospective attacks on his education in Lansonian "method" are invariably cited by historians of this period of French letters. Compagnon, for example, makes extensive use of them in his own critique of "Lansonism," while a recent bicentennial volume on the Ecole Normale, which devotes an essay to literary history and criticism at the institution, sets Péguy's characterizations up as an "ungrateful" settling of accounts with Lanson, who is described as one of the Ecole's most faithful servants; see Michel Collot, "L'histoire et la critique littéraires," in *L'Ecole Normale Supérieure* (Paris: Presses Universitaires de France, 1994), 247.

14. On Brunetière's "scientific" affiliations, see Antoine Compagnon, *La Troisième République des Lettres, de Flaubert à Proust* (Paris: Seuil, 1983), 36–38.

15. On event and repetition, see Jacques Derrida, "Psyche: Inventions of the Other," in *Reading de Man Reading,* ed. Lindsay Waters and Wlad Godzich (Minneapolis: University of Minnesota Press, 1989).

16. Alain Finkielkraut, in his *Le Mécontemporain: Peguy, lecteur du monde moderne* (Paris: Gallimard, 1991), attempts to reconcile this consequence of the proposition on the resonance of voices with what he adumbrates as Péguy's "pluriculturalism": "From the point of view of the rational mastery of the world, humanity is a unitary process and speaks in the singular. From the point of view of culture or meaning, humanity is a conversation and its law is plurality. . . . Péguy conceives humanity on the basis of culture. . . . And that is equally why he conceives, from the outset, universal emancipation in the musical mode as the opening to everyone of the concert of voices" (150–51). This is but one of the innumerable instances in which Finkielkraut's effort to redeem and reclaim Péguy as a "reader of the modern (but especially postmodern) world" betrays its tendentiousness and its refusal to risk reading beyond a superficial thematic level. It is symptomatic of this refusal that Finkielkraut follows Péguy in never acknowledging that the "resonance of voices"—whether singular or plural—is conditioned by the possibility of writing, as we point out below.

17. Lévy had been librarian at the Sorbonne since 1901 and the "bibliographical supplier" to the *Cahiers;* see Burac's "Répertoire des personnalités" in the Pléïade edition (1:1901).

18. That is, Eddy Marix, also a Jew and a Dreyfusard, a longtime friend of Péguy's and his legal adviser; see 1:1903.

19. Burac, *Charles Péguy,* 311.

CHAPTER FIVE: THE UNIVERSITY IN DECONSTRUCTION

1. Kant, "An Answer to the Question: 'What Is Enlightenment?'" in *Kant's Political Writings,* ed. Hans Reiss (Cambridge: Cambridge University Press, 1970), 55.

2. That the use of reason is never unrestricted or uncensored according to Kant has been argued in detail by Jacques Derrida in "Languages and Institutions of Philosophy," *Recherches Sémiologiques/Semiological Inquiry* 4, no. 2 (1984): 128ff.

3. This Kantian analysis of publicity is implied in Jürgen Habermas's notion of the "public sphere"; see, for example, Habermas, "The Public Sphere," in *Communication and Class Struggle: Capitalism, Imperialism,* ed. A. Mattelart and S. Siegelaub (New York: International General, 1979).

4. See Derrida, "The Principle of Reason: The University in the Eyes of Its Pupils," trans. Catherine Porter and Edward P. Morris, *Diacritics* 13, no. 3 (1983): "As far as I know, nobody has ever founded a university *against* reason. So we may reasonably suppose that the University's reason for being has always been reason itself, and some essential connection of reason to being" (7). In the preceding lines, Derrida refers to the *Conflict of the Faculties,* where Kant wrote that the University "should be governed by

'an idea of reason,' the idea of the whole field of what is presently teachable"
(6).

5. Richard Rand, ed., *Logomachia: The Conflict of the Faculties* (Lincoln: University of Nebraska Press, 1992), 161.

6. Ted Gordon and Wahneema Lubiano, "Statement of the Black Faculty Caucus," in *Debating P.C.: The Controversy over Political Correctness on College Campuses*, ed. Paul Berman (New York: Dell, 1992), 257. The "Statement" originally appeared in a different form in the *Daily Texan*, May 3, 1990.

7. Berman, *Debating P.C.*, 261. The editorial was first published in *Newsweek*, Sept. 16, 1990.

8. *New York Review of Books*, Sept. 26, 1991, 74.

9. The figure of "importation" from France runs throughout Paul Berman's introductory essay to his collection, and this foreign influence is made responsible for all the excesses of PCism. The latter, Berman implies, would have been avoided if the American left liberal tradition had not encountered French "cynicism": "Political correctness in the 1990s . . . is the fog that arises from American liberalism's encounter with the iceberg of French cynicism" (*Debating P.C.*, 24).

10. See in particular Bruce Robbins, "The Insistence of the Public in Postmodern Criticism," in his *Secular Vocations: Intellectuals, Professionalism, Culture* (London and New York: Verso, 1993).

11. Robbins remarks in his review of John Guillory's *Cultural Capital* that the author "tries to resituate criticism in relation to its public responsibilities." But, he adds, "This does not mean he addresses the public in whose name he speaks. As if in silent rebuke to those who are vain or silly enough to pretend they have the ear of the general public or common reader, Guillory's rich, strenuous, ferociously intelligent style makes no pretense of user-friendliness" (" 'Real Politics' and the Canon Debate," *Contemporary Literature* 35, no. 2 [1994]: 370). While Robbins would be vain or silly if he included himself in this rebuke, the fact that he hears it at all suggests that he has some difficulty with Guillory's "unfriendly" form of address.

12. One measure of the contrast between Robbins's and Bérubé's projects would be the different kinds of publications in which essays from each collection first appeared. Whereas Robbins's previously published essays all appeared in academic journals or in university press books, two of Bérubé's essays were written for the *Village Voice Literary Supplement* and a third appeared in a collection titled significantly *Wild Orchids and Trotsky: Messages from American Universities* and published by Viking Penguin. Given the question we're examining, this difference is not negligible nor is it negated by the fact that Robbins's and Bérubé's books would both be published, a year apart, by Verso.

13. In his introduction, Robbins does analyze at some length essays in mass circulation publications like the *New York Times Magazine*. These analyses are very cogent and persuasive, but their main concern is

with the symptomatic inconsistencies of the arguments being made there (or in the *New York Review of Books*). While a relation may well be implied or understood between these arguments and the conditions in which such magazines publish, that point is not stressed nor analyzed for itself.

14. Michael Bérubé, *Public Access: Literary Theory and American Cultural Politics* (New York and London: Verso, 1994).

15. Derrida has frequently referred to Benjamin's "proposition" and could even be read as having made it a watchword to some extent of his own writing practice: see "+R (Into the Bargain)" (in *The Truth in Painting*, trans. Geoff Bennington and Ian McLeod [Chicago: University of Chicago Press, 1987]), which begins by citing the Benjamin proposition, and "Ja or the *faux-bond*" (in *Points . . . Interviews: 1974–1994*, trans. Peggy Kamuf [Stanford: Stanford University Press, 1995), 56–65), where it is discussed at length. See also Tony Bennett (*Outside Literature* [New York and London: Routledge, 1990], 189), who cites Benjamin's proposition as the measure of a certain failure of recent Marxist criticism of the institution, particularly that of Terry Eagleton.

16. Walter Benjamin, ed., *Reflections*, trans. Edmund Jephcott (New York: Schocken Books, 1978), 228–29; the German text is found in Benjamin, *Versuche über Brecht* (Frankfurt am Main: Suhrkamp, 1978), 109.

17. Peter Demetz, "Introduction," *Reflections*, ed. Benjamin, xxxiv–xxxv.

18. Craig Karpel, "Vos concepts nébuleux ont conquis l'Amérique," *Actuel*, June 1991, 66–68.

19. Indeed, if the tactic can be described as charging an adversary with an empty use of language, with sheer repetition and so forth, then the history of its repetitions would have to go back at least to Plato's accusations against the Sophists. In the age of modern journalism and political parties, the tactic has flourished. In 1843, Balzac discovered all sorts of uses for it in his "Monograph on the Parisian Press," notably when he describes that species of essayist he calls the "Rienologue" ("Nothingologist"): "[He] spouts mechanically this frightful philosophico-literary mixture for endless pages. The page looks full, it appears to contain ideas; but, when an educated man sticks his nose into it, he smells the odor of empty cellars. It's deep, but there is nothing: Intelligence is snuffed out like a candle in an airless vault" (Honoré de Balzac, *Les Journalistes* [Paris: Arléa, 1991], 60). On Jean Paulhan's *Les Fleurs de Tarbes* (first published 1941), which remains one of the most probing analyses of the political and rhetorical uses of the tactic, see above, chapter 2, 71–74.

20. "La déconstruction rend compte des contradictions constitutives qui préexistent à la construction d'archisynthèses, ou infrastructures comme nous les appellerons plus loin. Les infrastructures représentent les lois de la distribution et de la disponibilité, des noyaux de concepts économiquement minimaux, des prolégomènes, des possibilités de contradictions, des niveaux de débat qui sont aussi des moments hétérogènes du discours. Le

nombre incommensurable de possibilités matérielles qui participent à ces synthèses et l'arrangement structurel qui y préside les rendent non unitaires, etc. . . ."

21. Mitchell Stephens, a professor of journalism, has questioned this kind of incoherence in his essay "Deconstruction and the Get-Real Press" (*Columbia Journalism Review*, September–October 1991). He cites there a number of journalist colleagues who have also criticized the American press for dealing so poorly with "ideas." Our hypothetical example is not intended to imply that no such critique has been offered by journalists and even in the newspapers themselves. But the point of Stephens's article is that this critical reflection is largely the exception in what he calls the "get-real press."

22. My own long letter on this incident to the group's founders did not receive a reply to the questions I raised.

23. The text of the manifesto places itself explicitly under Michael Bérubé's injunction to correct this inadequacy. There is no other attributed quotation in the text except the following, which, interestingly, returns the charge of writing "anything at all" about literary theory: "As Michael Bérubé has pointed out 'recent literary theory is so rarely accorded the privilege of representing itself in nonacademic forums that journalists, disgruntled professors, ex-graduate students, and their families and friends feel entitled to say *anything at all* about the academy without fear of contradiction by general readers'" (emphasis added).

24. Perhaps, however, what has shown up here is an instance of the "Sheldon Hackney" tactic to win public approval; Michael Bérubé, to his great credit, is one of the few literary academics who has denounced publicly the NEH chairman's rather shameful performance during his Senate confirmation hearings in 1992; see Bérubé, *Public Access*, 11.

PROLOGUE: THE IMPASSE OF LITERARY HISTORY

1. Timothy Bahti, *Allegories of History:* Literary Historiography after Hegel (Baltimore: Johns Hopkins University Press, 1992), 291.

MELVILLE'S CREDIT CARD

1. *The Confidence-Man: His Masquerade,* vol. 10 of *The Writings of Herman Melville,* eds. Harrison Hayford, Hershel Parker, G. Thomas Tanselle (Evanston and Chicago: Northwestern University Press and Newberry Library, 1984), 255; emphasis added.

2. The voluminous "Editorial Appendix" of the Northwestern-Newberry volume, which is several pages longer than the 251-page text of the novel it follows, is introduced by a note that carefully distributes editorial responsibility: "The first of the three parts of this *Appendix* is a note on the composition, publication, reception, and later critical history of *The Confidence-Man,* contributed by Watson Branch, Hershel Parker, and Harrison Hayford (who successively took primary responsibility) with the assistance of Alma A. MacDougall." But these four contributors also received as-

sistance from many other scholars, who are duly acknowledged, and their work was supervised by the series' general editors. In all, some twenty persons are named as sharing in the critical consensus that produced the volume.

3. A few minimal references here would include, in chronological order, Philip Drew, "Appearance and Reality in *The Confidence-Man*," *English Literary History* 31 (December 1964); Warwick Wadlington, *The Confidence Game in American Literature* (Princeton: Princeton University Press, 1975), 142–67; Henry Sussman, "The Deconstructor as Politician: Melville's *Confidence-Man*," *Glyph* 4 (1978); John G. Blair, *The Confidence Man in Modern Fiction* (New York: Barnes & Noble, 1979); Gary Lindberg, *The Confidence Man in American Literature* (Oxford: Oxford University Press, 1982), 20ff.; Michel Imbert, "Cash, Cant, and Confidence: Of Paper-money and Scriptures in *The Confidence-Man*," in *L'Imaginaire-Melville: A French Point of View*, ed. Viola Sachs (Paris: Presses Universitaires de Vincennes, 1992).

4. To give just one example of this effect, which has the merit of its ingenuousness, John W. Schroeder, in his "Sources and Symbols for the *The Confidence-Man*," after acknowledging that he has left some puzzles unsolved, writes: "Criticism, in these cases, must be content to explain as much as it possibly can and then *rest in the faith* that it will in time arrive at a level of interpretation which will resolve these questions" (quoted in *The Confidence-Man*, ed. Hershel Parker [New York: Norton, 1971], 315; emphasis added).

5. Derrida, *Given Time: I, Counterfeit Money*, trans. Peggy Kamuf (Chicago: University of Chicago Press, 1991), 28.

6. For a study of nineteenth-century American literature in the "context" of contemporary discourses on monetary and other kinds of value, see Louis Horowitz, *The Law of Nature* (Berkeley and Los Angeles: University of California Press, 1990). Even though he does not claim the label for himself, Jean-Joseph Goux's *The Coiners of Language* (trans. Jennifer Curtiss Gage [Norman: University of Oklahoma Press, 1994]) could be included within the principles of the "school" of American literary studies that has accepted to call itself "New Historicism." Goux isolates a certain sequence from the history of monetary forms and from literary history in order to see there two parallel developments: on the one hand, the abandonment of the gold standard throughout the West after the First World War and, on the other hand, the destabilization of reference in literary modernism (of which Gide's *Les faux-monnayeurs* would be the emblematic work). As Derrida has pointed out in *Given Time* (110, n. 1), this periodization tends "to naturalize and de-fictionalize gold-money, that is, to confirm an old and stable convention." To this one could add that Goux's periodization and historicizing also overlooks the differences between Old World and New World monetary conventions, the fact that paper money in various forms achieved wider acceptance earlier in the United States as compared, for example, with nineteenth-century and early-twentieth-century France, to which Goux limits his study. The problem, however, is not so much that

Goux's hypothesis would have to be recast to fit an American context, but that such recasting would also make apparent the tendency of literary convention to overturn the very sort of historical conjunction Goux seeks to establish.

7. The banker, it goes without saying and unlike the literary theorist, ought not to confuse the ledgers of credit and debt—at least not if she wants to keep her job for long. A bank that does not see the difference between owing and being owed, between those who owe and those who are owed is not fit to stay in business. Perhaps the savings and loan debacle of the 1980s is a massive illustration of precisely this axiom. What happened there, in effect, was a perversion whereby the richest parties were those who owed the most to the savings and loans and the poorest those who were the institutions' creditors, that is, their depositors.

8. See Cheryl Payer, *Lent and Lost: Foreign Credit and Third World Development* (London: Zed Books, 1991). Payer (whose name seems to herald the problem she treats) delivered in 1974, the year in which the crisis finally declared itself in an indisputable way, her first scathing critique of the trap laid for the Third World by Western credits; see *The Debt Trap: The IMF and the Third World* (New York: Penguin).

9. See Payer, *Lent and Lost,* in particular 16ff. The author explicitly evokes the swindles of a certain Charles Ponzi. In 1919 the latter persuaded an impressive number of investors to loan him sums of money that he promised to double on the market of International Postal coupons. He thus invented the kind of swindle that since bears his name: the "Ponzi scheme." It was quite simply a matter of reimbursing with a large profit the first creditors by means of the funds received from later investors who, as for them, never saw their money again. This con game, which is also called a pyramid, closely resembles, according to Payer, the series of loans, reimbursements, new loans, and finally crises of gigantic debt that, for the last forty years, has characterized the "development" of the Third World by Western capital. She writes in this regard that "the successive waves of these sources of credit have followed one another over the decades since the end of the Second World War in the grandest Ponzi scheme of all" (16).

10. For more details concerning the appropriations of this term by Melville's contemporaries, see *The Confidence-Man: His Masquerade,* ed. Hayford et al., 283–84.

11. Derrida, *Glas,* 219.

12. The editorial adviser for *Putnam's,* George Curtis, wrote after reading the story: "Melville's story is very good. It is a great pity he did not work it up as a connected tale instead of putting in the dreary documents at the end.—They should have made part of the substance of the story. It is a little spun out" (*The Piazza Tales and Other Prose Pieces, 1839-60,* ed. Harrison Hayford et al. [Evanston and Chicago: Northwestern University Press and Newberry Library, 1987], 581).

13. For a summary of this divided critical history, see Joshua

Leslie and Sterling Stuckey, "The Death of Benito Cereno: A Reading of Herman Melville on Slavery," *The Journal of Negro History* 67, no. 4 (1982): 300, n. 16.

14. Thus, the free indirect discourse floats the "black-letter" sentence between the two positions of character and narrator, as contrasted with the preceding sentence that identifies Delano's "thought": "Captain Delano thought he might extremely regret it, did he allow Don Benito to become aware that he had indulged in ungenerous surmises. In short, to the Spaniard's black-letter text, it was best, for awhile, to leave open margin."

15. After the failure of *Pierre* in 1852, Melville was in effect squeezed by his publishers, who refused the same terms of advance and royalties for the next novel. *Benito Cereno* and the other *Piazza Tales* were written for magazines at $5.00 a page.

16. For example: "Meantime, *as if* fearful that the continuance of the scene might too much unstring his master, the servant seemed anxious to terminate it. And so, still presenting himself *as a* crutch, and walking between the two captains, he advanced with them towards the gangway; while still, *as if* full of kindly contrition, Don Benito would not let go the hand of Captain Delano, but retained it in his, across the black's body" (97; emphasis added).

17. Concerning another Melville text, Tom Cohen has written: "Melville's 'Bartleby' . . . seems to ask how a text can pose as an event, a historical occurrence that alters or modifies signifying chains that pass through it. It does this not by choosing a rhetoric of action or representation, however, but by narrating and performing the dispossession of an entire mode of (re)production in which, technically, the reader is him or herself located as well" (*Anti-Mimesis: From Plato to Hitchcock* [Cambridge: Cambridge University Press, 1994], 152). Although Cohen would likely place *Benito Cereno* among those texts employing a "rhetoric of action or representation," the "dispossession" he points to is likewise at stake there in what we are calling the wager of its narrative performance.

18. With reference to *Billy Budd*, Barbara Johnson has already argued forcefully that "Melville seems to be presenting us less with an *object* for judgment than with an *example* of judgment. And the very vehemence with which the critics tend to praise or condemn the justice of Vere's decision indicates that it is judging, not murdering, that Melville is asking us to judge" ("Melville's Fist: The Execution of *Billy Budd*," in *Herman Melville: A Collection of Critical Essays,* ed. Myra Jehlen [Englewood Cliffs, N.J.: Prentice-Hall, 1994], 242). If anything, the scene of trial and judgment in *Benito Cereno* foregrounds even more spectacularly the way in which, as Johnson writes, "the law, in attempting to eliminate its own 'deadly space,' can only inscribe itself in a space of deadliness" (245). Johnson's essay, first published in 1979, is in many other respects congruent with the reading of *Benito Cereno* outlined here.

19. Among the several interesting divergences between the his-

torical Delano's original account, in his *Voyages and Travels,* and Melville's rewriting is the matter of payment promised to the American and his crew by the rescued Spanish captain if they are successful in retrieving his ship. The offer made of half the ship's worth, or about $50,000, is clearly an incentive to give chase. After seeing the *Tryal* brought to safe harbor, Cereno denies having made such an offer; Delano therefore undertakes to sue him in the Peruvian courts. It is not very clear in Delano's subsequent account whether the judgment in his favor eventually handed down there awarded him the promised $50,000 or merely cleared his name of Cereno's defamation. In any case, he did receive a gold medal from the Spanish king two years later in recognition of his meritorious service to the crown. He wrote that he expected to receive more. All of these dealings and transactions are omitted by Melville.

20. See the remarkably intense and beautiful reading of this self-allegorizing movement of Melville's writing by Philippe Jaworski: *Melville, le désert et l'empire* (Paris: Presses de l'École Normale Supérieure, 1986). Our own reading of *The Confidence-Man* owes many debts to this book, which begins with a certain decision to "seek out: *against* systematic analyses, interpretive practices, taxonomic madness—all of which illuminate, but destroy the fertility of shadow; they order, but by immobilizing the movement; they institute meanings, but by killing off the sudden appearance of sense, they apprehend truths, but freeze the question of Truth; they exalt the singularity of the Self, but by debasing, enclosing, or effacing the Other and its difference" (17).

21. The disturbing temporality of the sentence may be gauged by the difficulty translators have had rendering it. The French translation, for example, attempts to repair the disturbance by introducing an interval of succession: "A peine était-il apparu qu'on le vit monter à bord . . . [He had barely appeared when he was seen to go aboard . . .]" (*Le grand escroc,* trans. Henri Thomas [Paris: Editions de Minuit, 1950], 7).

22. Our reference here and there to French translations of Melville's language is one mark of the initial occasion for a first version of this essay, written in French for the colloquium at Cerisy-la-Salle (July 1992) "Passages des frontières, autour du travail de Jacques Derrida." But this circumstance of the French language is also already inscribed by this text whose narrative is carried along by a steamboat named *Fidèle,* which navigates between two cities also named in French and by French: St. Louis and New Orleans.

23. Michel Imbert, whose reading of the text is close to our own, has also explored this possibility. He compares the placard to the "Counterfeit Detector" that is featured in the last chapter, which, as its ambiguous name suggests, may itself be counterfeit. See his "Cash, Cant, and Confidence."

24. This is to suggest a parallel with the two kinds of laughter Derrida has made out in his reading of Joyce's *Ulysses:* the laughter of a

master-author who would survey with irony the calculated effects of a text all of which would return finally to him, or a laughter that breaks out at the point precisely where such calculation is necessarily inscribed by an irreducible affirmation of the other, coming from the other. (See Derrida, "Two Words for Joyce," trans. Geoffrey Bennington, in *Post-Structuralist Joyce: Essays from the French,* ed. Derek Attridge and Daniel Ferrer [Cambridge: Cambridge University Press, 1984], and "Ulysses Gramophone: Hear say yes in Joyce," trans. Tina Kendall and Shari Benstock, in *James Joyce: The Augmented Ninth,* ed. Bernard Benstock [Syracuse: Syracuse University Press, 1988].) As one might expect, the institution of Melville studies has largely held to the first, ironic version since only the concept of Melville's final mastery can ultimately guarantee its own. In a supplementary irony, it is this very form of institutionalized mastery that would have been generally unable to accommodate that which, in *The Confidence-Man,* justifies the comparison to any of the greatest works of modern writing, including *Ulysses.*

    25. "Saying" and "said" translate Emmanuel Lévinas's fundamental distinction between the "dire" and the "dit." See, for example, *Otherwise than Being or Beyond Essence,* trans. Alphonso Lingis (The Hague: Martinus Nijhoff, 1981): "Antecedent to the verbal signs it conjugates, to the linguistic systems and the semantic glimmerings, a foreword preceding languages, [saying] is the proximity of one to the other, the commitment of an approach, the one for the other, the very signifyingness of signification. . . . The correlation of the saying and the said, that is, the subordination of the saying to the said, to the linguistic system and to ontology, is the price that manifestation demands. In language qua said everything is conveyed before us, be it at the price of a betrayal" (5–6). This can suggest the considerable possibilities opened to a reading of the stepping movement of *The Confidence-Man* in this Lévinasian sense: nothing is finally said but the saying, in which nothing happens but the approach, proximity, and substitution of the other, the "signifyingness of signification," the pre-originary structure of the relation to the other that dictates the heteronomous subject, what Melville points to perhaps with the ineffaceable trace of "charity."

    26. A reviewer of *The Confidence-Man* in 1857 quite shrewdly put it this way: "It is of course very possible that there may be method in all this madness, and that the author may have a plan, which must needs be a very deep one indeed. . . . Whether Mr. Melville really does mean to teach anything is, we are aware, a matter of considerable uncertainty. . . . It may be a *bonâ fide* eulogy on the blessedness of reposing 'confidence'—but we are not at all confident of this. Perhaps it is a hoax on the public—an emulation of Barnum. Perhaps the mild man in mourning, who goes about requesting everybody to put confidence in him, is an emblem of Mr. Melville himself, imploring toleration for three hundred and fifty-three pages of rambling, on the speculation of there being something to the purpose in the three hundred and fifty-fourth" (quoted in *The Confidence-Man,* ed. Her-

shel Parker, 272). It should be noted that Melville's first critics, although uniformly unfavorable in their evaluations of the book, were nevertheless generally better attuned than succeeding generations, if only unconsciously, to the vertiginous possibilities of this writing on credit. To take just one more example from the reviews of 1857: "When we meet with a book written by Herman Melville, the fascinations of *Omoo* and *Typee* recur to us, and we take up the work with as much confidence in its worth, as we should feel in the possession of a checque drawn by a well-known capitalist" (ibid., 269).

27. This pattern was already in evidence when Elizabeth S. Foster wrote her watershed introduction to a 1954 edition of the text, where she argued most forcefully the case of the confidence-man's pact with Satan.

28. For a census of such critical identifications, see Mary K. Madison, "Hypothetical Friends: The Critics and *The Confidence-Man,*" *Melville Society Extracts* 46 (May 1981).

29. One could very reasonably and correctly argue that this frame is not so much imposed by reading as it is already put in place by Melville, who does little or nothing in this text to trouble confidence in sexual appearances. But this distinction would be pertinent only if one held to the notion that a text such as this is effectively contained in its author's design or by his calculation. We are suggesting here, however, that Melville is also from the first already a part of the calculation, a part that he himself therefore cannot calculate.

30. In French, both of these operations are covered by the expression *faire opposition*.

31. See above, p. 15.

32. On the figure of legs, see Cohen, *Anti-Mimesis:* "The feet or legs represent a prefigural moment in which the traces of anteriority conflate the material bearers of sense precedent to any metaphorization. They are the site not only of inscription, but also disinscription or reinscription. . . . If legs may be understood as a corporeal analogue for the material base of language itself, that entails the brute dependence of semantic relations on what precedes mimesis and figuration; on what, in the course of marking itself, gets woven into and alters meaning production; on what seeks and implements *a mimesis without models*" (7).

33. On this structure of giving what one does not have, see once again Derrida, *Given Time,* 2ff.

34. Cohen, *Anti-Mimesis,* 162, n. 9.

35. See Geoffrey Bennington's essay "Towards a Criticism of the Future," in his *Legislations: The Politics of Deconstruction* (London: Verso, 1994), which sets out clearly the dynamic of future writing we have attempted to elucidate in Melville.

EPILOGUE: A FUTURE FOR IT—

1. See above, the conclusion to chapter 1.

I N|D E X

255